Table of Contents

Plague of a Green Man

Plague of a Green Man

By

Ellen Foster

Valparaiso Indiana

2011

Lulu Press, Inc.

Copyright © by Ellen Foster 2011

First published in the U.S.A. 2011

Maps and cover photographs by Louis Foster

ISBN 978-1-257-12305-6

Library of Congress Number: PS 3606 .O88 P53 2011

http://blogs.valpo.edu/ellenfoster/

Foreword

In the thirteenth century, the River Exe was blocked by a weir, a small dam or obstruction placed across the river. It was built by the Countess of Devon, living in the time of Henry III, and was built to power her mills. She built the weir with a thirty foot gap in the middle to allow vessels to pass going upriver to Exeter. Her cousin and successor, Hugh Courtenay, blocked the gap between 1317 and 1327 and cut the port of Exeter off from its access to the sea, making the village of Topsham, down river from Exeter, the maritime port. In this novel, <u>Plague of a Green Man</u>, which takes place in Exeter in the year 1380, Exeter had lost its access to the sea. But the reader will allow, I hope, the author's resort to literary licence in describing Exeter as an important port city in support of her story. In all other details, she has tried to be faithful to the historical realities of Exeter in the year 1380.

Another Lady Apollonia Mystery
by Ellen Foster:

Effigy of the Cloven Hoof

ISBN: 987-0-39894-2
Library of Congress Number:
PS 3606 .O88 E44 2010

Acknowledgments

I have taken full advantage of the willingness of our friends and family members to read copies of the manuscript and share their comments with me. It is difficult to offer adequate thanks to everyone, but their suggestions have all been helpful to me. Our friend and neighbor, Mary Henrichs, and my PEO sister, Ellen Corley, were among the first readers of the draft of the novel. Katherine Adams, a journalist and writer, contributed many helpful suggestions. Kati Kallay added her teacher's insights as well her widely read experience of English history. Kathleen Mullen and her writers' group offered key observations and comments during the process of rewriting.

Valuable insights and questions have come from dear friends in Devon who continue to serve as stewards and guides at the 14th century Cathedral Church of St Peter in Exeter. Keith Barker was a willing reader who provided many knowledgeable ideas and corrections. David Snell helped me to keep awake nights, checking details of local Devon history, medieval architecture, and a variety of 14th century human wobbles.

Annette Aust has not only read the most recent manuscript, she has been among the first readers of both of the storied adventures of Lady Apollonia.

I especially wish to express my sincere thanks to my family. Our son, Ted, and his wife, Marilyn, have provided help in reading the manuscript as well as adding their loving support. Our son, Charlie, and his wife, Shelly, contributed their suggestions as important readers and punsters. Most of all, I am grateful to my precious "better half," Lou, for his computer skills and gracious willingness to reread endless rewrites.

Map of Exe Valley

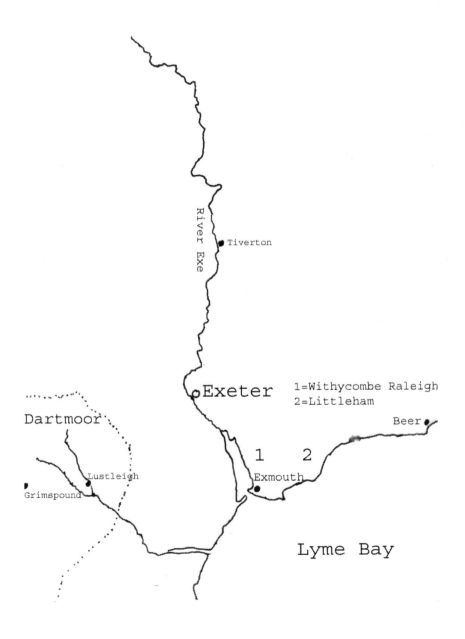

Map of Walled City of Exeter in 1380

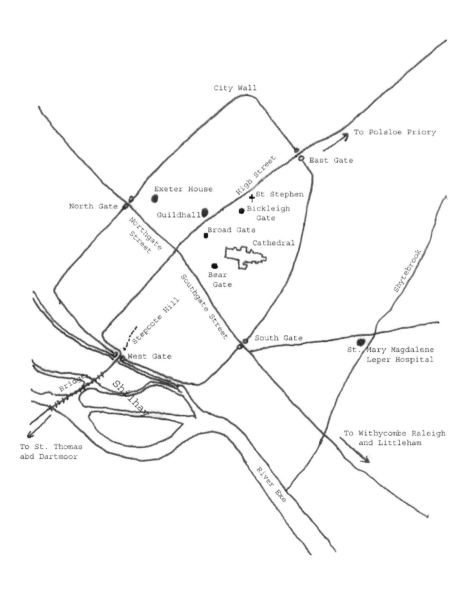

City Wall

To Polsloe Priory

East Gate

High Street

Exeter House

St Stephen

North Gate

Guildhall

Bickleigh
Gate

Northgate
Street

Broad Gate

Cathedral

Southgate Street

Bear
Gate

Shytebrook

Stepcote Hill

South Gate

West Gate

St. Mary Magdalene
Leper Hospital

Bridge

Shylhay

To Withycombe Raleigh
and Littleham

To St. Thomas
abd Dartmoor

River Exe

Prologue

Lost on the Moor

He should never have ventured onto Dartmoor! "Great God in Heaven," he hurled into the emptiness, "from what depths of Hell does one bid such fog?"

It had been well before the height of the noonday sun when Brandon Landow first ventured out towards the moor from Exeter's city wall. By now he had been wandering without visible guide or milepost for hours, his eyes filled with the featureless grey, oozing about him with his every movement. Absolution, his faithful mare, seemed as giddy as he, befuddled and blinded, with her eyes wide open into the meaningless depths swirling about her head. Fog had descended suddenly upon them; without winds, storm, or warning, the brightness of midday transformed into a silent, visual gel.

Growing more frightened as he rode but also angry at his own greed, Landow muttered to himself, "I should have known better! Why would anyone wish to meet secretly in Grimspound Village on this godforsaken moor, especially if he had some sacred relic to sell?"

Not able to refrain from smirking to himself, Landow had assumed from the first it was a stolen relic. The mysterious messenger who had approached him implied that it had come from the famous Hailes Abbey of Gloucestershire. He was no fool. Brandon Landow was a pardoner, albeit a very young dealer in indulgences, who was making the greater part of his wealth through selling relics. Hailes Abbey was known for one of the greatest relics in all of Christendom, drops of The Holy Blood of Christ.

His horse, Absolution, neighed fretfully, begging her master for some sense of direction. Landow jerked her reins irritably. At this moment, of all times they had ridden together, he had no patience for her occasional expressions of distress. More to the point, he had no idea where they were, neither which way they should be going, nor how in the world they could escape from the steadily darkening fog. It had been long hours earlier when they had sunlight to offer direction, but now in this iniquitous fog, Landow knew they could well have been riding in meaningless circles. Worst of all, he could see the fog was darkening; evening was closing upon them. Landow could feel night's damp chill penetrating his clothes; his great cloak seemed inadequate to warm him. He wrapped the immense, black garment closely around his chin and dismounted. Once standing on ground level, he began to search for clues in the granite strewn chaos that might offer a way out before total nightfall.

Landow kept a firm grip on Absolution's reins. She seemed to welcome his steady but gentle lead and followed willingly in his path, assuming her master must have some intended goal. They walked on together, but no matter where he turned his head or strained his eyes, Landow could find no hope of a trail or a mile marker, not the slightest sign of life nearby. The pardoner's eyes desperately searched in all directions, while darkness continued to leaden the dense fog about them. Suddenly, Landow began to sense his feet sinking. As he attempted to lift one leg, his other boot seemed sucked further into the spongy surface of the ground. Panic surged in his heart. When Landow reached to pull up that boot, he began to feel the other sink with his transferred weight. "Not a bog," he shouted into the night, "I shall never escape from a bog!"

The pardoner had only heard terrifying tales of travellers trapped in Dartmoor's bottomless pits of sinking, watery muck and vegetation, whose struggles against being pulled down only speeded their descent. They had proven to have been for him profitable tales of sinners being sucked down to judgement. Landow had frequently used such imagery to inspire fear for the increase of his sales. Frantically, now pulling to lift first one leg then the other from the moss covered ooze, he clung to his horse. Absolution seemed steadily unmoved and not the least frightened. Thanks to her powerful stance, he finally managed to get his left boot into a stirrup and hauled himself eagerly aloft into Absolution's saddle.

Visibly trembling, Brandon Landow realised himself to be abandoned in solitude, reduced from any possibility of his usual hauteur of the ecclesiastical official to terrorized infancy. But he forced his mind to think; he knew his only weapon against this blindness was reason. He must have a plan.

Absolution was a well-disciplined, obedient mare who responded to his command to walk backwards over the ground from which he thought they had come. Landow kept urging his mare with soothing voice, while patting her neck and stroking her mane. At last, when he was certain her hooves were striking solid earth, he paused. Sitting in his saddle, Landow bowed his head, crossed himself fervently, and offered his confession into the night, begging for some sign of forgiveness. Surely, as a confessed and truly repentant sinner, Landow told himself, God in His Mercy would show them a pathway.

He crossed himself fervently and turned Absolution's head to the right, dextra, away from the left, sinistra. All the while he recited to himself assurances from the twenty-third psalm. "Yea though I walk through the valley of the shadow of death, I will fear no evil for Thou art with me." Again and again, he repeated the words of the psalm as they walked on slowly to the right through the never ending fog. "Thou art with me. Thou art with me."

Then he heard it! Quietly gurgling in the near distance, Landow could hear the musical flowing of a stream. "Holy Mother," he prayed aloud, "lead us to safety, and I vow I shall grant a tenth of everything I ever earn be given to build your chapel." Dismounting once again, he strained to concentrate all his senses in his ears while he walked, slowly leading Absolution into the empty darkness towards the sounds of the falling water.

At last when he could hear himself to be nearer the water's gurgling flow, swiftly pouring over rocks in the river, Landow stepped towards it and suddenly found himself blindly sliding down a bank. He struggled frantically to catch his footing on the rocks while holding tightly to the reins of Absolution. Then bending down, Landow reached out his hand and touched the stream. "Praise God, this is it!" he shouted. This river, whatever its name, was their God given guide; they must go in the direction the water was flowing. Landow knew that all the rivers of Dartmoor flowed eventually towards the sea, sooner perhaps towards some place of human habitation.

"Thanks be to Thee, Great God Almighty; Holy Mary, Mother of Mercy, you have intervened to save me," he prayed in earnest gratitude. His breath continued to come in shaking, sobbing gasps, but he was indeed rejoicing! He knew they had been granted an avenue of escape, a hope of deliverance from the empty terror of Dartmoor.

Because of the constantly rocky, wandering curves of the stream, Landow continued to walk slowly along the fog shrouded bank, leading his horse while also using her strength to steady himself. At their tentative pace, time seemed arrested. They could make no progress in escaping from the dense cloud that constantly preceded them.

Absolution, now returned to confidence by her master's controlling hands, maintained her steady pace, never pushing nor demanding, but obviously grateful for his occasional soothing croon and reassuring stroke upon her mane. Still, it seemed an ongoing, dread filled passage of time for Landow. His ears alone led them by following the sounds of the waters; his eyes seemed worthless, blinded by total darkness offering no reassuring sight.

At first, Landow did not believe his eyes. Could that be a light? Was he actually seeing a flickering light far off in the distance? His heart raced to embrace the thought, while his feet began walking, pulling Absolution towards it. He moved tentatively away from the river, his only secure guide through the fog up to this point. He led Absolution towards the one thing he could actually see. With that, his horse seemed to sense his hopeful spirit and walked along faithfully, anticipating his pace.

As they moved forward, the light ahead seemed to be diminishing in its brightness, so Landow increased their pace. "Father in Heaven, do not allow me to lose this vision. Be Thou my vision! Thou hast led me to Thy guiding waters, Father; now sustain this holy light."

Landow's prayers grew more frantic as the light continued to dim. Then he heard a wondrous, tolling sound as a great church bell struck the hour. "Praise be to Thee!" he shouted aloud. "Praise be to God! Praise and thanksgiving for your mercy, gracious Queen of Heaven!" Landow felt tears pouring down his cheeks.

At long last, he could discern a now silent tower's outline, standing next to an ancient church in the swirling fog. The pardoner stumbled through the graveyard, then tied Absolution to a low branch near the church porch, and rushed to the door. Pressed by his driven weight against its handle, the ponderous door creaked open slowly to reveal a dark, fog free interior, lighted by a small bank of votive candles. Landow rushed to the altar, dropped to his knees, collapsed to the rush covered floor, and sank into the deep sleep of sanctuary granted at last.

* * *

"Sir, sir," the fearful voice said, while vigorously shaking the sleeping Landow. "Are you sensible? How may I serve you? How came you to this place?"

Slowly lifting his head, the pardoner's wits rushed to his defence as he drew himself up to his full, official substance and roused his body to seated position. He announced to the rustic cleric who stood before him, "Unhand me, simple parson, and know that I am Brandon Landow, pardoner by the appointment of the pope and Bishop Brantyngham of Exeter and official of Holy Church."

The parish priest stepped back in wonder at finding such an apparition lying beneath the altar on the floor of his church. "I pray thee, sir, forgive my presumption," he said humbly, folding his calloused hands into his sleeves. "I feared you may have suffered some injury. I meant only to offer succour and determine your need."

"Gratefully I thank you, father." Landow was now standing upright and spoke in a complete reversal of tone. "As you could see, I collapsed into sleep after finding sanctuary here in your church late last night, having wandered for hours on the moor in the devil's own fog. I was truly lost and would have died. But I saw the miraculous, heavenly light streaming from your church, and I heard from a great distance the Lord's own bell tolling from its tower. Can you tell me whence I have come?"

"Oh, my dear sir," the priest explained, "you have come to Lustleigh, and this is our parish church of St John the Baptist." Then the rustic parson chuckled a little and insisted to Landow, "But I must tell you, the heavenly light that drew you to our door was no miracle. Late last evening I was required to make a great fire in the back of the graveyard to burn away the rubbish of past months."

"No such unholy thought is granted you," Landow insisted. "Alone and dying on the desolate moor, I prayed for guidance and deliverance. In answer to my prayers, the Lord of Heaven brought me to sanctuary here! I say it was a miracle!"

Afraid to offer any differing opinion, the gentle parson said quietly, "Thanks be to God for His mighty blessings, indeed. But may I inquire what took you onto Dartmoor at such a late hour?"

Landow suddenly realised he now had some explaining to do to make his journey acceptable in the eyes of this village priest. "During this past month I have been offering my preaching services in Exeter from the Cathedral Close to the Church of Saint Sidwell. A messenger came to me, begging for my presence in the village of Grimspound on the moor. So with great haste, I ventured onto Dartmoor following the messenger's directions. I had begun my journey in glorious sunshine, but I soon found myself enshrouded in a mighty fog and totally lost my way until saved by the grace of God." Landow's voice had resumed its thundering assertion as he completed his tale. The priest of the parish was obviously impressed, but he could not help but continue his questioning tone.

"Dear sir, how could anyone send you to Grimspound? There is no village there! Only ruins remain of pagan dwellings, believed to have been used by the devil's followers in their ghoulish ritual since the days of Creation," he offered in humble correction.

Landow frowned and retreated into a frenzy of mental turmoil as he thought back to the messenger who had purposefully led him astray. In a matter of moments, he had composed himself once again. "Father, I am a stranger in Devonshire," Landow said with a dramatic sigh. "Someone has attempted to destroy my ministry, but God in his mercy has saved me from destruction! Will you not pray with me? We must give thanks and beg for the continuance of His Divine Protection."

As the parson and Landow knelt together at the altar of Lustleigh's church, one of their hearts was filled with words of praise and thanksgiving for God's mercy. But Landow's heart was boiling with fury. His mind continued to swirl in angry suspicion behind the rote repetition of his prayers. He would, he swore to himself, discover the identity of the person who had sought to lead him astray, and God help that creature when he was known.

Chapter One

Visitant to the Cathedral Green

She had come to live in Exeter in the early autumn of 1380 while her husband, Edward Aust, was required to travel first to Northampton, then to London. It had seemed such a good idea to the Lady Apollonia. Their family had never before lived for any length of time in an important town, and although they loved life in their tiny village, an important ferry crossing between England and Wales, she knew city life offered many cultural opportunities not found in Aust.

Lady Apollonia had brought with her their three younger sons to study in the school attached to the cathedral. She and Edward had always been unusual gentry parents for they insisted upon keeping their younger sons at home with them. Apollonia's mother had died at the time of her birth, and her father displayed no interest in her life until she had reached the marriageable age of fourteen when he sent her to the home of her first husband.

Edward had lived in the home of his merchant parents until they died. As an only child, he had buried them in the parish churchyard of Aust and sincerely grieved his loss, while cherishing his memories of family life. Apollonia had never known any expression of parental concern for her, and she felt its absence had created a wounding emptiness in her life. So after they married and were expecting their first child, she and Edward determined that although all their children must be well schooled, the sons would not be sent from home. Their children would remain with them until the boys' careers had been chosen. Their two elder sons, Hugh and Chad, now both in their teens, were serving in the household of her brother, Ferdinand of Marshfield in Gloucestershire, learning the skills of war and chivalric courtesy.

It had not been Apollonia's choice to select warfare as her sons' careers in life, but Hugh and Chad were devoted to the ideals of chivalry. They could only envision themselves as servants of the king. England required knights dedicated to its defence. The kingdom possessed volatile borders with Scotland and Wales and sought to establish English rule in Ireland. But since the reign of Edward III, England's monarchs had declared their birthright claim to the throne of France.

Lady Apollonia of Aust was a mature woman in her thirty-third year who still found herself inspired to pursue learning and inquiry. Unusually tall and long limbed, she was slender and graceful in her movement, but equal in height to her beloved husband. She had been named for the patron saint of those who suffer toothache, Saint Apollonia, and had been blessed since childhood with gloriously uncorrupted teeth. Her nobly sculpted face seemed constantly animated by an agile intellect, while her grey blue eyes and brilliant smile never failed to stir admiration midst those in her presence.

Apollonia had found few occasions to smile since they had arrived in Exeter. With Edward away in London, the Lady felt nearly disabled by loneliness, as if amputated by his absence. She frequently sighed from the depths of her innermost heart though there was no obvious cause for her distress. She and her household were now established in their town home, Exeter House, which stood well down from the High Street of this provincial capital of England's West Country. She had more than enough to occupy her days, overseeing their enlarged business ventures of wool carding and cloth weaving, and she had brought her most faithful servants with her to mind the running of her household. She had even brought their best cook from Aust to rule the kitchen and maintain Edward's expressed love of hospitality wherever they resided. But she so longed for his company.

He had been absent from her little more than six weeks. Yet his hearty laugh, his larking about with their boys, and his gifts for turning their long workdays into celebrations of accomplishment were all gone. Apollonia felt her world had grown void, empty without his presence to fill it. Edward Aust was Apollonia's second husband, but it had been he who offered marriage to her as a woman's greatest blessing in life.

Her first husband, from whom she was widowed, had been a nobleman, a garter knight, and a hero of the wars with France. He had been in every way a model of gentility, the perfect chivalrous knight. But in reality, Geoffrey of Montecute could only be remembered as a vengeful, controlling, malevolent spouse. She had been given to him as a bride of barely fourteen, and from the beginning of their lives together, he was determined to demonstrate that he valued her only as household chattel.

The Lady of Aust was aware that her second marriage was all that completed her as a wife, a mother, and an intelligent woman of business. Apollonia loved the popular story of The Loathly Lady. It was a moral tale of a beautiful, young princess, transformed into a loathsome hag. A gallant knight married the hag to gain from her the answer to the question, "What is it that women truly want?" The knight learned from the hag that what every woman truly wants is sovereignty in marriage. When he granted sovereignty to his wife, the ugly hag was transformed into a beautiful princess once again, and the knight was transformed by his gentle and virtuous love of her into a truly chivalrous gentleman.

Apollonia knew that it had been Edward Aust who gifted her life with that wholeness. He not only granted her sovereignty in their marriage, he actually admired her unfeminine gifts and was not the least bit intimidated by her intellect or advanced education. Edward was the son of a successful merchant who had achieved well in his own life, becoming a wealthy franklin, significant landowner, and wool merchant. Their love continued to grow from two hearts filled with mutual respect for the gifts each brought to their marriage.

Born into a noble family, Apollonia was a lady in her own right, yet she was more withdrawn when in fashionable company than was Edward. His "hale fellow well met" affability moved easily and companionably amongst all whom he encountered. Apollonia had never desired to imitate society ladies' craze for the newest fashion from Bruges or their love of gossip from important events at court. She hated discussions of war. She felt personally the English peoples' devastating sufferings through repeated visitations of plague and famine.

The Lady could feel a growing antagonism, expressed in ongoing clashes between those who laboured dawn to sunset and could still claim little in their lives, against those who possessed so much. She knew there was resentment simmering amongst the poor against the arrogance of the rich and powerful of the kingdom. And their King Richard, the second of that name, was a boy of thirteen, the same age as Apollonia's boisterous, bounding Chad. How could one fret over such flippancies as a horned headdress when everyone knew overmighty subjects were driving a faction ridden kingdom to the brink of chaos? Apollonia of Aust was a woman of her time; she regarded chaos as evil. She longed for calm, equilibrium, and balance to restore and maintain the hope of goodness in life.

Apollonia could do little but struggle with her misgivings and worry, without the presence of Edward's hearty balance in her life. She shamed herself for being so doleful. She repeatedly reminded herself, "All life continues one day at a time." In her mind, she would speak to Edward, promising him to find good company in their work until he had returned home once again. "It will be only a matter of months," she assured herself.

Nan Tanner, the Lady's personal maid, was sitting beside her in the solar, stitching enthusiastically until she noticed Apollonia's work lay untouched in her lap. The Lady's deep sighing did not go unnoticed, nor could Nan be unaware of her aching loneliness for her husband. She had served Lady Apollonia since her own early childhood and knew her to be a generous, energetic, well-purposed woman. But the past weeks of longing lethargy hung as a dense cloud about the Lady of Aust, and Nan knew this was not her mistress's usual life fulfilling conduct.

"You know, my Lady," Nan said casually, "Exeter is a bustling town. There are goods merchants here and a fine market, but also it has its own grandly built, new cathedral church. The people are right and truly proud of it, and no one comes to our door without some comment upon its glories." Apollonia nodded to her maid and picked at her embroidery disinterestedly. "Shall we not begin to explore the town to become better aware of all that it has to offer?" the little maid added, as she addressed the Lady more insistently.

Apollonia slowly raised her right hand to her chin and began to wonder aloud, "Truly, Nan, I should love to visit the cathedral, but how may we be introduced to it unless we have a knowledgeable guide?"

Nan moved to the edge of her seat and made the Lady look directly into her plain, earnest, little face. "Is it not possible that Master Edward's friend and man of law in Exeter, Philip Tropenol, might suggest such an introduction for us?"

"Oh, Nan," the Lady forgot her embroidery, "of course, the very one. I shall ask Gareth to carry a message to his chambers. Perhaps he will call upon us tomorrow. Please be sure that Stafford knows he must be present when we receive Tropenol. Oh, and tell Stafford I shall require his company as we explore the town."

The light in Apollonia's eyes seemed to Nan to be sparkling again. The Lady loved moving freely by herself about their small village of Aust in rural Gloucestershire, but she was now in a large, provincial English town. Apollonia surely did wish to see more of Exeter, but she was unacquainted within local society, and she also knew she could not go about unaccompanied. Normally Edward was her companion, but in his absence that role must be filled by Stafford, the steward of his household, an irascible old man who required patient prodding.

Nan's birdlike figure appeared to animate immediately as she carefully set aside her own embroidery and walked off to find the steward. The Lady's maid did not particularly enjoy Stafford's company, but she was well aware of the requirement of his presence at the Lady's side in public places. Nan's face grew serious, and her lips pursed together as she anticipated sharing her Lady Apollonia's news with the household steward. She knew he was certain to groan and protest at that which he considered to be the over burdening of his life and duties by his master's Lady.

Late in his forty-fifth year, Stafford complained constantly of his great age, aching rheumatics, and the growing failure of his eyesight and hearing. But Nan also knew Stafford always managed to place himself in the centre of the Aust family interests. He had a peasant's shrewdness in business, a keen eye for purchases or sales, and an ear always attuned to any household gossip. Stafford controlled members of the larger Aust household with an iron hand, allowing no one to shirk any assumed responsibility. He had been steward to Edward Aust when the master wed the Lady Apollonia of Marshfield; he knew his place and his responsibility to guard her every move during Edward's absence. One courtesy he could not manage, however; Stafford was incapable of any gracious response to a request for his services.

Nan found him in the kitchen, relaxing in front of the fire with one of his favourite kittens in his lap. Mistress Mary Mathe, the household cook, stood beside her massive table, powerfully kneading dough. Her kitchen wench, Emily, was cutting loaf shaped pieces of it for placement into the oven, already heated and prepared to receive them. Stafford's face immediately dropped to a grimace, seeing Nan enter the kitchen. It was as if he dreaded her interruption of his otherwise peaceful world. The pert, little maid greeted the household cook and Emily but walked directly to his chair and officiously announced her message of the Lady's will.

Stafford moaned deeply but continued to note carefully all of Nan's instructions. Then as she finished, he announced he would await the Lady's pleasure in the morning after breaking their fast. "But," he added pointedly, "Oi shall be eavily burdened to complete this day's tasks."

With a very small smile on her face, Nan promptly left the kitchen to return to her own embroidery that she lovingly worked with an artist's eye and skillful hand. Whatever the days ahead should bring for them, she was pleased that her Lady was restored to anticipation, happily looking forward to the morrow when they would begin to plan their exploration of Exeter's new cathedral.

* * *

Stable master and cherished member of their household, Gareth had come to Aust as a former servant of Apollonia's deceased first husband. He thought he had been about eleven years then, having begun his full-time service in Lord Montecute's stables at the age of seven. By now a mature man, Gareth was an experienced handler of stock but especially skillful with horses. He returned from delivering the Lady's message to Philip Tropenol's chambers and walked into her hall the following morning, just as she was receiving the Mayor of Exeter. The mayor had come in full estate to officially acknowledge the Lady's residence in her town dwelling, but also to express his gratitude at the increased commerce Aust wool enterprises brought to the town. Gareth stopped at the hall entrance as soon as he realised the ceremony in progress. He was never at ease in company with "the betters."

Lady Apollonia received the mayor near the great fireplace of the hall, seated in her armed chair with the steward of the household, Stafford, standing officiously at her side. She had called for a chair to be brought for His Honour and was extending carefully chosen words of welcome to their home, as well as her personal gratitude for this opportunity to make his acquaintance. When at last the mayor took his seat across from her, Apollonia could not help but note that he presented an enthroned vision of substantial mercantile success.

He was a grotesquely heavy man, made larger by his furred mayoral robes and chains of office, so that his body seemed to overflow the chair in all directions. The great, furred hat he held in his hand had been doffed immediately in his awareness of Lady Apollonia's blood lines, dating back to the Norman families of the Conquest Period. Although her present husband was a wealthy franklin, the mayor knew Edward Aust had made an excellent marriage to a lady of superior standing in society. His serjeant-at-arms stood next to the mayor, bearing the local staff of office. He said nothing but kept his own bared head held high as the knob of a goiter in the front of his neck seemed to bounce with his constant swallowing.

Gareth was immediately aware that he could not speak to his Lady in the midst of this audience. He signaled to Nan, ever present at her side. The petite lady's maid had noted his return and walked to speak quietly with him. Together they hurried behind the hall's beautifully carved, wooden screens passage.

Gareth was a strikingly blonde man of medium height with a powerful body, daily maintained through his exertions with the livestock of the household. Nan had known Gareth since their earliest days of service to the Lady Apollonia and always remained conscious of his presence. She also knew he was far more at home in the barn and stables, being painfully shy. Gareth hated to be caught up in any perceived function of society. His message to Nan was brief as ever. Leaning down to speak into her ear, he simply said, "Tell m'Lady ee's coomin." With that he placed his hat firmly on his head, spun round to leave the great house, and return once more to the company of his favourite creatures.

Nan returned to Apollonia's side opposite that of Stafford, as the mayor droned on in his speeches of welcome. They all listened politely until his prepared words seemed complete; then the Lady of Aust rose to extend her hand. Of course the mayor of the city must stand when she stood, but the effort of rising was a far greater struggle for him. His serjeant-at-arms held the staff of office in his right hand only and extended his left arm to the mayor to assist his rising.

All the while he struggled to his feet, the mayor continued speaking. "Surely, my Lady of Aust, you must visit the Close and see our city's renowned cathedral church. It has been newly completed, after the labour of many decades, and required the treasure of our bishops and our entire diocese. His grace, our revered Bishop Brantyngham, is the Lord High Treasurer of England," the mayor said proudly. "He has seen to it that young King Richard has confirmed all previous royal grants to the church of Exeter. And, my dear Lady, you must see our Guildhall. It, too, is of grand design, standing on the High Street not far from the Broad Gate's majestic entrance to the Cathedral Close," the mayor said with beaming, gasping pride.

Lady Apollonia smiled her warmest appreciation for his gracious welcome and assured him of her sincere desire to see the city's greatest jewel. "Indeed, Your Honour, I treasure your suggestions." The mayor seemed to swell in the aura of her smile. "Our younger sons are being schooled with the clerks of the cathedral's school," she said, "and thanks to your gracious encouragement, I am truly looking forward to viewing its magnificent design very soon."

* * *

Apollonia had begun the new day, as was her practice, with prayers conducted by the family chaplain just after dawn. As well as receiving the mayor of the city, she had been about her morning's pursuits for hours with Stafford at her side, maintaining his deeply muttering, moaning presence.

The man of law presented himself later that afternoon, vociferously promising to Nan his enthusiastic willingness to assist her Ladyship in any request she may have of him. Nan brought her visitor into the hall with a flourish, knowing that her Lady was keenly anticipating his arrival. Apollonia looked up from examination of the cloths recently received from Crediton. "Master Tropenol, God give you good day. I do welcome your presence, but I must confess I have rather frivolous need of your advice."

"Truly, my Lady," he continued in his best courtly manner, "thy merest need is my command. I shall plead your case with the utmost of my proofs; I shall provide legal remedy to restore entente in any dependency."

"Gramercy, Master Tropenol," Apollonia continued. "I am well aware that my husband relies upon your steady counsel and learned advice; therefore, I too shall seek to employ your knowledge of the city of Exeter. I wish to find some well-informed, local gentle who will help me visit the new cathedral church with educated and inspired eyes."

"Gracious Lady, speak no further," Tropenol urged her. "I am acquainted with the best of men to inspire you. He is a canon of the cathedral who has travelled the world viewing great churches from Constantinople to Compostela."

"I knew you should be the perfect source," Apollonia said. "How grateful I am for your acumen; pray tell us of whom you speak."

"I shall do better than words, my Lady; I shall arrange your meeting."

* * *

It was the following day, early in the afternoon, when Philip Tropenol returned to Exeter House with Baldwin Chulmleigh, canon of Exeter Cathedral and fellow native son of Devon. Tropenol could scarcely conceal his delight in being able to bring his long time friend into the presence of the Lady Apollonia of Aust. "Our comity began as school boys, my Lady. Allow me to present Canon Chulmleigh, my dear friend Baldwin, whose path in life led to the church, whilst mine rose divergently into the law."

"Canon Chulmleigh," the Lady said, "I bid you welcome and offer my sincere expressions of gratitude for the privilege of this meeting. Master Tropenol has expounded upon the worldwide nature of your travels but, more pointedly, to your intimate knowledge of the masonry and design of Exeter's glorious, new cathedral church."

"Alas, my Lady," the canon replied, "I shall never be able to prove equal to the heights of Philip's praise. But I have been blessed in my long life to observe many wondrous constructs to the glory of God, and I should be honoured to proffer all that I am able in the way of your introduction to our new cathedral."

Apollonia was thrilled. She could barely believe their good fortune to have a canon of the cathedral as their guide. Smiling eagerly, she attempted to keep her enthusiasm subdued. She truly did not wish to appear a total rustic, experiencing the wonders of a cathedral city for the first time. "I should be grateful to appear on the Cathedral Green at any opportunity granted according to your convenience," she said quietly.

"Then let us away!" the canon responded. "*Carpe diem*!"

Lady Apollonia immediately signaled to Nan and of course to Stafford, whose long face lengthened further with a low voiced moan. Nan rushed to collect the Lady's cloak and gloves. When all were dressed against the early autumn weather, they proceeded out of the hall, their party swiftly formed, yet enthusiastically joined in purpose.

Nan was thrilled to be accompanying her Lady. She knew she was going to be allowed to share in the Lady's tour with an important priest and canon of the church. Stafford would complain of the walk, the need to stand for long periods, and especially that which he felt was his endless requirement to accompany his Lady in the absence of their Master Edward. But he also knew he would gain much insight into the construction and meaningful religious decoration of the cathedral. He would assume his superior position amongst the staff and, in describing to them their tour of the cathedral, emphasize to everyone in the household once again his mastery of everything!

Chapter Two

Green Men of the Cathedral

Canon Chulmleigh led Apollonia's party up Northgate Street to Exeter's High Street, walking with the Lady at his side, Stafford and Nan following close behind them. Nan strained to hear all that the cleric wished to share. He pointed out several important parish churches along their route, but the canon also urged Apollonia to visit Exeter's Guildhall during her stay in the city. "It is the beating heart of commerce and trade in Exeter, your Ladyship, and the guildsmen have spared no expense in building the finest of its kind in the West of England." Chulmleigh was rightfully proud of his native city, so as the group reached the High Street, he first turned their attention towards the east, where they could look down towards the covered exterior of Exeter's Guildhall.

The canon, having brought them to a full stop, next turned their attentions to admire the Broad Gate, principal entrance to the Cathedral Close. "I have been informed of your fine mind and devotion to study, my Lady; therefore, I will tell you that the Cathedral Close is a walled community within a walled city. Exeter was founded as a legionary camp of the ancient Roman Empire. Its city walls were first built by the soldiers of Rome. And," he said with a flourish, "as we enter here, we are treading back in time into Exeter's ancient heart."

Apollonia made little effort to disguise her interest in the history Canon Chulmleigh wished to share with her. She was aware, as a student of Latin, that their little village of Aust also traced its origins back to the days of the Roman occupation of Britain. But she tarried before entering the Broad Gate. She was moved by its massive portal, through which they must pass. Shading her eyes from the bright sunshine of the early afternoon, she looked up to examine more carefully this monumental, stone entry gate. Two tall levels of chambered floors were built above the gate's pointed arch portal, outlined by massive voussoirs, arcing grandly upward from ground level stone pillars on either side. Two side towers, each as tall as the combined gate and its upper floors, framed the sides of the arch and pointed the massive stone structure upward.

Apollonia could not help but think the Broad Gate had been built in imitation of the gates of heaven.

"What a glorious entry you have chosen for us, Canon Chulmleigh," Apollonia told him enthusiastically.

"Well then, my Lady," he responded, "you shall not be disappointed in all that lies beyond. But I have purposely brought you to enter here because this is the gate into the Close for all important guests. Kings, bishops, and nobles enter here. I wish you to share their introduction to the mother church of our diocese."

Thus, grandly encouraged, Apollonia and her party walked with the canon through the Broad Gate and found themselves standing in an area of the city unique to its purpose, the Cathedral Close. As she entered the Close, Apollonia's first anticipation of heavenly vision was utterly dashed by the disorderly collection of buildings, brawling pedestrians, and rowdy games they found within. An open ditch ran around a grass covered cemetery, the Green. Within this space of sanctified ground, rowdy prentices were playing a contentious ball game, while citizens of all classes stood in groups, arguing, gossiping, and laughing at the latest bawdy joke.

The Green was bordered by a tree lined lane, leading to a collection of fine homes that had been built as residences for the cathedral canons. "If you look just there, beyond the Treasurer's house, built into the wall of the cathedral's north tower, you will see my house," the canon told them proudly.

Chulmleigh began to call their attention to several churches and chapels, in addition to the cathedral, built within the Close. "But since the eleventh century, our cathedral has maintained the sole right of sepulture within the city, excluding the monasteries of course. Other parish churches in Exeter have no graveyards. All funerals and burials in the city must take place here," he told them proudly.

With the canon leading, they walked down one of the paths through the graveyard past the Church of St Mary Major. Suddenly they could see the west front of the cathedral. Apollonia felt stunned by the vision before her. Her group found themselves looking upon an extended series of exquisitely carved figures running the full width of the cathedral.

"This is our new image screen, my Lady, and it continues to progress," the canon said, using his right arm as he guided their attention. "You can see angels in the lower level supporting an upper collection of regal carvings of the kings of England, as successors to the kings of the Old Testament. But, my Lady, please note each king reigns in his own royally carved niche."

"What a magnificent work of art!" Apollonia gasped. "The carvings of the kings and their garments are presented in regal colour, enhanced by the gold of their crowns and silver of their armour. What a wondrously glorious gallery of kings Exeter Cathedral has achieved."

"And it is yet to be finished, my Lady," Chulmleigh responded. "One more level of saints and fathers of the church will be added atop these completed stages, offering inspiration to all who will gaze upon it. But of signal importance," the canon assured them, "the carvings of the west front image screen will offer to those, who are unlettered within our community, an understanding of the promises of Holy Scripture, the history of holy church, and the attributes of the saints."

Nan drew in a great breath. The little maid had seen nothing of such princely design in all her life. As they walked past the screen, she could not keep her hand from touching the carvings and scratching some of the stone from this sacred place under her fingernails. Once returned from their tour, Nan knew she would carefully clean the stone dust from her nails and place its sanctified particles into a small cup. When needed, she believed she could add water to the cup and drink it for its healing properties, if ever severe pain might return to cloud her vision.

Canon Chulmleigh led his party around to the cathedral's north porch, where they would enter the nave of the great church. Again, Apollonia was shocked by a squabble of argumentative noises, meeting them in the porch and issuing out of the great, vaulted nave. The nave was full of groups of merchants, guildsmen, and their underlings, using the cathedral as if it were a town hall meeting place where each sought his personal pursuits, none of them of sacred purpose.

Nan was shocked to see two townswomen walking within the nave, surreptitiously selling cheaply made church ornaments to visitors. And, as the men of Exeter used the nave for their business, spurious groups conspired near pillars or seated themselves in small groups next to the walls. Nan could see that one young woman walked near to them and quietly lifted her skirts to display a naked, shapely ankle. She did not wear the yellow hood of the prostitute, but Nan was convinced this girl was soliciting. Nan felt outraged! Something must be done about such disgraceful behaviour in the cathedral, but no one else made any notice. The cathedral custor was fully occupied by his efforts to expel a feral dog out from the nave, and he rushed hither and yon in a frantic effort to herd it towards the doors.

The canon urged Apollonia and her servants to follow him to the far western end of the nave. Standing there, not one of them could fail to lift his head in dumbstruck awe at the hundreds of foot lengths of heavenly vision soaring above them. The cathedral's tierceron vaulting stretched eastward, arcing overhead from its western portals towards the high altar. The stone ribs of the vaulting seemed to spring, as if giant bouquets of stems vased within clustered columns, and reaching to an unbroken, central rib stretching the length of the cathedral from west to east.

Lady Apollonia, Stafford, and Nan, now totally unaware of her concerns for cathedral propriety, were unable to speak words adequate to the moment. The lavishly decorated nave offered a miracle of the masons' craft, not only in the overall design of the master mason but even more in the exquisitely carved details. Elegant carvings decorated every roof boss of the vault. Every corbel flowed upwards from the pillars while their decorated capitals completed two long streams of pillars that separated the aisles of the nave. And, every walled surface was painted and brilliantly presented to inspire, within all worshipping souls, a vision of the glory of God's house.

"I call upon each of you to direct your eyes upward to the inspiring roof boss that secures the vault above our heads." Canon Chulmleigh pointed their gaze to the ceiling. "We call this our Becket Boss, as it presents for us the entire drama of the martyrdom of St Thomas in Canterbury Cathedral two centuries ago." The canon crossed himself reverently but continued, "Our Bishop Grandisson, of venerated memory, whose tomb chapel stands directly behind us within the walls of the west front, was devoted to the memory of St Thomas and wished to enable everyone who enters our cathedral to acknowledge his martyrdom."

"Pray, Canon Chulmleigh," Apollonia said, with her head tipped back awkwardly to continue looking upward, "why choose a roof boss so far above us to portray the details of the martyrdom?"

"My Lady, you are twice observant, but I must remind you that the murder of the blessed Thomas occurred within the cathedral of the lord archbishop of our English Church. It was a brutal act, committed by minions of King Henry, the second of that name. This boss seeks not only to memorialize our blessed Thomas but to require remembrance of all who enter here. For as the roof boss serves as keystone to the vault above our heads, so also does St Thomas's martyrdom serve as key to the sovereignty of our English Church."

Apollonia could not help noticing that Stafford had ceased his perpetual groaning. He stood quietly with hat in hand, his head lifted back and eyes wide open to the human miracle of creation and construction displayed before them. Nan appeared to shrink slightly into a realm of childlike visions of saintly glory. Neither of them noticed that the lady and the canon had moved on until Apollonia called to them.

Leading his party to the south aisle, Canon Chulmleigh invited them to gaze across the width of the nave and look upward towards another surprising feature of Exeter Cathedral. Above the arcade over the fifth bay from the west on the north aisle, Apollonia could see an elegant balcony featuring carved angel musicians, each the size of a small child and holding a familiar instrument as if playing for them. One angel held a gittern, another played the bagpipes, while others played a citole, a harp, a trumpet, a portative organ, a shawm, tambourine, pipes, and cymbals. Every instrument was known to members of the Aust household as one that might be played by minstrels in their own hall. Nan put her hand above her eyes to focus upon the painted and gilded angels who seemed to be quietly gazing down upon them, while offering their songs to all those gathered below.

"We call this our Minstrels' Gallery," the canon told them, "for on high holy days of the church year, one portion of our choir sings from that gallery, filling our cathedral nave with their angelic voices."

Apollonia had read about great churches and their furnishings but had never thought to find a Minstrels' Gallery placed above the gathered congregation in the nave. Still it was perfect for the space, she thought, especially as music proclaimed the glory of worship in the church. Uniquely here in Exeter Cathedral, music was portrayed as heaven sent to the people of the nave, as well as sung in God's praise from the exclusive quire of the bishop and clergy.

The Lady was somewhat prepared to understand all that was being shown them because she was aware of other great church building projects throughout the cathedral cities of England. But Nan could not take in enough; her eyes flashed from the bosses of the vaulting overhead, to the gallery, to the pillars and corbels. Her small face seemed constantly tipped upward throughout their visit to allow her eyes to see more, while her mouth gaped in wonder.

The canon took them to the crossing, and they walked to its centre to stand in front of the intricately carved quire screen separating the quire from the nave. "Look now upon the corbels of the four central pillars of this church," Chulmleigh told them. "Here you see portrayed the four cornerstones of every great cathedral: the king, the queen, the bishop, and the master mason." Stafford was stunned, not only by the beauty of the colourful, carved portraits but more pointedly by his sudden awareness of the inclusion of a member of the commonality amidst such an elevated group of the highest in the kingdom. He continued to study the handsome face of the master mason upon the southeastern corbel, totally unaware that the canon had moved on.

They had begun to walk through the south aisle of the church, next to the quire, when Apollonia noticed a strangely carved roof boss in the lower aisle vaulting overhead. It appeared to be a human face, but one that was composed of leaves from which she could see menacing eyes glowering down upon them. "I beg your pardon once again, Canon Chulmleigh," she said to their guide, "would you inform us of the meaning of such a face filling this boss above us?"

The canon paused to look overhead for a brief moment, grimacing as if he did not wish to address that carved feature. "Oh, dear Lady, you will find many such foliate faces here in the cathedral. The masons love to carve them and suggest they are ancient symbols of renewed life, commoner's symbols of the Resurrection, I fancy," he said, hurrying on. "Please, let us away to the Lady Chapel before the next masses must be sung."

But before they could continue, a very agitated cleric came to the canon's side and whispered a message into his ear. "I must beg your leave, Lady Apollonia," the canon said, halting their progress. "A message has come requiring my immediate attention. Would you be so kind as to excuse me whilst you continue your visit?" And without pausing for the Lady's answer, Canon Chulmleigh quickly walked away with the messenger, a growing expression of concern creasing his face.

Not knowing what to think of their guide's hasty departure, Lady Apollonia, Nan, and Stafford continued walking slowly by themselves along the south aisle to the east towards the Lady Chapel. They paused to admire several beautifully carved knights' effigies and an elegant table tomb displaying the brass image of a bishop. But just after turning into the ambulatory and before entering the Lady Chapel of the Virgin Mother, Apollonia saw in the vaulted ceiling more of the disturbing bosses she had mentioned to Canon Chulmleigh. Over her head, just before the entrance to the Lady Chapel, Apollonia noticed there were several kinds of foliate faces, some with facial features composed of leaves, others with stems protruding from their mouths or eyes.

She said nothing to Nan or Stafford, as they were obviously thrilled with the beautifully sculpted saints in prayer niches at eye level. But Apollonia could not help feeling disturbed by the carvings in these bosses. "Why are such images used as symbols in Christ's Church?" she wondered uneasily to herself. "If faces of leaves or faces with stems are truly ancient symbols of new life, then why have I found no reference to them in the Holy Gospels or in the lives of the saints?"

Apollonia continued to ponder her questions until their party had returned through the length of the north quire aisle to the crossing, where a life-sized statue of St Peter stood near to the North Door. It was called Old Peter and held in its hands a large collection box. The Lady deposited her coins into Peter's box as they turned to leave. She had truly enjoyed her first walk about the new cathedral, but she could not help feeling disturbed by some of its symbolism.

"We shall consider these foliate faces further, Canon Chulmleigh," she thought to herself. "There must be a better reason for their inclusion in this place than merely the whimsy of the masons."

* * *

During their stroll home to Exeter House, Nan continued chattering aloud of her growing sense of wonder at all they had seen. The lady's maid was a village girl who had known little in the way of impressive buildings larger than a parish church and who was now convinced that Exeter's must be the greatest cathedral church in the world! "My Lady, Exeter has truly built the most beautiful of God's holy churches, such grace in its soaring vaults, such heavenly inspired decoration. Have you ever seen its equal?"

"Truly, Nan, I have never seen such a church before, though I have encountered descriptions in my readings of even greater churches in Paris, in Rome, and in Spain at Compostela. But, dearheart, the greatest of all churches is said to be in Constantinople, built centuries ago by a Roman Emperor." Nan listened politely to her mistress, but as she was not quite certain where Compostela and Constantinople were to be found, she decided to remain constant in her opinion that they had seen in Exeter that day the most beautiful church in all of Christendom.

Stafford's reflections upon the new cathedral were never expressed. The old steward had returned to his usual "in charge but complaining" composure. He continued to groan as they walked. His rheumatics were worsening, he mumbled, because he had been required to stand for interminable periods, and he was grateful to be escorting his Lady home at last.

* * *

When the canon arrived at the deanery, whence he had been summoned, he found the dean and several other members of the chapter significantly disturbed by the most recent appearance in a series of mysterious, threatening messages discovered that morning in their cathedral. This time, Chulmleigh was told, the grotesque threat had been found in the chapel of Bishop Grandisson, bishop of the diocese when the cathedral had been completed. His tomb chapel was built within the main portal entrance to the cathedral, and only persons of importance were allowed entry through that portal. Several of the canons opined how unlikely it was that anyone of the town could have gained entrance there.

"Canon Baldwin," Dean Walkyngton said as Chulmleigh entered the chamber, "what do you make of this?" He was holding in his hand a copy of an official indulgence issued through the church but one with the seal of the Bishop of Exeter wickedly cut away. It had been replaced with a large face of green leaves, its angry eyes and snarling mouth spewing out the words, "NO FORGIVENESS JUDGEMENT IS MINE!"

"This," the dean continued, "was found rolled into the eye of a skull, God protect us, left sitting upon Bishop Grandisson's tomb." The dean was obviously distressed and displayed a sense of growing urgency in seeking Baldwin's counsel, as student of religion and history as well as canon of the cathedral. Canon Chulmleigh carefully examined the mutilated document but could only shake his head in disbelief.

"You have suggested in the past that these warnings, we continue to find, are the work of a demented mind. But who is this person, what does he seek, and how does he have access to the chapels of the cathedral after the gates of the Close are closed and locked each evening?" the dean asked.

"In all my years," the canon was forced to admit, "I have never encountered anything to compare with such bizarre threats. I can neither reason what such messages portend nor the intent of the perceived threat. Worst of all, I have no idea of how we are to answer it. I am truly sorry, Dean Walkyngton. I frankly confess these mutilated indulgences are completely baffling to me. Surely they are the creation of a literate person and one who may have a connexion with the church in some frenzied way. We must be prepared to act in our own defence. This is not only the work of a demented mind but also one who may be in a position to do us harm."

The dean made some effort to conceal his personal distress, but he spoke with emphatic direction in his voice as he addressed all the assembled chapter members. "You and your households will remain on alert to any unusual person seen about the Close after evening services have ended, indeed, at any time of the day. Raymonds, the custor, who lives above the north porch, must be shaken to his core. It is he who locks the gates of the Close. Tell him we require him to be instantly aware of anyone moving about the cathedral during the nighttime hours. I prefer that we shall not call upon the civil authorities for assistance in this matter. Instead, we will be on our guard and look to discover the culprit ourselves. Then we shall learn the real reasons for his threats against us."

* * *

That same afternoon, Brandon Landow returned to Exeter from Lustleigh and was riding towards the Franciscan friary, located just outside the city wall, where he had taken rooms in the guest house and arranged stable privileges for his horse, Absolution. By this time the pardoner had regained his usual arrogance after his terrifying exposure on Dartmoor. He had achieved modest success in sales of indulgences amongst the gullible parishioners of the village of Lustleigh where he had found refuge. He had also noticed while in the village that a significant number of indulgences had been stolen from his great leather wallet. The thief must have sent him on the wild goose chase to Grimspound to keep him from noticing his loss. "Stupid churl," the pardoner told himself, "whoever you are, you shan't be able to sell them, and their replacements will be easily forged for me."

As his purse was jingling with coins, he preferred to forget that it had been his own greed that had driven him onto Dartmoor. He continued instead to nourish his anger against the thief, while trying to pinpoint in his mind just where in Exeter he had encountered him, and what had the man looked like. Landow remembered it had been a strong but very poor creature who approached him humbly as he finished preaching on the step of the north porch of the cathedral. The pardoner realized that surely the poor man must have been sophisticated enough to possess some insight into Landow's baser motives. The man's clothes were old, and he had worn a hood round his face to shade his features. But he had spoken as a gentleman, so probably had fallen in estate and was possibly someone who had returned from war.

"Yes, that is it!" Landow said to himself. Normally he did not care enough to remember the faces of those who sought his help, but this man was distinct. "His face was scarred between his eyes, across his nose, and into his right cheek," the pardoner remembered, "as if from old sword wounds." He could recall little of the thief's colouring, but he was certain he was of similar height to himself. And he would recognize that scarred face if ever he encountered the man again.

Leading Absolution towards the friary stable, the pardoner decided he would remain in the neighborhood for the evening, going to an inn with alehouse where he knew he would find a meal, lusty company, and possibly caresses with those who ask no questions. His horse walked willingly with the stable hand as if she felt grateful to be returned to civilized accommodation, while Landow strode off to his room to create a marked transformation in his personal appearance.

He removed from his shoulders the great walet, especially designed to hold his collection of indulgences and then took off his heavy cloak with the veil of Veronica sewn across its back. Taking some of his favorite apparel from his bag, he pulled on a fresh pair of striped hose to display the length of his elegant legs. As a final touch, he changed from his travel boots to his favourite, long pointed poulaines.

Once his ensemble was complete with a padded blue jupon, he left his room, now presentable for the evening as a young dandy of the town. His long, yellow hair was freshly combed to his shoulders, and a smart, feathered cap angled towards his right eye. On his way to the tavern, Brandon continued to assure himself that the search for his unknown enemy would be pursued. He knew that many people despised pardoners, especially those who judged their purposes as less than truly religious. But Brandon never forgave an offense against himself. "For now I require jollier persons of a looser sort," he snorted to himself. With that, he turned a corner to the lane leading away from the main streets. Within a matter of minutes, Landow could hear the rowdy roar of the public house.

He entered the low beamed tavern and shouted out an order for his ale. His penetrating, nasal voice announced his arrival to everyone in the room, but it was from a group in its far corner that a returning shout of welcome begged him to join them. They were brightly dressed, young men sitting round a table. Not one of them shared his name, but their trifling eyes and rouged smiles intensified his erotic feelings of congeniality. Little time passed before Landow became aware that several in the group were actors.

Their early evening hours together passed in varieties of rowdy, bawdy exchange until closing bell, just before curfew at nine of the clock. Landow was invited to accompany several of his new companions to their humble abodes. Finally with the dawn breaking, he left the chambers of one newfound Exeter mate and staggered back to the friary and his celibate bed.

* * *

In the darkness of the early predawn hours, a large, round, iron lid, carpeted with grass, was lifted slowly upward from the lawn of the Cathedral Green. No one was about to witness his movement, but the figure, still below ground, was patiently cautious in all of his moves. He carefully searched first in every direction, before pulling his lithe body up and out from the entrance to the underground tunnel. He was a man of medium height but one of great strength; his muscular body moved with quickness and awareness, his powerful legs obviously knowledgeable of where they intended to go in the unlighted darkness.

Proceeding directly to the north porch of the cathedral, the shadowy figure walked past the steps to the porch, going into the darkness at the place where the walls of the porch met the cathedral wall. There he dropped to his bottom and sat against the stone wall of the cathedral; he drew up his knees and covered himself with his dark, woollen cloak. When the cathedral bells began to toll the hour of five of the clock, the figure waited until all citizens who were gathering for the early morning office had been allowed to enter the Close through the gates. They approached the north door, and the dark figure moved silently from the shadows to join them and entered the cathedral nave with the morning faithful.

* * *

Midmorning, the head custor was proceeding down the south aisle of the cathedral to see to the dozens of candles lighted by people leaving early mass in the Lady Chapel. As he walked past the tomb of Bishop Berkeley, he was startled by a grotesque smear of overturned candles pressed upside down onto the table tomb and fouling the brass image of a well-loved bishop. Lying upon the tomb was a wreath of rotting leaves holding an indulgence. The official seal and signature of the bishop had been ripped from it and replaced by a foliate head spewing forth the words, "BEWARE THE ANCIENT REVENGE!"

Chapter Three

Friar Francis Faces Expulsion

Lady Apollonia was having Nan dress her with care this morning. She had selected her husband's favourite gown and had her hair combed into a perfect coif, designed to receive its complementary headdress and veil. On any normal day of business, the Lady of Aust would never fuss so with her appearance; a simple wimple with veil would have sufficed, but this was no ordinary day. Lady Apollonia was preparing herself to be received by the Mayor of Exeter in his official capacity in the Guildhall on the High Street. Her visit was not merely in response to the mayor's call upon her. His invitation, received the day before, suggested that he wished to be her guide on her first visit to the structural improvements of the recently enlarged Guildhall. Finally assured that she was elegantly prepared for this official call, the Lady asked Nan to summon Stafford, so that with her steward, their party might begin the relatively short walk up the hill from Exeter House towards the High Street.

The Guildhall stood proudly in the centre of Exeter's growing merchant community. Within its walls, a woollen market hall proved to be the meeting place for many men of business, active in the important cloth production of southwest England. But it was also the meeting place of the city council, and it housed the mayor's chambers where he might entertain his guests. The Guildhall was an old building of the city and had undergone several periods of rebuilding, most recently in 1330. As if in counterbalance to the ecclesiastical enlargement of the new cathedral, the Guildhall had been transformed.

The mayor had placed one of his servants on watch for the arrival of the Lady of Aust and her party. So it was that, as they approached the central entrance beneath its covered way, he rushed forth to meet them and begged to be allowed to escort them to the mayoral chambers. The mayor's servant led them into the lobby, up the stairs, and down the foyer where the mayor awaited them. Various citizens and officers of the city stepped back, bowing to allow them passage.

One aggressively prominent member of the group refused to bow, simply removed his hat in greeting to the Lady, and positioned himself in her path. Thus he required her party to pause, separated from their guide, so that he could take advantage of his position and speak directly to her. "My Lady of Aust, I shall be first to bid you welcome to Exeter." He spoke forcefully and with an aggressive tone in his voice, as if implying some kind of threat.

He was a small, bony man, less tall than she but dressed in the height of luxury. In total disregard for sumptuary laws, he was garbed in an elegant tunic with tailored sleeves, sculpted and cut from his wrists to flow near in length to his ankles. Most surprising of all, though a skeletal man, his thinness was buttressed all round his body with linings of ermine. The Lady stood before him to offer a greeting but acknowledged that she knew him not.

"My willing thanks for your kind welcome, sir, but I regret we remain strangers. May I know your name?" Apollonia spoke with politeness, but from her superior height, she continued to look down upon him.

"Oh you shall know it, my Lady, for I hold prerogative here and shall always be your most severe competitor." He spoke loudly in an obvious attempt to display a kind of contempt for her before the gathering of well-dressed merchants moving about the hall.

Stafford moved to his Lady's side, as no one could mistake the attitude expressed in the words of this particular merchant. Apollonia had never encountered such discourtesy in her life, but she refused to be intimidated by his words.

"I repeat, sir, I have no response to you for I have no idea who you are." Pointedly looking down upon the man, she simply said, "Now you shall let me pass," and as she continued to walk, she forced him to back away.

"Wolfson is the name," he shouted after her, "and I have powerful friends in Exeter!"

The mayor's servant returned to her side, obviously embarrassed by the encounter he had just witnessed. "My Lady, pray do forgive Master Wolfson's enthusiasm. He is indeed one of our most successful merchants, but he does allow his spirit of competition to get the better of him." Then he led the Lady to the entrance of the mayoral chambers and grandly announced her arrival. The mayor struggled upward, lifting himself in boisterous greeting from his chair behind a great table near the tall windows.

"Ah, my Lady of Aust, welcome, welcome. I am delighted that you have deigned to grant us your presence on this glorious morning." The mayor's hugely extended middle seemed to disallow any rapid movement by him. Clad in his official robes, he doffed his great hat, bowing slightly with the chains of office clanging upon his chest. His ever present serjeant-at-arms stood at his side, always prepared to offer an arm or simply to provide liveried substance, enabling his master to stand with dignity.

"Gramercy and heartfelt thanks for your gracious invitation, my Lord Mayor," the Lady said. "With this, our first entry into your Guildhall, I am stunned by the grandeur of your civil estate."

"Oh, you have seen nothing, nothing at all, my Lady. Allow me to walk with you throughout my chambers but also to extend your view into our great hall where all important meetings of the courts and council take place. It will demonstrate for you that our Guildhall is one of the most impressive buildings west of London!" the mayor said, nearly bursting with pride.

Lady Apollonia could hear Stafford groaning deeply into his high collar, but she knew he would be more than pleased to describe to their entire household his personal knowledge of every detail of the construction and decoration of the Guildhall. Nan stood in wide-eyed wonder, but she remained silent. She moved closer to her Lady, as if her small body would provide defence against any further threatening words. The mayor walked slowly, speaking in ponderous tones of the increase of trade bringing wealth and growth to their fair city of Exeter. He was obviously pleased to encourage the Lady to recognise that the expansion of the Aust investments here had indeed been a wise choice.

The mayor's extended walk about the Guildhall with her party was truly helpful and informative to Apollonia. She immediately replaced the insults of Wolfson with the gracious welcome of the mayor and proceeded to forget the sinister, little man. Her dear Edward had already informed her of the importance of this building to them as merchants, as well as active members of the wool guilds of Exeter. But as he had not yet seen its interior chambers, market hall, or cells, she would now have much more to share with him at his return. When their tour was completed, the mayor escorted her party back to the main High Street entry. The Lady thanked him sincerely, with heartfelt enthusiasm for his courtesy to her. With Nan and Stafford in her wake, she left the Guildhall, walking on to the High Street once again.

They were walking past the Broad Gate entrance to the Cathedral Close when Apollonia noticed a noisy crowd gathered in front of the

Broad Gate. Amongst the mob were clerics, some with their arms raised in anger, while other lay persons pushed rudely at a very young Franciscan friar who seemed woefully unprepared to deal with the shouting and accusations being hurled at him. One of the most aggressive members of the mob was immediately known to the Lady. She had not seen him for at least five years. And she did not approve of his relentless shouting towards an elderly Grey Friar, whom he seemed to be urging to bring charges against the young brother, now so broken and humiliated.

Lady Apollonia drew Stafford to her side and pointed out to him the presence of Brandon Landow, the young pardoner, and his role in agitating the crowd. With a grunt of recognition, her steward immediately acknowledged the young man as a former member of the Aust household. Nan, too, gasped as she recognized Landow. If they had been given their preferences, both of them expressed a desire to avoid any reacquaintance with the young man. But Apollonia felt strongly that she must be informed of the causes of this very one-sided but heated commotion. Before she and Nan left the turning to walk down the hill towards Exeter House, she directed Stafford to move into the crowd and speak with Landow.

"You shall tell him I command his presence in my hall this day, or I shall be speaking again with the civil authorities!"

* * *

It was later that same afternoon when the young pardoner appeared at her door. Nan brought him into the hall. She moved to join Stafford, each standing either side of the Lady, who was seated behind a great table. Apollonia not only wished to create distance between herself and Brandon but to suggest to him a setting of judgement. Landow swept off his hat in a disdainful bow and spoke before she could utter a word.

"We meet again, my Lady of Aust. But of course, now I am on an entirely different social level than when you expelled me from your household," he smirked.

Lady Apollonia remained stoic and calm but refused to greet him. "You will tell me why you were agitating against that young friar on the High Street!"

"You may not have noticed that I am now a pardoner of Holy Church," Landow responded. "You may call in civil authorities all you like, my Lady; I may now claim benefit of clergy!"

"Brandon Landow, every member of my household knows well your thieving habits. You, of all members of my affinity, earned your own expulsion from it. I congratulate you upon the canonicity of your position as pardoner, but you will tell me now why you were agitating against that young friar. If not, I shall see that your presence in Exeter is endlessly complicated for you by major charges of theft." The Lady paused to allow her words to penetrate Landow's presumed indifference.

Finally, after having seemed to consider all his options, he said simply, "Friar Francis is accused of stealing from the poor box in the church of the Grey Friars."

"And why are you his chief accuser?" Apollonia continued to press him.

"Simply, because I am the chief witness to the theft," Landow said nervously, wriggling his hands together in discomfort with her persistence.

"Look directly into my eyes, Brandon," Apollonia's voice continued to rise. "You will now describe to me the precise manner of your witnessing his theft," she said with distinct pronunciation of each word.

"My Lady," Landow began to whine. "I found him alone in the church, and the box had been emptied."

"But you already knew the collection box was empty, did you not, Brandon?" the Lady insisted. "You knew simply because you had already stolen its coins and were searching for another victim to suffer for your crime." Lady Apollonia suddenly stood her full height and pointed her arm's length directly towards Landow's face. "You are the thief, Brandon Landow. I command you now to return to the friary church and restore the money you stole from it. Then you will report to the young friar's superior and announce that this entire episode has been a most regrettable mistake."

Landow stood silent for several moments, still trying to reason his way out of this cloud of dilemma the Lady had cast about him. Not a word was spoken by anyone in the hall as he pondered, but the discomfort of his wriggling silence seemed to scream his guilt.

"My Lady of Aust," Landow spoke at last, again restored to his loftier tones of address. "I regret to inform your Ladyship that I am required to leave Exeter early on the morrow and must now return to the friary to pack my miserable belongings and sing through the service of Compline this evening. As you suggest, this 'regrettable mistake' will be shared with the head of the order, and the pitiful sum of money will be discovered in a corner of the offering box. Thus, I shall bid you adieu, fair Lady, until next we meet." Landow bowed deeply once again and seemed to begin to leave the hall.

"Before I dismiss you, Brandon," the Lady continued to employ his boyhood name, "I suggest you see to it that the sum of money 'discovered' shall be a substantial one. I am also pleased to remind you, Brandon, that as you have achieved position in Holy Church and may claim benefit of clergy, your office will always make you locatable for me."

"Beg pardon, my Lady, by your leave?" Landow whined. He wished to have this audience cease and be on his way.

"Yes, Brandon," Apollonia responded, "now you may go."

Soon after the pardoner had departed the hall, Nan returned from seeing him to the door and announced angrily, "Thanks be to God, my Lady, he is gone. That wretched Landow has not the slightest sense of guilt or remorse. He was arrogantly flippant with me, boasting of his profits made from abuses of the ignorant poor."

"I believe we can do little to alter his patterns, Nan, but we may be able to restrain some of his evil intent. Will you please find our chaplain and tell him I wish to speak with him before evening prayer?"

* * *

Apollonia was sitting in her solar late that afternoon, when Nan brought Chaplain Anthony to her and urged the elderly man to take his chair next to the Lady, near the fireplace. When they were seated together, the Lady smiled and welcomed him to her side. "You have always been a good friend and spiritual advisor to us, Anthony. Edward and I would never have achieved such balance and goodness in our marriage without your counsel."

Anthony had baptized their five sons and prayed with them through the loss of two infants, one whose life would have begun between the birth of Chad and Thomas, and the other infant born dead between Alban and David. The chaplain's strong faith in times of celebration, as well as suffering and loss, had enriched their marriage and sustained their family. Apollonia was especially grateful for his ministry when she found her own spirit troubled.

"Father Anthony," she began to tell him, "Stafford, Nan, and I passed a dreadful scene on the High Street today, just before the Broad Gate entrance into the Cathedral Close."

"I am truly sorry for it, my Lady," Anthony replied. "What may I do to ease your concern?"

Apollonia shared with her chaplain the entire tale of witnessing the street bound humiliation of a young friar. She described for him her personal dread that Brandon Landow, formerly of their household, had instigated the accusations against the friar after having robbed the friary church himself. Finally, she recounted to him her personal charges expressed to Landow's face, with her requirement that he return to the friary and release the innocent friar from all accusations.

"Father, I must be assured that Brandon did indeed fulfill his promise to me," Apollonia said pleadingly. "Can you go to the Franciscan friary tomorrow, speak with the head of the order that we may know the truth, and I may be at peace?"

The chaplain began to chuckle, his deep voice expressing his own remembrance of having been placed in such situations before. This was not the first time his Lady Apollonia had sent him to intercede in behalf of someone she felt to be wrongly accused. "You have a very kind heart, my Lady, but are consistently moved to protect innocent young men as if they were all your sons, I vow."

"But no, Father Anthony, can you not see I have every reason to feel responsible for the actions of Brandon Landow against an innocent victim who is also a servant of God?" Apollonia pleaded to justify herself.

"My Lady, of course I understand your grasp of responsibility. I shall indeed speak with the members of the friary who lead the order here in Exeter, but you must know other monastic leaders in the city do not feel constrained to defend Franciscans at all. The local Benedictines regard them as insolent intruders who insist upon preaching wherever they wish, even when they have been forbidden to do so. Beyond that, the Franciscans may be somewhat suspicious of my motives as I am unknown to them," Anthony said in cautioning tone. "However, Brandon Landow left your household to become a sorry example of one in service of the Church. I resent all that he stands for, and tomorrow I shall certainly discover whether or not he has undone his wickedness against the young friar."

* * *

Late in the morning of the following day, Chaplain Anthony returned to Exeter House with a new guest. As they entered the hall where Apollonia was working with Stafford, her chaplain brought into her presence the young Franciscan whom she had seen so distressed and humiliated earlier in the week. "My Lady Apollonia of Aust," Anthony began, "may I present a very enthusiastic mendicant. This is Friar Francis who says his call to this order has guided his life since the day he was born."

Friar Francis, wearing the simple robe of his order tied with a cord around his waist and shod only by the poorest sandals, literally dropped to his knees and placed his arms across his chest in a gesture of total submission. "My Lady of Aust, you have saved my reputation, my calling, and my life! How can I ever thank you?"

"Bless you, Brother Francis, I have done nothing beyond an earnest pursuit of truth," Apollonia said, pleased to meet him at last. "I am grateful to learn that your innocence of wrongdoing has been declared, and your calling has been vindicated." She turned to dismiss Stafford so that he might carry on with other morning tasks. Meanwhile, she asked the young friar to sit with her and Chaplain Anthony that they may learn to know one another better.

"My Lady," Francis told her as they seated themselves, "I have been declared innocent of all accusations against me and have been allowed to return to my ministry to the poor. My parents prayed that I would devote my life to him for whom they named me, for our dear patron saint. I am a mediocre student and have proven myself unable to achieve great study or become a teacher. But I do joyfully dedicate my life to Lady Poverty, as St Francis did, in imitation of the life of our Lord Jesus Christ."

"And my Lady," Anthony told Apollonia, "young Francis has chosen to serve the poorest of the poor. He is preparing to work outside the city wall of Exeter in the Leprosarium of St Mary Magdalene."

Lady Apollonia could not suppress a shudder at the possibility of such a calling. Leprosy was, in her mind, the most horrible of disfiguring, tissue rotting diseases. Lepers were not only declared unclean, they were required by law to be kept away from any contact with the human community. Their hospital stood outside the city wall, and individual lepers, when on the streets, were forced to maintain their distance from everyone, warning aloud of their presence. They were regarded as the living dead, allowed to possess nothing, not even legal protection.

Francis could not help being aware of her shuddering reaction. "Oh, dear Lady, please do not allow yourself to be frightened by the residents of our leper hospital. I have found those who live within St Mary Magdalene to be the most patient, most faithful, and most loving of all God's children. Even when they no longer have fingers or whole hands, they continue to raise their arms in praise of God."

"Friar Francis," Apollonia begged, "pray, forgive me. My ignorance of the lepers' disease and their wretched condition in life is my only excuse. I shall try to observe your ministry as the most perfect imitation of the life of our Lord Christ, and I truly hope you will continue to visit me, bring news of your patients, help me to see them as you see them, and show me how I may support you in all that you do."

Friar Francis was thrilled by her declared interest in the leper hospital. He gladly promised he would find ways to bring her news of his life at St Mary Magdalene. "My daily prayers to St Giles will be that all people may come to a greater understanding of this dreadful affliction. But, my Lady, I shall also offer my prayers to St Apollonia in thanks for you, for your willingness to help me in my time of trouble, and your gracious goodness in seeking to establish my innocence. You alone have preserved my life's calling, and I shall always be your willing servant."

Chapter Four

Phyllis of Bath

The Lady of Aust was pleasantly surprised to find Canon Chulmleigh awaiting her in the hall of Exeter House after morning prayers. He seemed his usual congenial self, offering his greetings but also adding, "I could not fail to return and express my heartfelt apologies for abandoning your party during our tour of the cathedral."

"Canon Chulmleigh, we were overwhelmed by the grandeur and beauty of the cathedral; we could not possibly take it in through one brief visit. Exeter's cathedral church is wondrous beyond our imagining, but you were able to help us focus our eyes and our understanding upon especially meaningful detail. Pray be seated. May I continue to probe your accumulated knowledge of the cathedral's building and design?"

"Gracious Lady, ask any question, pursue any idea, and I shall be your most willing library." With that, the canon sat back in his chair as if prepared to remain as long as needed.

"I have enjoyed learning more about the grand churches of France and England," Apollonia began. "Through my French studies, I have heard of the great cathedrals of Chartres and Paris, earlier built in the newest style. Yet the French churches have significant differences in their overall design and construction from our great English churches such as Exeter Cathedral."

The canon lifted one eyebrow at her surprising observation. "I must tell you, my Lady, none other amongst the laity has ever noted these differences to me, much less asked about them. I presume you are referring to the variations in height and length between great churches in France, when compared to our English cathedrals?"

"Your insight never ceases, Canon Chulmleigh," the Lady smiled. She enjoyed the company of this scholarly man who was willing to share his intellectual observations with a woman. "Indeed, I have been told the great French Cathedral of our Lady in Chartres is built to extraordinary height, that its vaulting soars beyond a hundred and twenty feet overhead, whilst I could not help but be aware that Exeter Cathedral's vaults fly to little more than half of that height. Yet, when I observed the great length of Exeter's cathedral church, you told us that its vaulting continues unbroken for more than three hundred feet."

The canon sat back in his chair and drew a great breath, furiously exhaling! "I shall try to speak adequately towards the insightful points that you raise," he said. "But perhaps it will be helpful at first to point out some differences between the French and English interpretations of liturgical use of the new style of church building. Clearly, the new style of design comes to us from France, as it was first inspired by the writings of Saint Denys, the Areopagite. He wrote of a quest for geometric planning in church building that was combined with a desire for luminosity. In other words, the great churches of the Isle de France sought to achieve harmony in proportion, while flooding their interiors with divine light. Therefore, their vaults soar to great height, whilst their walls are transformed into huge glass windows." He paused and looked to the Lady to gauge her grasp of what he had said.

He could see that she not only followed his reasoning, she seemed enthusiastically expectant for that which would follow. Therefore, he continued, "Here in England our great churches are also built to achieve mathematical proportion and balance, and we also construct them with great stained glass windows to fill their interiors with light and luminous colour. But the height of the vaulting is not considered liturgically required. We prefer to address the importance of clerical procession throughout our great churches. We stress harmonious construction filled with sacred design and story, so that every heart may be uplifted, and every eye filled with a sense of heavenly vision here on earth. Even more, as we process from west to east, we also seek to symbolize the length of our earthly lives striving towards the universal hope of achieving the heavenly Jerusalem." He looked to her once again and asked, "Am I being helpful or merely adding layers of confusion to your thoughts?"

"Canon Chulmleigh, you are a learned teacher. Thanks to you, I can envision, within my feeble imagination, comparisons between English and French cathedrals. But you have also granted me better understanding of sacred meanings within the design and sacred carvings we experienced yesterday," she said sincerely.

"Of course," the canon continued, "we must also be aware that Exeter Cathedral's great length of unbroken vaulting is made possible by the lack of a central tower. Exeter built upon the footprint of its earlier Norman cathedral and is therefore unique amongst our English cathedrals. It is constructed with two side towers, surviving from the earlier Norman church, now opened to create its crossing. The vaulting continues unbroken because there is no central tower between the nave and the high altar of the presbytery to interrupt its flow."

"Of course," she said, "I had forgotten Exeter's lack of western towers. Thank you for sharing your insights with me, Canon Chulmleigh, but may we also return briefly to our discussion of the foliate face?" Apollonia asked him. She could see the canon's expression darken.

"I fear you have been somewhat arrested in your study of religious symbols, my Lady," he sighed. Then the canon suddenly sat forward in his chair and changed the subject of their discussion completely. "Pray, allow me to reveal to you yet another reason for my visit this morning?"

Lady Apollonia lifted her eyes towards him and with a gentle nod encouraged him to continue. "Is there any way in which I may be of service to you?" she asked.

Canon Chulmleigh inhaled noisily and expelled breath, as if to express his frustration. "Indeed, my Lady, my fellow clergy and I would be most grateful for your helpful advice regarding a troubling matter within the diocese."

"Pray continue," Apollonia encouraged him, "but I must confess that I feel most inadequate to deal with any theological discussion."

"My Lady, we the clergy of the diocese request your assistance with a human difficulty of which I am certain you are the singular person to help us." Canon Chulmleigh cleared his throat, thought silently for several moments, and then continued, "Have you encountered a woman of substance living in nearby St Thomas parish, who has been most successful in our growing cloth industry? Her name is Phyllis of Bath, and she worships regularly in the Chapel of St Thomas on the far side of the bridge cross the River Exe."

"Truly, I have heard her name mentioned in the markets, and she seems to have achieved considerable respect from those with whom she deals," Apollonia replied.

"The young curate of her parish chapel has complained to the bishop, and the bishop has consulted the dean and chapter. The curate is unable to contain her!" the canon exclaimed.

"I pray thee, Canon Chulmleigh," Apollonia said with a grimace, "what is it the young curate complains must be 'contained' regarding Phyllis of Bath?"

"In a word, my Lady, it is her speech, her free and open descriptions of her lustful physical behaviour with five different husbands!" Canon Chulmleigh said, most uncomfortably. "The young curate has often spoken forcefully with her, he tells us. He is certain that her assertions can only lead the young girls of his congregation into lives of great impurity. But Phyllis responds that his choice of celibacy only makes him unable to advise any woman. She says Holy Scripture insists that humans must reproduce. She quotes religious texts telling us of Old Testament fathers who had many wives, and whom God blessed." The canon paused to wipe his forehead.

"As you may guess, my Lady, I am most uneasy in speaking of such things, but I know you are a mature lady of reputable family. May I ask if you have any suggestions as to how we may respond? This woman has proved the intensity of her Christian faith through accomplishing many pilgrimages, including those to Jerusalem in the East and Compostela in the West. I feel we must tread very carefully in this matter."

Apollonia did not respond immediately. Nodding, she lowered her eyes briefly and smiled inwardly, as she could indeed sense the canon's personal discomfort. After a matter of several minutes, Apollonia addressed her friend with positive enthusiasm. "Canon Chulmleigh, do you think it might be helpful for me to extend a hand of friendship with Phyllis of Bath, from one woman to another who shares common interest in the local cloth markets?"

"Oh, Lady Apollonia, could you consider making such a gesture?" the canon said with a slight pleading in his voice.

"I shall indeed be pleased to make her acquaintance and exchange ideas that may be profitable to both of us. But I cannot promise to correct her lusty speech or control her enthusiasm," Apollonia assured him. "Nor will I promise to 'contain' Phyllis. I can only attempt to help her be more considerate of her young curate's keen embarrassment."

"Gramercy, my Lady, I know you will endeavor to speak with her in friendship but also with discretion," the canon said, rising from his chair.

As Canon Chulmleigh offered his good day and prepared to leave the hall, Apollonia sensed that he walked slightly taller, perhaps relieved of a sense of burden or even enlarged by some hope of improvement. He had never personally encountered Phyllis of Bath, but he had heard of her earthy speech, even in company with members of the cathedral clergy. He would continue to pray that such a meeting might never occur.

* * *

The following day Apollonia called Nan to come to her from the midst of other household duties. As Nan came into the hall, she found Apollonia and Stafford finishing their morning's tasks and preparing to go off somewhere. Whenever the Lady planned to leave her home, Nan knew she could never proceed alone; the Lady must be accompanied by some members of her household, usually Stafford, her steward, and Nan. So the petite lady's maid asked with some small sense of adventure, "Shall we be travelling this morning, my Lady?"

"Yes indeed, Nan, but we shall not venture far, merely to St Thomas parish across the river to make a social call." Lady Apollonia was busily reassembling a collection of contracts for Stafford to return to their proper shelves when she continued to instruct Nan. "Would you kindly speak with Gareth and ask him to bring our horses round to the mounting block in front by ten of the clock?" The Lady looked up from her collection of documents. "And would you also bring my cloak and be prepared to join us for our journey at that hour?"

As always Nan was pleased to be sent to speak with Gareth, who could easily be found in his favourite realm of the barn or stable. Nan barely understood her true feelings for the stablemaster, but she never questioned them. Most people who encountered him thought Gareth to be an extraordinarily handsome man but one so painfully shy that no one else in the household knew him personally. Nan respected his preferred withdrawal from others, indeed from much social contact at all. She knew and treasured the occasions when he would always welcome her as Lady Apollonia's messenger.

In truth, she enjoyed seeing Gareth on any occasion, to be quietly allowed to admire him, while always thrilled by his respectful acknowledgement of her as the Lady's closest personal servant. Nan thought herself to be of similar age with Gareth, but whereas he was comely and well built, she was petite, thin, and hopelessly plain. She expected no favours of Gareth, but she treasured his awkward friendship and regarded him to be the nearest person she had ever known of godlike proportions.

Walking into the stable first, she found him teaching one of the new lads how best to clean and refresh the horses' stalls. He used few words and preferred to demonstrate how to do it, but once done, he expected a careful repetition by all who served under him. As soon as he noticed Nan had entered the barn, he put his rake to one side and swiftly doffed his broad brimmed hat.

"God's blessings upon you, Gareth," Nan greeted him warmly. "I do admire how you manage to keep the barn as clean and tidy as any dwelling."

Gareth blushed but was truly pleased when anyone noticed how orderly and well kept his outbuildings always were. "Wha brings ye, Mistress Nan?" he asked.

The little maid felt her heart leap as he spoke her Christian name, but looking down towards her folded hands, she quietly responded. Nan told him that their Lady requested mounts be prepared for herself, Stafford, and Nan. They should be ready and waiting at the front mounting block by ten of the clock that morning.

Without another word, Gareth replaced his hat and strode away.

* * *

Gareth was waiting with their horses at the appointed hour. He deferentially removed his hat while holding the Lady's palfrey steady to assist her mount. "What a lovely day, Gareth," Lady Apollonia said, mounting the block and slipping into her side saddle. "You have groomed Patience so beautifully; she seems ready to be presented to the world." In truth the lady's horse, Patience, seemed to have an extra bounce in her step as she moved from the block. Gareth's face reddened with pleasure at the Lady's expression of appreciation for his hard work. Apollonia's horse, as if grateful for her momentary celebrity, lifted each hoof smartly and carried Apollonia in a large circle about the road in front of Exeter House.

After Nan and Stafford were mounted and ready, the Lady called back to her stablemaster. "Please tell Mary Mathe we shall return before sunset, Gareth."

With that their party started up the hill on Northgate Street towards the High Street, trotting single file to avoid the sewer drains. They continued by way of Smythen Street and began to descend Stepcote Hill, down from the plateau of the city centre towards the river. Soon they approached Exeter's city wall and rode on to leave the town through its West Gate.

It was a radiant day with sun's rays burnishing the landscape while white clouds scudded across the blue heavens. Apollonia could not help rejoicing to inhale the sheer beauty of venturing out to the countryside, so welcome to her rural soul. But a grotesque panorama of disgust assailed them as they had to ride beneath a collection of body parts, chiefly heads and limbs of criminals, decaying on poles above the city gate. Carrion birds screeched to pull away pieces of rotting flesh. Apollonia lowered her head and closed her eyes until they had passed through the gate. They could see the River Exe ahead of them, marked by its meandering mud banks, shaped and manipulated by the flooding and receding of autumn rains. Suddenly, as they rode, the winds shifted, blowing towards them from the South.

"Dear God have mercy!" the Lady gasped. She exhaled noisily, and her hand flew to her nose. She was not alone amongst the party to lower her head as the winds' currents from down river enshrouded them in a great cloud of stench. The filthy odour issued about them with the wind from Exeter's Shytebrook, an ancient stream used to provide a flow of sewage and excrement from outside the city wall of Exeter, downhill and into the larger, flowing currents of the River Exe.

The blessing of a dramatic shift in the direction of the wind allowed Apollonia's party to lift their heads and take in the view once again. "Oh, my Lady," Nan gasped in amazement, "do look at that marvelous bridge across the river." She held her hands above her eyes to gaze ahead at eighteen massive arches, built of local volcanic stone, reaching across the entire width of the River Exe. From their distance, the Exe Bridge could be seen to have a chapel built at each end of it, and although the bridge was narrow, each pier was complete with a recess built on its top to allow the groups of people on foot to tuck safely aside when wide carts were drawn past them.

Stafford said little but was obviously taken with this bridge as he too had never seen anything like it before. He pressed back his hat, put his hand above his eyes to shield them from the sun, and slowed his horse to a halt to take in the entirety of it.

Apollonia slowed to see the entire bridge from the height of the roadway, before they began the descent to cross it. "Truly, Nan, I can not believe there are many bridges such as this anywhere in the kingdom except London, certainly few others in the West Country."

The Lady led the party in their turning towards the bridge and, as they approached it, stopped to admire the chapel of St Edmund's, built upon two of the eastern arches. Narrow houses were built upon the bridge, too, so that its surface always seemed alive with the to and fro movement of people, animals, carts, and horsemen. Once they had begun to cross the central arches, they could look down upon the river.

As they reached the western end of the bridge, they found the chapel dedicated to St Thomas a Becket that served as parish church to the small community on the St Thomas side of the Exe. Apollonia stopped her horse and dismounted quickly to enter the church and light a candle, while Nan and Stafford waited outside holding Patience's reins. The Lady did not remain long inside the chapel, but she wished to have some idea of its interior because she knew it was the church of their intended hostess, Phyllis of Bath, and her tormented vicar.

* * *

Stafford led them easily to the lane leading to Reliant Cottage, as it sat upon a small rise in the lowlands of rich alluvial soil on the west side of the River Exe. It had been built as an imposing three room, cross passage house with outbuildings in the rear and lovely gardens, their beds lined in green hedge, across the front. Tying their horses to a wooden pole fence, Lady Apollonia and her party began to walk through the garden's path towards the main entrance. Nan preceded them and pulled the bell. A tidy, young maid appeared at the door and admitted Nan, who had been instructed to introduce the presence of her Lady and express her desire to call upon the mistress of the cottage. The Lady Apollonia of Aust, she was to say, had learned from several members of the cloth guild of Mistress Phyllis's fellow membership and wished to be allowed to make her acquaintance.

Within a matter of minutes, Phyllis of Bath emerged with a great flurry of welcoming arms and hospitable assurances. "M'Lady o Aust," she shouted in greeting. "Oi too ave eard o yer presence in o'r city an ave longed ta meet ye. Yer successes be th envy o many a mann in Exeter, whilst Oi vow em ta be th pride o ev'ry female in th wool trade, sech as Oi be. Please ta grant us th pleasure o yer comp'ny."

Stafford walked behind his Lady and Nan into the cottage, and the group found themselves standing within a darkly paneled parlor, warmed by a great fireplace reaching through the roof. "As ye see afore ye, th fireplaces be moi newest betterment o Reliant Cottage," Phyllis said enthusiastically. She also seemed pleased to call their attention to the beautifully painted, wooden screens passage dividing the parlor from the hall.

"Ifn ye can imagine sech a primitive construct, m'Lady, th all behin dis screens passage ad in th centre o its floor a great open arth! Jus think on th smoke flowin inta th all afore goen up an out thru th thatch," she said, laughing at the idea. "Th roof timbers o moi all be still smoke blackened! Bu Oi ave built two new fireplaces ta warm th rooms an draw th smoke directly up'ard thru th chimneys," she said, with obvious pride. "Bu enuf o me rattlin on. Oi pray ye, please do seat yerse'ves an alow us ta bring ale. Ye mus ave a mighty thirst awfter yer ride from Exeter."

Lady Apollonia sat in the chair offered her, near to another where Phyllis would sit. Stafford and Nan stood on either side of her chair until Phyllis had stools brought for each of them. A large, drooping hound pulled his extended stomach across the floor on very short legs, and Lady Apollonia bent to pet his head. He not only slathered her hand with his long, wet tongue, he settled himself next to her chair and seemed content to remain.

"Ye mus nay mind Arry, m'Lady," Phyllis said, noticing the hound's preference to sit near Apollonia's chair. "Ee be a great lover, bu Oi do keep im on short lead an, Oi confess, do overfeed im reglar."

"Mistress Phyllis," Lady Apollonia began, "pray, accept my thanks for your gracious welcome. As you seem already aware, I am newly arrived in Exeter and am struggling to acquaint myself with all that it can offer us in the woollen trade. My husband, Edward, and I have our home in a very small village called Aust on the banks of the Severn River in Gloucestershire, but our interests in cloth making require us to establish a presence here in Devon."

"Ow be it den dat ye coom ta Exeter alone, m'Lady?" Phyllis continued to probe. "Do'n ee, yer usband Oi mean, rule th roost? Wher be ee?" she asked, as if unaware of the impertinence of her question. Apollonia could hear Stafford groan and sniff noisily.

"You are very keen in your observations, Mistress Phyllis," Apollonia replied. "My dear Edward is required to be in London, whilst I am here to represent our interests. Edward and I share equally our work, as well as our profits, and we each bring different strengths to complement the other's contributions to our ventures."

"Praise be, m'Lady, ye be blessed ta ave zo educated yer mann. Ow many wives as ee ad, an ow many usbands did ye take afore ye cou'd create dis mawsterful union?

"I am first wife to my dear Edward, but I confess that he is my second husband."

"Oh aye, bu ye ave coom early to sech unnerstandin. Oi ave ad five usbands an th fifth on, ee wer th best. Bu we did war again each udder many a day, til at last ee granted me person'ood an freedom ta be mese'v. Oi loved im very well," Phyllis said with some longing in her voice, "bu Oi wou'dn min findin yet anodder sixth!"

Apollonia smiled warmly and confessed that she too missed her husband while he was forced to be apart from her, but she told Phyllis that whilst he was gone, she must get on with their work. "Would you be willing to share with me any recommendations you have gained whilst working with the members of the cloth guilds here in Exeter?"

"Aye, m'Lady, dere be sev'ral thin's Oi wou'd recommend ta elp ye." Their conversation went on to discuss the finishing of cloth, so central to the businesses of Exeter. Thanks to the city's abundance of water and the group of mills already built along the leats on the island called the Shilhay, Exeter was growing into one of the most important cities of the West Country. Mistress Phyllis recommended that Apollonia seek the services of her favourite fulling mill.

"Tis all due ta th excellence o th miller oo directs it, m'Lady," she said assuringly. "Ee'll ne'er look down pon ye as a woman, nor try ta cheat an take advantage. Martyn th Miller do kno is craft, an ye can trust all that ee says. Ee ne'er drinks when ee's workin, an ee ne'er lets th women o is piss carts drink when dey be gatherin u-rine from th taverns an inns!" she said with complete confidence.

Apollonia was well aware of the importance of the use of human urine to prepare cloth for fulling, and she was grateful for Phyllis's recommendation of a good fulling mill. But as she noticed the afternoon was passing, she decided to alter their conversation slightly.

"I was able to stop in your chapel of St Thomas Becket as we made our journey across the bridge," Apollonia told Phyllis. "It is my custom to light a candle in thanks of all God's gifts to our lives, whenever such opportunity presents itself. I could not help noticing what a lovely chapel you have to serve this parish."

"Oh aye," Phyllis agreed with her, "th bridge chapel o St Thomas do serve us well, bu o'r young vicar, ee needs ta grow up a bit."

"How so, Mistress Phyllis?" Apollonia encouraged her. "Is he not well prepared to serve as your priest?"

"M'Lady," Phyllis paused as she spoke. Then she began again, "We, ye an Oi, be women o th present day, bu we also kno's well th ancient truths o life. Can ye follow moi meanin?"

Apollonia nodded, so Phyllis continued, "O'r vicar be nay on'y foolishly young, ee as no unnerstandin o real life. Celibate ee be fur Oly Church, bu ee's kno'en nay uman life neither. So when th young maids o St Thomas Parish go's ta im fur confession, ee angs eavy penance pon der souls fur doin wha th Lord in eaven created us fur doin. When dey comes ta me, Oi tells em straight out, th Virgin Mary does nay wish dey be virgin. Oi tells em dey mus do th penance bu den think ne more bou it. Spread yer legs an gather in th seed, whilst ye be young and merry, Oi says!"

Nan and Stafford could be seen feeling some discomfort at the frankness of Phyllis's speech, but Apollonia thought she could discern her good intent. "Do you have any idea of the age of your vicar?" she asked.

"Oh aye, m'Lady, Oi swear ee be on an twenty," she responded, "bu do'n ye see, ee nay be offerin spiritual guidance an blessin, on'y judgement pon t'ese young maids. Ee may be true ta is callin in th church, bu dcy mus be readyin ta ave babies!"

Apollonia was silent a moment and then said to their hostess, "I have been blessed as the mother of five sons, Mistress Phyllis. The two elder are already striving to prepare themselves to serve the king as warriors. But two of my younger three sons may, I believe, eventually find themselves in the church. My husband and I agree wholeheartedly with you that anyone who seeks to enter the church must be made aware of the matters of 'real life' as you put it. But as your young vicar seems unprepared to understand the needs of the young maids of your parish, perhaps he needs to be told some facts of 'real life.' May we not suggest that he seek guidance from an older man of the church?" Apollonia asked her.

Phyllis's face brightened at the thought of a helpful solution. "Indeed, m'Lady, oo may th churchman be?"

"I know a very fine canon of the cathedral in Exeter who would willingly serve as your vicar's counsel." Apollonia went on to tell Phyllis of the location of the residence of Canon Chulmleigh in the Cathedral Close. Then she recommended that when Phyllis next would speak with the young vicar, she should also mention that he tell the good canon, "Lady Apollonia of Aust has encouraged their meeting."

"Oh truly, dis be th bes ope fur im," Phyllis said.

"But also, Mistress Phyllis, we, you and I as women of age and experience, must seek to be sensitive when in the presence of young churchmen. As you have noted truly, their celibacy does limit their experience of 'real life,'" Apollonia reminded her.

"Be dat as may be," Phyllis winked at the Lady, "we 'women o age an experience' do kno o some in th church nay so celibate nor so unaware o 'real life,' ain't it be zo?"

* * *

There was no one about the Cathedral Close in the early dawn hours. There were no ears to hear the small, metallic creakings of the great, round, grass and weed covered lid and no eyes to see as it was lifted from its surroundings. On many earlier occasions, too, the same hands lifting the iron cap pushed it slowly upward, so that the eyes below it could peer in all directions to assure that the visit would go unobserved. Then, powerful arms pushed the heavy cap to one side, and a lithe body lifted itself onto the surface of the graveyard.

He moved quietly across the grass until close to the walls of the darkened cathedral but this time did not seek a hiding place to conceal his presence near its doors. Instead, the shadowy figure walked silently between the west front portals of the cathedral and the Church of St Mary Major. Once past the church, he stole towards the smaller walled area of green, surrounding the deanery. Nimbly and easily he climbed the locked gate and darted swiftly into the deanery garden. Pausing again to assure himself no one was about, he darted on into the shadows beneath the deanery's stone window arches. Then he continued to walk the perimeter of the dean's ancient lodging.

Suddenly from the darkness, a harsh growling and barking began snapping at his heels. It was a small watch dog but one who took its responsibilities to guard and protect as loudly as possible. The dark figure bent over, lifted the dog into his arms, and closed his hand around its muzzle. The dog grew silent, unafraid of the kind hands gently petting it, so the intruder continued his exploration of the dean's garden and carried the dog with him. Looking to take something personally meaningful to the dean, the dark figure tried windows and doors but could find no access.

Chapter Five

Apollonia's Chapel

Father Anthony closed the morning office of Lauds for the Aust household with his blessing and sent them all out into their world in peace. Lady Apollonia rose from her knees, crossed herself reverently, and returned to her seat, feeling neither peaceful nor spiritually calmed by her daily renewal through worship. The Lady realised that she too was longing for their ancient family chapel at home in Aust, where all the members of the Aust affinity retreated several times each day. Here, in Exeter House, they could only gather for worship in a large storage chamber just off the great hall. Her chaplain, Father Anthony, had consecrated the altar and continued to offer each of them the offices of the day, the mass, and regular confession. The Lady knew she was not alone. Everyone in her household seemed to be missing their ancient chapel, and as one of the boys from the stable was heard to object when leaving service, "T'aint like goin ta church, is it?"

Apollonia remained seated in his presence, but she looked towards her chaplain. "If you please, Father Anthony, may we speak together?"

Anthony, anticipating some personal fear or religious quandary may be troubling, sat himself beside her. "I dorste swear, my Lady, I shall remain gladly."

With no further introduction, she looked up from her missal and asked him pointedly, "Father Anthony, how may we build a chapel here for our private use, whilst we live in Exeter House? You are priest to each and every one of us, but I fear we as a household are struggling in our worship together, because, as young Liam just said, we do not feel ourselves in church."

"My Lady, you are better instructed than most to know that God lives in the hearts of all His children and will hear them wherever they call upon Him," Anthony said carefully. "Why should you feel stranger to His love, simply because we have no chapel here in which to worship?"

"Oh not alienated from God, not at all, Father Anthony, I have misspoke," Apollonia said. Then she added quickly, "I sense that members of our household gather here to fulfill their obligation to me but are not finding a true spirit of worship, because of our lack of sacred space. It seems to me that our family, household, or affinity, however you wish to call us, is losing its sense of oneness. We are devoted to each other as nearly as family, but we must feel ourselves to be Christ's servants first. That is how we begin every day and celebrate closing every evening. That is what calls us together, defines us, and comforts us." Apollonia stopped speaking. At loss for further words, she looked into Anthony's eyes, asking for his understanding of the problem she sensed and his help in finding its correction.

Father Anthony had always found his residence in the household of Aust to be his personal ministry and more. Lady Apollonia and her husband, Edward, sincerely felt their responsibilities to offer sustenance to the poor, healing to the sick, and comfort to all those who were in mourning. As their chaplain and priest, Anthony was enabled, through their generous support to provide alms, visit the sick, as well as those who mourned, and still spend time in his personal devotion to study. Edward and Apollonia were grateful for the priest's willingness to serve as early educator to their sons and moral counselor to their household.

"As priest and teacher, my Lady, I am aware there are many families of means these days finding themselves desirous of a private chapel. Is it not possible to transform this space? Do you not think we could slightly alter the design of this high ceiling chamber, with its great exterior wall, to create a more perfect sense of sacred space here? It is certainly large enough to become a chapel."

Apollonia looked about herself at the chamber in which they sat together. It had previously been used only for heavy storage by the merchant who originally built Exeter House. But its sheer size began to fire her imagination. The space was a basic cube, but she could envision some glorious possibilities: the installation of oak ribbed arches, reaching upward from a series of pilasters built onto the two side walls; niches for their name saints; and, most especially, an elegantly traceried rose window, showering its stained glass lights upon the altar below.

"I should love to create a chapel dedicated to Our Lady in memory of my mother," she said. "Do you think it may be possible?"

"Bishop Brantyngham is known to be very encouraging to families within his diocese who seek to do that," Anthony told her. "I would think that we must seek his licence first and then call in the masons."

"Father Anthony, will you consent to be my guide as well as our spiritual advisor in this venture?" Apollonia asked him. "I am thrilled to consider building our chapel, but I have no experience and feel truly unprepared to take on such a project."

"Lady Apollonia, my first call is to serve my God and minister to His people." Anthony seemed animated by her request. "But I shall be delighted to assist you, in any way that I can, to build an extension of holy church here within your household."

"First, I must write to Edward and share our ideas with him," Apollonia said with obvious enthusiasm.

Anthony noted with a smile that she said, "Share *our* ideas."

Then she went on, "We shall pursue the licence and seek the bishop's blessing. How soon do you believe we may call in a master builder?"

* * *

Canon Chulmleigh was waiting in the parlour of the deanery, because he had been summoned by the dean. The canon suspected that there must have been another threatening incident of the noxious green man image. He could not believe how any person continued to gain access within the walls of the Cathedral Close and still not be observed by any of the canons, clergy, vicars, or staff who constantly walked within its precincts. Chulmleigh knew that the custor, who lived in the little flat above the north porch entrance to the cathedral and was present every day and through every night, had been warned after each incident that his vigilance must be increased. The custor defended himself rigorously. He was, he insisted, always on the alert, but he had never seen the slightest movement during those nights when vandalism was done or scurrilous acts were performed.

Disturbances within the Close were not unusual during daytime hours, as young people and ruffians from the town enjoyed using the graveyard's space between cathedral and the churches of the Close for their rowdy games. Fights often resulted, so that the dean and chapter would sometimes have to call for assistance from the city officials to help calm the fray and arrest the unruly. Canon Chulmleigh was never entirely comfortable with the idea of seeking help outside the Close, but he was well aware of a kind of working balance that had been in place for decades between the city government and the cathedral chapter.

Nearly a hundred years before, an incident of great violence had occurred just outside the door of one of the canon's houses within the Close. In a quarrel between the then bishop of Exeter and the dean of the cathedral, citizens of the town had been charged with striking down and murdering the chapter precentor as he left the cathedral after Matins in the early morning hours. Legal proceedings against those charged progressed slowly until two years later, the King of England, Edward I, came to Exeter to settle the case in person.

After the trials were over, King Edward encouraged the cathedral clergy to surround the Close with a wall and series of gates. Since that time the Cathedral Close had been a "walled" precinct within the walled city, and the dean and chapter had felt confident in the added protection. Not only the cathedral canons, but all of the churches and chapels of the Close shared that sense of protection. "But what has happened to our defensive walls now?" Canon Chulmleigh muttered to himself. "We seem to be as vulnerable to violation as any slum of the city."

Dean Thomas Walkyngton came into the parlour with a dolorous grimace set rigidly upon his face. "I feel unable to deal with this endless onslaught," he said to Canon Chulmleigh. "Last night the demon killed the deanery watchdog and left this hateful message strung upon his body."

The canon took from the dean's hands yet another official indulgence with the bishop's seal, replaced by a foliate face spewing forth the words, "NORMAN DOGS MUST SUFFER."

"Dear friend, I am truly sorry it has come to this," Chulmleigh said with sincere disgust. "If this malevolence has now become a personal threat against you, perhaps we must reconsider. Is it not time for us to seek the protection of the sheriff and his men?"

"Chulmleigh, you know as well as I relations between the chapter and the town have often been tense. I do not wish for that to reoccur. We must determine for ourselves the identity of the possible enemies we face. It may very well be some official from the town. But who would use the image of the foliate face upon an indulgence, or who would wish to declare ongoing terms of judgement against the clergy of the cathedral with the accusation 'Norman Dog?'"

"Well, Dean Walkyngton, in truth nearly all of us in chapter have some relation to old Norman families. The King himself claims descent from William the Conqueror. But in these days, do we not all think of ourselves as English, not Norman? Must we seek some surviving Saxon line that lives on, determined to exact revenge for the Conquest?" the canon asked.

"Can we really be speaking of a grudge that survives from hundreds of years in the past?" the dean said in total exasperation. "William the Norman conquered England more than three centuries ago!"

"I dorst swear it seems beyond all belief, yet I must wonder," Chulmleigh went on. "Is it incumbent upon us to warn local people of Norman heritage that there may be some mad man going about uttering threats against them?"

"Stay my friend and colleague; let us not act rashly," the dean cautioned. "But I require of you to apply your scholarly mind to a careful examination of our cathedral records. Have we ever received such threats before, and, if so, from whom, why, and what was done about it?"

"Indeed, I shall remove at once to the library, but do you not think it wise to enlist some of our stronger vicars choral to patrol the Close through the nights ahead, as some small display of force?" Canon Chulmleigh asked.

"I shall speak with the precentor straightaway. It would seem that our vigilant guard must now become aggressive and more muscular."

* * *

It was midmorning the following day when Apollonia and Stafford were working through stacks of woven cloths. They had been brought to Exeter House from the collection of individual weavers living in shires throughout the West Country. Apollonia was instructing Stafford to have the cloths transported to the fulling mill of Martyn the Miller on the Isle of Shilhay. "Accompany the lads in this transport, Stafford, and make clear to the miller that we expect quality work from him, based upon his recommendation to us by our friend, Mistress Phyllis of Bath. But," she added to her Steward, "also imply that the investment from Aust enterprise here in Exeter may grow significantly, if we find the excellence in his craftsmanship we have been promised."

Stafford stood next to the Lady, nodding to Apollonia while wiping his nose and bending in deference to receive her instructions. "Yes, m'Lady, it shall be done as you say," he sniffed. But when the young lads arrived in hall to begin carrying stacks of folded cloth out to their wagon, Stafford reassumed his full height, not only asserting his superior position in their errand, but also determined to inform the party just who was issuing orders. "Keep those bundles orderly, and mind how you stack them!" his deep voice commanded, as he stomped out to the waiting cart.

Apollonia had seated herself behind the hall table with quill and a large sheet of parchment at hand. She used a straightedge to outline the bare walls of Exeter House's storeroom, intended to become her new chapel. She began to sketch her ideas of a series of elegantly carved, wooden arches pointing upward from stone pilasters she intended built along the walls. The arches would create a sense of church like vaulting within the chapel ceiling. Then with a string, she encompassed a beautifully, round opening in the exterior wall where she hoped to place a rose window above the altar. She was in such a state of concentration that she did not hear the approach of her maid, Nan, and was startled by the sound of her voice.

"My Lady, Canon Chulmleigh has asked to be received," she said in her usual quiet manner.

"Oh, my dear Nan, pray do forgive my inattention. I am always delighted by the canon's visits. Please bring him to the hall and see that another chair is placed near to mine."

As Nan left, Apollonia covered over her drawing and stood to greet him as he entered. "Welcome, Canon Chulmleigh," she said enthusiastically. "It is my favourite surprise to welcome you and wish God's blessings upon your day."

"Benedicete, my Lady of Aust. I bring blessings upon you and your entire household. I do hope I have not interrupted important matters of commerce," he said, as he seated himself across the table from her.

"Your arrival is perfectly timed and many times welcome," Apollonia said. "I have a number of concerns I wish to share with you."

"Our concerns shared will surely become accomplishments if I may assist you in any way," the canon said. He had long ago devoted his life to the service of God, but Canon Chulmleigh enjoyed the company of the Lady of Aust. As a gentleman, he had never lost the gracious courtliness of his manner with ladies. He possessed no desire to suggest flirtation or inspire coquetry; he simply revealed his early upbringing in a household devoted to the gallant ideals of chivalry. In truth, he had grown to admire the Lady Apollonia, not because of her beauty but because of her intelligence and open hearted honesty.

"I have called upon Phyllis of Bath," Apollonia told the canon, "as I told you I should do, and found her to be an extraordinary woman. She has succeeded, through her own wit and hard work, to achieve an admirable position of earnings and place amongst the local merchants. And she is so entirely open as to how she did it."

Chulmleigh only responded with a slight cough, as if reluctant to comment further upon her "openness," but he did ask Apollonia if she had determined how they might control her bawdy speech when in the presence of her young vicar.

"Mistress Phyllis has offered an inspired idea to help her vicar," Apollonia told him. "She suggested to me that he must be informed of real life, as discussed in the Old and New Testaments, so that he may be enabled to minister to the realities of his young maiden parishioners. I recommended to her that she send the vicar to speak with you, not only as his father in the Church but as a father figure able to cure him of extraordinary innocence."

The Lady looked down into her lap and then added, "I truly believe you are the man to help him, Canon Chulmleigh. But please know that I also urged Phyllis to strive to become more sensitive in her speech when she is with the young vicar. She told me that she is aware of the limits his priestly, celibate life requires of him, and I believe she will not only try to become less bawdy but may even attempt to become more motherly in his presence."

"My Lady of Aust, you will have achieved wonders in behalf of our young vicar, should all this come to pass," Canon Chulmleigh enthused. "Of course, it was good of you to suggest that he be sent to me, as I believe I may share some personal, masculine experiences helpful to his dilemma. But if you are able to encourage Phyllis of Bath to become more gentle in her speech, I think you will have solved a great problem for all the clergy in the diocese."

"You credit me far too generously, Canon Chulmleigh, but I do thank you for your willingness to speak with the young vicar in this matter. And I hope my friendship with Mistress Phyllis will continue to grow." Then the Lady reached to the edge of the large parchment, covered over on her table, and slid it towards the canon for his perusal.

"There is yet another matter I wish to discuss with you. Dependent upon the advice of my chaplain and his counsel, I am beginning to consider ways to transform a large storeroom here in Exeter House into our family chapel. Chaplain Anthony has taken our request for such a licence to Bishop Brantyngham in the sincere hope that his grace will grant it."

"Hmmm, does this represent some of your ideas to guide the masons when they begin their design?" The canon reached into a pocket of his robe for a pair of lenses he kept there for use in his studies. The lenses were framed in a wooden *V* and attached to a central hinge, allowing the frame to open as needed when placed upon his nose. With the lenses then suspended in front of each of his eyes, he was able to look very closely at her drawing and see it well.

"I have these marvelous lenses from Naples, and they do strengthen my failing sight," he said, while continuing to scrutinize all aspects of her drawing. At last, he looked up with a question. "Are you certain that this wall is adequate to support such an opening for the rose window you propose above the altar?"

"Gramercy, canon, indeed I am not," Apollonia replied. "But when we begin, I shall put your question to the mason and ask if such an opening can be adequately buttressed."

"I am not well informed in techniques of building, but I do admire your design and will do all I can to encourage the bishop to speedily grant your licence. Many of the great families of Devon have sought to include a chapel within their homes. I have not always been convinced that their faith drives them to such purpose. Does it simply represent a further expression of their pride?" Then Canon Chulmleigh looked directly towards Apollonia and spoke in a more somber tone, "Can you tell me your reasons for creating such a chapel within your home, rather than seeking religious service in the cathedral or any number of churches and chapels nearby within the Close?"

"It is only right that you should question my motives, Canon Chulmleigh," Apollonia said quietly, "but I confess that my husband, Edward, and I are in complete agreement. We feel we need a chapel to serve as the religious heart of our household. Chaplain Anthony has maintained a high level of divine worship and confession for us whilst we have been in Exeter, but worship is enhanced when we gather in dedicated, sacred space with Christ's crucifix and the holy saints to inspire us. Do you not agree?" Apollonia looked to him for his response.

The canon nodded his head, so the Lady continued, "We are a household of twenty persons living together here, serving in the house, the kitchen, the stables, and the barns, more when our sons return from school. When we come together for chapel services, we are made aware of our shared status as children of God. This sense of being God's family defines us through the day, while reminding us that the love of Christ requires us to share His love with others. Forgive my theological limitations, Canon Chulmleigh, but my husband and I do believe the presence of a household chapel will encourage us all to be better servants of God."

"My Lady, I truly hope you do not feel that I was suggesting you or your husband is merely seeking some enhancement of status or an expression of family pride. But when we invest in God's House for our personal use, I believe we must be clear as to our motives. Few within my acquaintance would have expressed your household's needs in better theological terms," the canon told her honestly.

"But I also have very personal reasons," Apollonia went on. "I long to build a chapel dedicated to the Virgin Mary as a memorial to my mother."

"I take it your mother has died?" the canon asked.

"Her name was Mary, and she died when I was born," the Lady said. "My only images of her are those shared with me by my brother, Ferdinand, eight years my senior. He remembers how pitifully our mother endured ceaseless pain caused by toothache during her pregnancy. The midwives told her she would be unaware of the painful extraction of the offending tooth during her greater suffering of childbirth. It was she who dedicated my life to St Apollonia, and to whom, my brother told me, she continued to give thanks even during her own death throes."

"I can only encourage you to proceed as soon as you have received Bishop Brantyngham's licence," the canon continued. "And if I may, I should also like to recommend to you a young mason living here in Exeter. He has done outstanding work in several of our churches but is currently without employment. His name is William of Wedmore, and I believe he will be sensitive to all your desires in the construction and interior decoration of your new chapel. More importantly, he has travelled to Paris to study the methods of the masons of Sainte-Chapelle, and he can recreate the most beautifully designed and widely admired rose window in all Europe."

"How do you manage to anticipate my thoughts?" Apollonia asked. "Would you kindly pass on the name of Master William to

Chaplain Anthony? I am personally inspired to begin as soon as we may." She rose from her chair, as she could see the canon was about to take his leave. Extending her hand to wish him farewell, he held it warmly within both of his own.

"My Lady Apollonia, will you allow me to inquire how your husband has assured protection of you and your Exeter household in his absence?"

Apollonia could not be certain of the purpose of the canon's question, but she replied straightforwardly, "Edward and I regard ourselves and our affinity as rural people. I must add none of us has felt threatened by anyone in the city. Indeed, I have been most cordially received by the mayor, members of the guilds, as well as lady wives of several of our neighbors. Nearly everyone here has expressed welcome and hospitality to me. Should we worry ourselves about protection?"

The canon seemed to retreat into a spasm of generalities. "I do not mean to alarm you, my Lady, but your wealth, your ancient heritage, the well known excellence of your household, and your husband's continued absence could inspire some criminal jackanapes to seek to take advantage."

Apollonia thought to herself for a few moments and then spoke aloud, "I must confess I have never been concerned for my personal safety, Canon. Certainly, whilst we lived at home in Aust, I never gave the slightest thought to locking our doors. But perhaps you are correct to remind me that as we are now living in a city, I must remember to be more cautious. Thank you once again, Canon Chulmleigh. You are very kind to express your concerns, but as you know, I never go anywhere without the company of our steward, Stafford, and my personal maid, Nan. If I feel any of my errands require additional male force, I may call upon Gareth, our stablemaster, to accompany me."

The canon seemed relieved at the list of persons surrounding her. But in his heart of hearts, he wished she, and especially her Norman heritage, were not so well known in Exeter during recent days.

* * *

In the darkness of the early predawn hours of that following morning, the iron lid in the grass of the Cathedral Close was lifted tentatively, while eyes below peered furtively beyond its circle.

Singing voices, sharing bawdy tunes, seemed to be walking between the Church of St Mary Major and the cathedral graveyard. These were young men on guard in the Close. The powerful arms holding the cap allowed it to fall silently back into its place on the ground. "Not this night," he whispered to himself in the darkness. He struck a flint to light his candle, waiting for him in its usual holder, and made his way back through the underground passage.

"They will grow tired of watchfulness," he continued, "and I can wait."

Chapter Six

Tale of the Tumblers

Late each afternoon, the younger sons of Edward and Apollonia would return from the cathedral school, crashing into Exeter House through the kitchen door, simply because they were always ravenously hungry. Apollonia would be waiting there in the realm of her cook, Mary Mathe, to enjoy the explosive energy of their entry and their chorus of shouts, sharing the day's news and gossip as they gobbled warm bread and swallowed great gulps of watered wine.

"Mamam, Mamam!" Thomas at age ten always assumed leadership of the younger boys, though he had not been able to move beyond his early childhood mispronunciation of "Madame." "Mamam, can you imagine? There has been some sort of devil roaming about the Cathedral Green during the late night hours!"

"Coom naow, Thomas," Mistress Mathe scolded him gently from behind the great bowl she was beating furiously in preparation for their evening meal. "Ye mus nay frighten yer dear Lady Mother wit dem outlandish tales! Do have some o t'ese tasty figs. It wer a miracle, bu Oi was able ta find dem in th market dis morning."

"No, no Mamam! I only share with you truth. The men of the vicars choral have been on watch every night looking for some sort of devil in the Cathedral Close. My friend Colin, one of the older choristers, told me there have been evil signs and threats left after its visits. But no one has seen it, and no one knows how it is able to enter when the gates of the Close are locked after Compline."

"I do thank you sincerely, dearest Thomas, for I know you would never share falsehoods," Apollonia assured her middle son. "And I am also certain that the cathedral dean and chapter will be vigilant against any threat. They will seek out the perpetrator who is probably more human than demon."

"I shall take my sword and join them each night," young Alban said, with the assurance of a soldier. "No such creature threatening Christ's church shall escape my vigilance." At age seven, Alban thought of himself as a man and was longing to join his elder brothers, Hugh and Chad, who had already entered the household of their Uncle Ferdinand to be schooled as knights.

"Your sword must rest for the moment, Alban, my love," Apollonia said pointedly. "You know your father and I desire you to apply yourself first to your studies with the clerks. We believe your display of warrior's prowess will wait until you are older." Passing on some figs to her son, she could not miss noticing the scowl wrinkling his freckled face. Alban slipped away, with one fig in his cheek and several more in his hands, as he walked out through the kitchen door towards the stable.

"I learned the most lovely story today, Mamam," little David said to Apollonia as he pulled gently upon her sleeve.

"Come hither and tell me all, Davie," Apollonia said, as she lifted her youngest into her lap. "You know I do love a good story."

In every way, David still seemed so much her baby; Apollonia found it difficult to send him off to school each day. But early in his young life, it had become obvious that David was blessed with an especially sweet, clear boy soprano voice. The choir master of the cathedral was sparing in his words of praise, but he was obviously pleased to hope that David would join his youngest group of brilliant voices.

"It was Vicar Clarence who showed us where to find the Tumbler's Corbel in the big room of the cathedral today," David told his mother.

"That 'big room' is called the nave, Davie," she said, "but please do tell me; what is the Tumbler's Corbel?"

"It is one of those great, carved stone shelves between the arches, on top of the columns, Mamam," David went on. "It is a carving of a tumbler doing tricks on top of his fiddler's head."

Apollonia smiled at her little boy's advanced knowledge of cathedral design. "I think I know where you say it is, but I must have missed seeing it during my tour of the cathedral. Why in the world, my little love, is a tumbler doing his tricks on top the head of a fiddler?" she asked.

"That is the story, Mamam. It is all about this tumbler and his fiddler who decided to enter a monastery. When the day of Christ's masses came, they found that they had no gift to give to the Christ Child, for they could not write nor paint nor draw. So, they decided to do their tumbling tricks for Baby Jesus!" David seemed proud of their ingenuity. "But," he went on, "the other monks got angry for they did not think it was proper; so, they told the tumbler to stop because it was not nice in the church. And you know what?" he said with eyes wide and wonderful awe in his voice. "The Virgin and Child smiled. They liked it. They told the tumbler and fiddler to go on; so, they did!"

"Really, Davie," Apollonia smiled at her little boy's obvious sense of wonder. "Then what happened?"

"Well, Vicar Clarence told us that the moral of the story is clear. Whatever we can do, we must do it as best we can in the service of God!" David looked up into his mother's face. His great blue eyes were beaming, and his blonde hair seemed to be a golden halo of curls. Apollonia loved to watch his angelic face. Still she always reminded herself that though David was a beautiful child, beneath that precious aura lay a spirit all boy!

"What a wonderful story, Davie. Will you please save it in your heart and share it with your father when he comes back to us?" Apollonia hugged his little body closer to her. Of all her sons, David was the most gentle and most giving. He could not pass a begging child in the streets without insisting that he must bring him home for his care. "Do you think you shall be a tumbler or a fiddler?"

"Oh, Mamam, I cannot play the fiddle, but I can sing, and I can tumble; just look upon this." David jumped from her lap and began to do a series of somersaults around the kitchen.

"David, you must stop that," Thomas called to his littlest brother. "You know Mistress Periwinkle tells us 'no jumping about indoors!'"

Apollonia turned to her responsible middle son and in a voice grateful for his care of his brother simply said, "Not to worry, Thomas. Mistress Periwinkle would not mind jumping about in the garden, and next time we shall do our tumbling there. Please take Davie with you and find Alban. You must all be on you way upstairs to let Mistress Periwinkle know you are safely returned from school."

"Alb will be in the stable with Gareth," Thomas said to his mother. "He is never difficult to find." Taking David's hand, he walked out from the kitchen, reassuming his role *in loco parentis* once again.

Apollonia turned to her cook to continue their discussion of the meal for that evening and said, as if thinking out loud, "Have you heard anything of this demonic invasion of the Close before this afternoon, Mary?"

"Nay, m'Lady, it mus be child's tales out o school. Children do luv ta share sech wild yarns."

"Hmmm, yes," Apollonia agreed. "You must be correct."

Nan found her mistress before she could leave the kitchen and placed an elegantly sealed invitation into her hands. "This has just arrived for you, my Lady." Nan seemed to have an added sparkle in her eyes as she spoke. The Lady's maid could not help but rejoice in the recent transformation of their social life. From earlier depths of depression due to her longing for her absent husband, the Lady Apollonia was continuing to find life in the city full of amicable people whom she could happily receive, and upon whom she was invited to call.

"The messenger told me this bears the seal of the Lady Prioress of St Katherine's Priory in nearby Polsloe," Nan said as she pointed to the elegantly embossed envelope. "I have heard tales of her noble birth from gossips in the market. It would seem that many of the local gentles are now aware of your residence in the city, my Lady, and wish to make your acquaintance. But surely, as the prioress is cloistered, she must request you to come to her."

Chapter Seven

St Katherine's Wheel

The following morning, Nan accompanied her Lady as they rode together with Gareth from Exeter House, up to the bustling High Street, and left the city through the East Gate. Gareth was the perfect, strong-armed guard for ladies riding alone outside the city wall; his manner with them was one of friendly silence. Lady Apollonia had known Gareth before her second marriage to the franklin, Edward Aust, and had brought him and Nan into service at Aust. They were all comfortable in each other's company, but Nan especially loved being in Gareth's presence. He would remain with their horses, once they arrived at the nuns' priory, and not be moved until his Lady required them to return to Exeter.

They joined the Pinhoe Road, going in the opposite direction to most of the traffic which was moving into the city. The country road was busy with many local farmers travelling into Exeter's market day. Apollonia of Aust rejoiced for this opportunity to be riding out from the city and into the nearby countryside. A country woman at heart, she especially enjoyed riding outside the city wall into the welcome, early morning sunshine and fresh breezes of the autumn day.

It seemed no great stretch of time, after turning onto the lane leading to St Katherine's Priory, that they found themselves at its gatehouse. The convent was a daughter house of Benedictine nuns that sat amidst a great rural deer park. It had recently been rebuilt from its earlier wooden buildings into grander constructs of the local sandstone. Its four main buildings were built around a quadrangle, but the entrance to the Priory Church of St Katherine occupied the entire south side and opened its south doors into the further quadrangle of the covered cloister. There was no other access to the cloister from the courtyard, except through the church. This allowed the nuns to walk from their dormitory, through the cloister, and into the church, completely hidden from public gaze.

Gareth led their party as they rode through the gatehouse into the public courtyard of the convent, past a large tithe barn to their left, next to a great kitchen full of the pother of servants, tenant farmers, and priory groundsmen. Nan dismounted first. As one of the members of the priory staff approached to meet them, she announced the arrival of her Lady of Aust, come to call upon the prioress. She extended the sealed invitation that had been received a day before.

They were obviously expected. After assisting his Lady's dismount, Gareth took the horses to the stable to wait there. The Lady and Nan were led towards the largest buildings of the convent complex which housed the guest apartments and the prioress's chambers. They were taken into a stately hall where a table had been laid and chairs placed to allow intimate conversation. With a gentle but enthusiastic welcome, they were greeted by the Prioress Clementine.

It required several minutes before Apollonia could determine that the prioress was speaking to her in French. Her grammar and pronunciation were manifestly alien, best described as somewhat battered anglicizing of the language of Paris. Without hesitation, Apollonia returned her greetings in French and expressed her personal appreciation of the prioress's gracious invitation. At that point in their conversation, the prioress suddenly switched to English.

"Now, let our chatting express more intimate acquaintance between us, Lady Apollonia," the Prioress Clementine said. "I rejoice to have your company and would have invited you sooner, but I have only just returned from Tiverton, guest of my dear friends, the Courtenays. Surely, you know them, the Earl of Devon and his countess?"

The Lady of Aust smiled at her new acquaintance's presumptions of the nature of her social life, but expressed her sincere regrets at having been denied such an honour. As they walked together to their chairs in the hall, Apollonia's keen eye could not help noticing their hostess's habit was elegantly styled of expensive fabric with long sleeves lined in silk. The prioress was a shorter woman than she but one who, Apollonia thought, expressed an aggressive sense of her importance in the chamber. She could also see that the prioress had plucked hair from her forehead to emphasize the high, white, oval shape of her forehead, so desired by all ladies of fashion and framed within her perfectly cut wimple, designed to emphasize her aristocratic forehead. Even more striking to Apollonia was the jeweled necklace that graced Clementine's bosom and fell beneath the breast of her habit.

"Your visit brings the sunshine and the glory of a perfect day," the prioress said to Apollonia. "I pray the journey has not overly tired you, my Lady of Aust?"

Apollonia assured her that she too had enjoyed the brilliance of the day and found it to be a relatively short ride from Exeter House to Polsloe and the priory. Again, as they entered the Prioress Clementine's hall, she could not help but wonder as she looked at the costly decor and dignity of the prioress's private accommodation. The walls of her hall were hung with Burgundian tapestries, the delicate chairs upon which they sat were probably imported from France, and the linen draped table presented a collection of delicacies beautifully presented on silver trays. Apollonia was startled by the sheer opulence displayed before them, but the prioress surprised her further by suggesting that the delicacies on offer were created by her personal French cook.

"Several of the sisters here have their own servants, of course," the prioress told them, "but, as I am of most delicate constitution, I am required to eat with great care only those things prepared for me."

Apollonia could see Nan's eyes grow wide with astonishment. The maid had never seen such a display of elegantly prepared food. Apollonia was compelled by courtesy to compliment her hostess upon the excellence of her table, but silently Apollonia noted to herself that the prioress may well have already consumed too many of the luxurious treats prepared for her. When Clementine bent in her chair to collect the yapping little lapdog at her feet, her middle was bulging against the stretched seams of her habit.

"Your call upon us this day is most pleasing, my dear Lady Apollonia," the prioress repeated her earlier comment with a more personal address. "You have no idea how difficult it is within the cloistered life to maintain any degree of society. Please do share news you may have from London. I hear that your husband is there at present. Is he serving at court?"

"Gramercy, my Lady Prioress, for your gracious hospitality and expressions of interest, but I fear you may have been misled. My dear Edward has no position at court. He was in Northampton representing our shire in the Commons of Parliament, but then he travelled on to London to establish our overseas banking services," Apollonia said. "I have come to Exeter to manage the expanding demands of our woollen investments in Devon."

"Ah," the prioress sniffed slightly, "you are in trade?"

"Indeed, we are. Edward and I have found great success in the excellence of the growing cloth market of Exeter," Apollonia responded enthusiastically. She was truly proud to speak of their successes in a market that was carefully regulated and controlled by officers of the king.

"At least here, upon our shores, you may pursue commerce without being forced to expose your Christian souls to the evils of Jewry."

Apollonia was startled by such a proclamation. She could only assume the prioress was referring to the expulsion of the Jews from England a century earlier. Even Nan could sense her Lady's discomfort with this undisguised display of religious prejudice. Apollonia was well aware that many Christian people in England continued to express their personal judgements against those whom they referred to as the "killers of Christ," but she did not wish to share their partiality.

"My husband and I have been pleased to deal with the honest and well-intended assistance of Jewish moneylenders, allowed by the church, to enable our business contacts cross the Channel." Apollonia spoke quietly but with obvious purpose. "Truly, my Lady Clementine, I have no experience of that which you describe as 'the evils of Jewry.' I believe we must remember that our Lord Christ was born a Jew; the first Bishop of Rome, St Peter, was a Jew, as was also the great messenger of our faith to the Gentiles, St Paul."

The prioress then drew a deep breath and added hurriedly, "Oh yes, yes, of course one must address such realities. But dear Lady Apollonia, do bethink you of the sufferings of our gracious, little martyr, St Hugh of Lincoln, his body discovered in a well." Tears flooded into her eyes, while the prioress fed her lapdog several more of the dainties from the table. "How can one absolve those responsible for ritual murder, confessed by the Jew, Koppin? It is too dreadful; I may not think on it further."

"Pray God, allow none of us to think further on such things," Apollonia encouraged her to change the subject. Her dear friend, Abbess Clothilde of Wiltshire, would have begun their visit by sharing news of her most recent readings. The highly literate leader of Lacock Abbey was one of her favourite conversationalists, who could always stimulate Apollonia's intellect by sharing the recommendation of a new writer or a new copy of the work of an ancient one.

The prioress continued to caress her little dog, speaking to it as if it were an infant in her lap; then she looked back to the Lady of Aust with a completely different inquiry. "How do you find society in Exeter? I understand that you have a notable townhouse there. Are you able to find adequate servants? I hear that one must import them from the country."

Apollonia responded calmly. "There are fewer hands available in the countryside as well, my lady prioress. Indeed many villages in the West Country have been devastated by repeated visitations of plague. But with God's help, we must continue to pray for some hope of cure." The Lady looked at Nan, meaningfully, and then she completely changed the subject and tone of their conversation to announce their departure.

"I believe the hour may be approaching for the office of Sext, my Lady Prioress. We can detain you no longer from your devotion to the *opus Dei*. Nan," the Lady said to her petite servant, "would you kindly seek Gareth? Please ask him to bring our mounts?" Apollonia spoke with a sense of urgency, not only because she could see the passage of daylight hours, but also because she felt they had fulfilled the propriety of their social call, and she was more than ready to return to Exeter House.

Reassuming her dreadful French, the prioress stood to bid them safe journey. Apollonia replied with courtesy's required expressions of thanks and esteem. The two ladies embraced each other, and the prioress lavished her guest with her joys of their acquaintance. Neither noble lady wished to see the other again. They knew they shared little in common. Each assumed, however, she had gained the measure of the other.

* * *

Apollonia's party spent no time exploring the priory church, as the Lady would normally have done when paying a call in a religious community. She seemed to Nan somewhat agitated and more than ready to depart Polsloe Priory. Gareth was ever prepared to return to his own stable domain and be certain his lads had followed every instruction left for them, to the letter.

Nan, as the Lady's constant companion, was accustomed to sit near her Lady during such calls upon neighbors and friends and silently listen to their conversations. But she could not free herself from the troubling contrasts she recognized between Polsloe's Priory of St Katherine and the convent community she remembered visiting frequently with Lady Apollonia at Lacock Abbey in Wiltshire. The

Abbess of Lacock and her sisters warmly expressed honest simplicity of hospitality and personal humility through their dress, their service, and constant acknowledgement of their cloistered calling. Nan would not think to judge the lady prioress's behaviour, but the Lady Clementine's personal devotion seemed to Nan constantly expressed through worldly concerns.

Apollonia did not wish to share her thoughts with Nan as they rode together, but she felt somewhat misused by the lady prioress's condescension. As leader of an important convent, she knew the Prioress Clementine bore a critical role directing the religious life of her community. Yet, Apollonia could see that her apparent concerns of charity and ministry were more urgently expressed to the lapdog she cherished than to the poor of her parish. Clementine's priory had been known as guesthouse to many noble people of the realm, but the prioress herself felt no requirement to remain cloistered there.

"Well," Apollonia groused to herself, "I have not been called to the cloistered life; therefore, tis surely not my place to criticize." Still, she could not help but wonder if the wheel of this St Katherine's Convent was dedicated to a martyrdom of travel. Smiling, while also admonishing herself for such frivolous thoughts, she decided to pursue other concerns with Gareth. So, she turned back in her saddle to face him. "Gareth, would you object to helping me with an inquiry?" she asked.

Startled by her direct question to him, Gareth immediately doffed his hat, rode up to her side, and responded straightaway, "Oi shall do moi best, m'Lady."

"Our son, Thomas, brought home a most unusual tale from the cathedral yesterday. He told me that the young men of the vicars choral have been patrolling the Cathedral Close throughout the nighttime hours this past week in search of some sort of devil."

Nan gasped audibly. "Oh, my Lady, this can not be."

"I suspect they are more likely searching for a human invader of their sacred space," Apollonia said to her, "but I believe local gossip may be discussing this episode, and I would be very grateful to you, Gareth, if you could gather any of it for me. Do you and the lads ever visit the Bishop Blaize on the Shilhay of an evening?"

Gareth nodded his head to acknowledge the Bishop Blaize as one amongst several of their favourite alehouses and promised to try. "Tis nay moi ken ta reckon udder's tales, m'Lady," he said to Apollonia. "Bu me an th lads'll open o'r ears."

Chapter Eight

Fullers, Tuckers, and Nosy Parkers

"The odious aulnager! He is destroyer of all my profit! He examines my cloth, elegantly offered for sale, and condemns it as inadequate to the requirements of the law," the small man shouted angrily. "He declares my dozens to be weak, our cloth of assize to be inept! I shall cow his arrogance. He will serve my will, or I shall remove him!" The boney man, whose luxurious garments could not soften his skeletal limbs or increase his scrawny neck, was breathing heavily as if strenuously active. Yet his only movement was that of pacing to and fro, while his steaming anger continued to char the air within the cave like darkness of the wine cellar. "I swear I shall make him submit! I have noble friends; I have influence! But my intent must not be detected, you hear me; no one in the town must know of my role. You shall continue as my instrument of diversion."

He was speaking disparagingly to a well built man of military stature, significantly taller than he, but one who's bent shoulders and bowed head, covered by a hooded cape, emphasized his demeanor as that of supplicant. "What is it you wish from me, master? I have followed your orders." As he spoke, his face was concealed by the heavy hood drooping downward from his lowered head. "But whilst the vicars choral roam the Close during the darkest hours of the night, I can not continue to place your threats against the dean and chapter in the same manner. I must not risk injury to the young clerics, even if they are armed against me."

"You will do as you are told." The angry one stomped his foot. "I shall drive the dean to call upon the mayor and authorities of the city for protection. They will be unable to provide it, their ancient suspicions of each other will be reawakened, and you shall make it happen. Then, whilst the town looks to defend against a threat presumed aimed at the cathedral, I shall find ways to bring the aulnage to my will or be rid of him! You, a knight's squire," he scoffed in belittling tones of mockery, "but one who is unable to defend against choir boys?" He pulled the hooded head down to his level and shouted into his face, "You will continue to compel the dean to fear that his church, his clergy, and all those residing in the Cathedral Close are mortally threatened! Do you hear?"

* * *

After combing, feeding, and settling the mounts into their stalls, Gareth suggested to two of his stable lads it was time for a flagon of ale. They had four hours until curfew, so the trio strode out of the stable, laughing and jesting as they walked together up hill to the centre of town and eventually down through the west gate of Exeter's city wall towards the river and the Shilhay. Their goal was the Bishop Blaize, a popular alehouse located near to Exeter's Quay.

Always filled with sailors, some from abroad, whose ships remained anchored until their next sailing, it was also a great favourite with a variety of locals. Because it was located in the Shilhay, the Bishop Blaize was not far from the drying fields of racks for the woollen trade, so it was also used as a gathering place for local fullers, tuckers, and the occasional mill owner. Even some of the younger, more boisterous members of the minor clergy of the cathedral knew the Bishop Blaize could offer them an evening of rollicking adventure, shared with members of all classes within the city. By the time Gareth and his lads approached the alehouse, flaming torches lighted its presence while music and drunken singing continued to pour from its doors.

Gareth retreated with his drink to a stool nearly hidden in the darkness of a corner, close to the fireplace. He was always a shy, withdrawn man, but Gareth knew he was required on this evening to serve his Lady's purpose. Lady Apollonia wished to know if any tavern gossip spoke of "threatening things" happening within the Cathedral Close. He may hear nothing worthy to share, she had told him. But if he did overhear even a few comments of menacing happenings on the Cathedral Green or threats towards the cathedral clergy, or if anything was said describing trouble on the Close, she begged him to bring such words to her for study.

The younger stable lads had seated themselves near a small table, attempting to wrap their arms and hands about the body of a buxom serving wench who seemed prepared to enjoy their attentions simultaneously, until she would be called away. Pushing back their caps and running her fingers through their hair, she kept saying how she would "teach them good manners," while leaning across the table to reveal a generous bosom nearly bursting from her bodice.

Across the main room from Gareth, a group of clerks were gathered, drunkenly singing lewd songs even though they were all in holy orders. Gareth quietly moved his stool more closely towards their revels while continuing to remain within the shadows of the low, dark beamed ceiling. Their speech and behaviour were disgusting, Gareth thought, but he forced himself to listen to their bawdy language and sexual jests. Time passed and he could find little being said of any value to his Lady's purpose. He was about to move to another side of the great fireplace when one of the local Tuckers' Guild staggered up to the clerks and asked them straight out, "Why be ye nay guardin th Close from th devils, den?"

They roared with laughter and shouts until the apparent leader of the clerks announced haughtily, "The choir boys will deal with such things, my man. We," he hiccupped noisily, "are the guardians of the intellectual powers of the Close!"

"Wha be th devils wantin wit an oly place?" the tucker continued to ask.

The clerks' boisterous laughter roared once more as they held their sides and ridiculed their interrogator as a simpleton. "Oh aye, my man," said their leader, "surely even you can see it is 'oly places' that the devils be 'wantin' most!"

His group shouted boisterously, this time at their leader's mimicry of the tucker, whilst he turned to call for another drink.

The tucker began to walk away, muttering some words concerning "th waste o learnin," but then he stopped and turned back to try another tack.

"Oi've eard yu'r all fearful o th green mann," he taunted back at the clerks.

Their rowdy shouting stopped suddenly, and the offensive member of the group turned sharply to the tucker and demanded, "What could you possibly know of green men, my man?"

"Oi ne'er be yer 'mann,'" the tucker said with apparent disgust in his voice, "bu Oi kno ye be lookin fur some jack o th green oo means ta do ye ill.'" And with that, the tucker turned his back on all of them and walked away.

Gareth was near enough to hear the entire exchange between the clerks and the tucker. He could make little sense of it, but did not miss noticing how seriously quiet the clerks had suddenly become. Remaining in the shadows, he moved slightly nearer to their huddled figures. Their exchange of comments was reduced from shouts to murmuring amongst themselves, and he could hear only the occasional phrase.

"Nothing more, for the dean wishes no interference from the city," said one voice.

"What is wanted?" questioned another.

"Is this an ancient Saxon envy?" was added.

"Nay, I say, tis the heathen spirits of the Druids that have been summoned. Holy Mary, Mother of God, save us!"

Gareth could hear less and less, for the clerks continued to converse more privately within their group. He kept his patient watch, as he would have done with any troubled filly in his care, but their group began to break apart. It was well before curfew and an hour before closing bell; still one slipped away, then several more. Finally, the most offensive of the clerks drank down his flagon, looked to several other flagons sitting about, and drained them. Gareth continued to watch when the clerk pulled the hood of his monk like habit closely round his face, lifted his lantern to light his way, and slipped through the portal of the Bishop Blaize into the night.

* * *

Edward Aust's man of law had come to Exeter House early the following morning. He came largely to honour his promise to his friend that he would be sensitive to any assistance the Lady Apollonia might require during the months of her residence in a strange town. Also, Philip Tropenol wished to assure himself that the Lady was finding life in his city as balanced and buoyant as it could be for her during her husband's extended absence. When he was shown into the hall, he found her already hard at work with Stafford and Nan, as they continued comparing the stacks of woollen cloths with the ledgers of receipt.

"Ah, God's blessings upon you, Master Tropenol," Apollonia greeted him. "It is always my pleasure to welcome you, and I have yet to thank you properly for your introduction to Canon Chulmleigh. He has been a valued companion. His knowledgeable discourse, preface to Exeter's beautiful cathedral church, surpassed all that I have read of cathedrals in France or England. We could never have been so well prepared by anyone else."

"My Lady, it is your intellect and learning that inspired the comments of my dear friend to me after his tour with you and your party. But I am truly grateful that your cathedral visit was a success, and that you have enjoyed sharing the acquaintance of my oldest friend." Turning suddenly, he began to examine the cloths displayed before them. "I say, these are truly impressive," Tropenol exclaimed when he moved towards a great stack of the dozens lying tidily arranged on the great table.

"Our collection from the weavers is at last complete, Philip," Apollonia said with a brilliant smile. "It has been a very successful year, but we must now engage the oversight of the aulnage to add the official stamp of approval before we present them for sale."

"Well, dear Lady, I can assure you that our official supervisor of the cloth trade is the most honourable and esteemed member of our local gentry. We must arrange transport of these cloths to the market hall, whence I shall personally introduce you to him. He is Sir Moreton Molton, and his reputation for excellence in examination of cloths is unsullied." Tropenol's gaze continued to move along the displayed cloths as he spoke.

"As you can see, we have a majority of the smaller 'dozens,'" Apollonia continued to point out to him, "but you will also see there, near the end of the board, our collection of the larger cloths of assize." She felt a sense of real achievement, not only because she had been able to oversee the enlargement of their woollen interests in Exeter, but also because Apollonia knew they would do very well that year. She could hardly wait to tell Edward the potential extent of their profits. But first, all cloths must be submitted to the examination of the aulnage, Sir Molton, that they may be affixed with his official stamp.

"Shall you be able to present these to the market hall on the morrow, my Lady?" Tropenol asked her. "I will gladly accompany you as representative of Aust interests here."

"Gramercy, Philip, you will do me the greatest of favours if you will join us then," Apollonia said. "I fear I am unprepared to handle all of this on my own. I shall be most grateful, not only for your introduction to the aulnage, but also for your continued counsel in these matters." Apollonia was speaking with an honest sense of relief in her voice, which did not pass unnoticed by the man of law.

"Always at your service, my Lady of Aust," he said, and with a graceful bow, he bid her farewell till the morrow.

* * *

After a busy but well-accomplished morning, Apollonia had retreated to her solar, welcoming a chance to rest her feet for a few moments. Nan entered her chamber and told her that the stablemaster, Gareth, wished to speak with her at her convenience. "No better time, Nan," Apollonia said to the maid. "Send Gareth to me now, if you please."

Nan hesitated, as if not quite certain how to continue. "You know, my Lady, Gareth does not feel at his best, even in hall. It would be painfully uncomfortable for him to join you here." As she paused, Apollonia looked with questioning eyes towards her faithful maid. So Nan continued, "My Lady, could you not speak with Gareth below in the main barn. I am certain he will feel far more at ease there, and he will send the other lads off to assure your privacy."

"Of course, Nan, what was I thinking? My thanks for your kindly prudence and insight." Apollonia stood up from her chair, straightened her wimple, and made ready to walk down towards the barn. "I shall join Gareth in his realm at once, but I should prefer you to remain with us. Gareth appreciates your reassuring presence and will feel more comfortable speaking with me, if you remain."

It was a matter of minutes before Apollonia could descend into the main barn, so she sent Nan ahead to find Gareth and tell him where the Lady would meet him. Apollonia entered the barn alone and looked overhead towards the large loft of hay. In truth, she could not help wishing to climb up and throw herself into it. She would have done in her childhood, rolling about until her dress, her face, and hair would be full of the pungent strands projecting in all directions. Instead, the Lady decided to preserve some decorum and found a wooden bench where she sat to await the others.

Gareth walked ahead of Nan into the barn and noticed her Ladyship sitting patiently. "Do beg pardon, m'Lady," he said hurriedly, "Oi did nay wish ta keep ye waitin."

Nan walked to take her place next to the Lady, but Apollonia responded with real enthusiasm, "Oh Gareth, say no more! I do love being in the barns. I love the scent, the tidiness, and the well-worked care of our animals always found feeding here. You must never try to hurry me away."

Gareth blushed to the skin beneath his blond hair, but could not help smiling at her honest enjoyment of his favourite place. Pulling up a small stool, he sat down near the Lady's feet to speak quietly with her.

"We did as ye asked, m'Lady," he said carefully, for her hearing alone. "Th lads an me, we went ta Bishop Blaize."

"Did you hear anything of note?" Apollonia asked him straightaway.

Nan was aware of the source of her Lady's worry. Apollonia was mother to three sons attending the cathedral school and felt a possible need to protect them. The little maid moved closer to the Lady's bench, and the three of them seemed to put their heads together.

"T'were th strangest ta'k, m'Lady. Oi do'n roightly unnerstan ani o it."

Lady Apollonia leaned more closely towards him, looked directly into his eyes, and laid her hand upon his arm. "I pray thee, Gareth," she said earnestly. "Tell me everything. I will be truly grateful to you for helping me learn from any of the 'strange talk' you were able to overhear."

Gareth nodded his head to acknowledge her purpose and then said to her quizzically, "M'Lady, do ye kno anithin bout a jack o th green?"

Chapter Nine

Bloody Fraud

He had not planned to leave Devonshire so speedily, but the young pardoner, Brandon Landow, had been somewhat discomposed, shortly after his arrival, to find the household of Aust so well established in Exeter. He felt largely secure in his protection, through canon law, against any charge the Lady Apollonia may conspire to bring against him, but he preferred to secure his personal comfort through significant distance between the Lady of Aust and himself. Past that, he had convinced himself of an inspired way to achieve his heart's desire, a way to multiply his profits. He was guiding his horse, Absolution, through Gloucestershire on the road towards the Manor of Hailes. The goose chase he had been sent upon into the fogs of Dartmoor by an unknown villain was proving to be the source of his inspiration.

Brandon Landow wanted to become rich. A significant theft of indulgences had been stolen from his walet in Exeter, probably at the hands of that same unknown adversary. But Landow had swiftly forged an additional collection of indulgences to sell, and they had produced reasonable profits as he passed through Somerset. But indulgences, Landow thought, were slavish booty for limited sums, even if always dependable. His great vision of hope on Dartmoor had altered his thinking completely. He would fret no longer as to how he might put paid to a foolish vow of charity; instead, Landow chuckled to himself, he must look to miraculous possibilities for huge profit. He would see it with his own eyes, examine it as closely as he would be allowed, and study the entire presentation of the famous Relic of the Holy Blood at Hailes Abbey. Any fool could obtain great riches if he possessed such a relic as the Holy Blood of Christ to sell.

What man or woman in all of England would not beg to acquire personal possession of a drop of Christ's Blood? Think of it, he urged himself, just how many relics known to have touched the Divine Presence are there in the world? One could list Christ's shroud, the wood of the True Cross, the Crown of Thorns, the Roman Spear, a few nonage teeth, or the foreskin when the infant Christ was circumcised. Having ticked these items off in his mind as he rode, the pardoner went on to remind himself of other possibilities. "Oh yes, I must add the swaddling clothes, a bit of the wood of the manger, and, of course, the chemise of the Virgin worn at the time of the Birth."

His calculations soaring, Landow began to notice how heavily travelled the road to Hailes Abbey had grown. He could see that he was passing large groups of pilgrims. Some were walking barefoot, some crawling on their knees, many enabled by crutches, the most helpless being drawn in carts.

"The gathering throng," Landow thought, smirking to himself as they crowded around him, "they are all moving towards the hope of experiencing a miracle by placing themselves in the Presence of Christ's own blood! Perhaps I can create a way to make the miraculous seem more accessible to a wealthy but desperately gullible pilgrim."

He was riding along the Salt Way coming from the South, when suddenly the roadway flowed over a dramatic ridge. Looking down from the top of its descent, Landow could see the extensive abbey site, lying throughout his view, spread over acres of land below. Cistercian Monks had built Hailes Abbey after it was founded and endowed by the Earl of Cornwall in fulfillment of his vow. But a son and heir of the founder had brought an even greater gift to the abbey in 1270. Processing with a worshipful crowd of people into the abbey church, the heir had placed the Relic of the Holy Blood into an ark, set high upon a stone shrine in the far eastern chevet of the church. Pilgrims began coming to the abbey immediately thereafter, daily filing through the long aisles of the nave, waiting patiently for the moment when they would approach the shrine, fall to their knees to offer their prayers and supplications in the Presence of Christ.

The pardoner's excitement stirred as he rode through the main abbey gate. Crossing the expanse of courtyard, Landow could not help admiring the elegant residence of the Abbot of Hailes. These Cistercians had grown rich! The abbot's private house filled one entire side of the courtyard. It was several stories tall with a grand entry portal at its centre, surrounded by six large stained glass windows, three on each side. But from Landow's perspective, the best revelation of the wealth of the abbot's dwelling could be seen through a covered passageway leading to the stables. The pardoner laughed aloud as he could see there a prized array of kennels full of baying hounds.

At the far end of the courtyard, Landow arrived at the west front of the abbey church. He secured Absolution and walked to the north porch where he entered the majestic nave. He joined a stream of pilgrims who were passing reverently over a beautifully tiled path in the church floor, leading through the north choir aisle. The pardoner spent no time pausing to admire stately tomb effigies of the Earl of Cornwall and his wife. He expressed no interest in the five chapels surrounding the eastern chevet. The pardoner went directly to the central chapel of the shrine and remained as long as he could, while the guardian of the shrine revealed the relic and repeated the narrative of its origins before the gathering of wide-eyed pilgrims.

Landow repeated his approach to the shrine many times that day. On each occasion, he looked specifically for the relic within the ark. He made mental notes of the reliquary's size, shape, colour, and how much of the Holy Blood could actually be seen by the penitent. All other pilgrims except the pardoner approached the shrine, consumed with contrition and remorse, begging God's forgiveness. Landow was irritated that he and the endless line of pilgrims were allowed to spend relatively little time looking at the relic, before being forced to move on.

In order to touch the reliquary of the Holy Blood, nearly every pilgrim to the shrine also brought some gift to endorse his petition and, when near the ark, reverently placed his gift on or near the shrine. Landow brought a beautiful silk scarf, lined in gold thread, that he would hang upon the altar, then sneakily pull it back into the sleeve of his cloak when he was forced to keep moving.

The pardoner retreated to his room in the pilgrim's hostel that night and by candlelight carefully drew, according to life-size, the transparent, jewel like, beryl sphere. It was secured by a stopper and bound in continuous circles of silver. At the top of the sphere, he added to his drawing a Cross, because the Guardian of the Shrine told every pilgrim it was there that the reliquary contained a sliver of the True Cross. At the base of the sphere, the dark red colour of the Holy Blood lay between two of the silver circles.

Landow was certain the reliquary could be duplicated, and it would be simple enough to fill it with a drop or two of red dyed honey, so that the "Holy Blood" would miraculously never desiccate. Any small splinter of old wood could recreate the relic of the True Cross. "I can pry as much old wood as I need from any abandoned barn and shape a whole collection of holy 'slivers of the True Cross,'" he chuckled to himself.

One further item must be acquired before he prepared to leave Hailes Abbey the following morning. Landow went to one of the older monks in the scriptorium to ask for his help in seeking, he said, to rededicate his life more fully to the teachings of Christ's Gospels. He told the monk that he was a poor man, but he would give all he had to obtain the special papal indulgence granted to Hailes. From the scriptorium, Landow was directed to one of two brothers of the Confraternity of Hailes. They heard his confession and accepted his small money gift to the abbey; then one of the monks gave Landow an indulgence showing on its Latin seal a monk holding the flask of the Holy Blood.

Bowing his thanks to the monks, Landow walked back into the courtyard, rejoicing aloud to all who were gathered there. He proclaimed that God, in His Mercy, had granted him all he could hope for from Hailes Abbey! Bystanders interpreted his joy and thanksgiving as his having been granted a spiritual gift. In truth Landow's joy was in his deceit, that all he carried with him from Hailes would enable his creation of a perfect fraud. He walked to the stables to reclaim Absolution, and with his baggage stowed carefully, he leapt into her saddle. "To Chester!" he shouted in his exuberance. He knew some practised forgers there.

* * *

It had become part of Lady Apollonia's morning routine to examine the progress of the building of her family's private chapel in Exeter House. She and Edward had received a licence to build from Exeter's Bishop Brantyngham and had engaged the services of a young and enthusiastic master mason. By this time, she found it personally inspiring to witness the carving of the arches of oak ribbed roof beams. The arches would eventually arise from the course of stone pilasters, now beginning to stand along the walls of the chapel and each crowned by an elegantly carved stone capital.

Apollonia's young mason, William of Wedmore, had proved to be especially skilled in the creation of stained glass window tracery. The exterior stone wall of the former store room, being transformed into household chapel, was covered in poles of ash and alder, anchored into putlogs in the wall and laid across with planks to provide walking space for the masons to pursue their work. The framework of scaffolding on the eastern wall had already enabled the masons to construct two strong, triangular stone buttresses against the exterior wall. William was just beginning to pierce that eastern wall, between the buttresses, to open a great circle. It was sized to hold the frame of the rose window, which would rise to central focus above the altar in celebration of the Virgin Mary.

A special niche, to the left of the central altar, was being carved in stone to receive the statue of Saint Apollonia. To its right, a second carved recess would present a new carving of Saint Edward the Confessor. And in alternating levels beneath the rose window, special niches were already in place for the statues of St Hugh, St Chad, St Thomas, St Alban, and St David. Apollonia had made it known to William that she and Edward wished to place the patron saints of their sons within the aura of the Rose, the Virgin of Mercy.

As the Lady walked into the chapel work area with Nan at her side, William's dog ran up to leap at her skirts. "Get down, you sorry, little mutt!" Nan commanded, as she attempted to force her own skirts in defence against the barking, dog's attack upon her mistress. Everyone knew the little dog meant no harm but did insist upon being the focus of human attention within his master's work space. He would not stop barking until Apollonia reached down to caress his head and rub his tummy. Once he had achieved his desired attention, he would retreat to his favourite blanket, lie on his back, and scratch a flea niggled ear before resuming his watch.

"Blessings of the morning, William," Apollonia called to the mason perched high upon interior scaffolding against the east wall. He was well focused upon his work, striking precisely at the stones of the wall to enlarge the opening circle.

Realizing the Lady had come to the work site and approached to speak with him, William quickly placed his tools upon the scaffold, pulled away his leather apron, and jumped to the floor in greeting. "God give you good day, my Lady," he responded, as he doffed his leather hat. "By my troth, the work goes well, and I have much to share with you." William led Apollonia and Nan to the south aisle where he had placed his most recent design, sketched into the plaster of the floor. "Pray tell me, do you find this rose tracery to offer the inspiration you seek in your family chapel?"

The Lady paused to examine the design of William's tracery closely and to see how the radiating sections of stained glass would swirl together. William's design seemed so totally new. It was a circular tracery but presented in a pattern spreading outward, full of fluidity and movement. He had employed none of the static, wheel shaped devices in stone Apollonia had seen in many older churches. She not only liked the design, she was proud of her young mason's inventiveness. "I believe you envision a hope of heavenly glory on earth, William. There is shimmering movement in all that you have done. But in this, I suspect you are a magician, transforming stone into lace and light."

William's face flushed with pleasure. "I have sought only to follow your wishes, my Lady. But do you really feel this pattern for the tracery will fulfill your hopes for the chapel rose window? It must be the central focal point of worship and praise in this space."

"Indeed, this design is most seemly. When may we have it done? Do you have a master of stained glass able to complete it for us?"

"Thanks be to God, there are still adept glaziers completing the glazing of the cloisters in Exeter," he said, obviously encouraged by her praise. "If you please, I shall retreat to their workshop with my design and set their hands to our work as well."

"May we discuss the choice of colours you have selected?" the Lady persisted. "I should love to have blue predominate, so that when the sun rises, our chapel may be filled with the colours of heaven and heavenly love."

"I dare swear," William enthused, "you are a mind reader, my Lady. As you will dedicate this chapel to the Virgin, blue is the colour of her mantle. So, indeed, blue shall fill the greater portions of the tracery. But to enhance the blue, I plan to use green, the colour of vegetation and spring, suggesting regeneration of the soul here, here, and here. But, purple must also fill these panels as the colour of royalty, God the Father, King of Heaven and Earth. And violet, symbolizing life and truth, passion and suffering, will complement this area, while golden yellow will enhance the small but sparkling rays of the swirling rose at its ambit. What say you?"

"I say your comprehension of colour complements well your miracle of movement in stone. But may we also add a small touch of red to remind us all of the suffering of martyrs, most especially my patroness, Saint Apollonia?"

"For aught I know, my Lady, you have completed my hope of heavenly glory." William propped his left hand on his hip while placing his powerful right hand to his chin, as if completing at last within his imagination the entire colour plan. "Once the glaziers have assembled the design, I shall accompany you to their workshop for its final approval, my Lady. But I do believe we have created a vision."

"It cannot be denied, William; you are a designer of genius." Her glowing smile completed his moment of joy filled accomplishment.

* * *

Edward was having difficulty sitting in his saddle. He was not an accomplished horseman. Even at his best, he could not sit on horseback as his wife, Apollonia, who seemed to ride totally at one with the beast. He tended to bounce about, trying to remind himself of all the recommended concepts Apollonia would suggest to him when they were riding. "Use your knees, Edward; hold the body of the horse firmly with your legs. Strongly position your feet in the stirrups to lift yourself into the movement of the animal's gallop."

Edward Aust was not well. He had been having great difficulty stirring any appetite within himself of late; worse yet, many things he ate soon vomited back up. At first he had simply blamed the food of London. The inn where he stayed was an adequate accommodation, but God only knew where the food they served came from—obviously not from the gardens and fields of his native village of Aust. And the good fish pies he could always count on at home, fresh from the Severn, were never so dependable here in the capital. Any seafood served here seemed to come with a suggestion of foul odour, too many days from the sea. Edward was desperate to return to the West Country, back to his wife, his sons, his household. He had stopped eating anything, other than broth and dry bread, and forced himself to drink whenever possible to slake his desperate thirst and calm his innards.

Jude Dennish, Edward's yeoman, rode as near to his side as possible. They had been on the road from London for three days, and Jude knew his master could not ride much further. He felt desperate to get some word to Exeter where the Lady Apollonia was in temporary residence and would need to be informed of her husband's sickness. Jude knew she would insist on caring for him herself. And, she would be prepared to find proper doctors of physic for him. There had been no one in London Jude felt that he could trust. Every recommended physician seemed only to bleed Edward further, while charging a great fee. Edward's healthy, rugged body was visibly weakening, not only from the effects of his illness but from the assaults of the doctors as well. As they approached the cathedral city of Salisbury, Jude made his decision. They entered the courtyard of a roadside inn, and while his master waited, Jude hired a room he and Edward alone would share, while also gaining adequate stabling for their mounts. Once he had put Edward into bed, he strode downstairs to find the inn keeper and ask him for his best recommendation of a courier who could ride straightaway to Exeter.

When the messenger was introduced to Jude as a known and reliable, local Salisbury man, he gave him a walet containing an urgent message to be delivered into the hands of the Lady Apollonia of Aust in Exeter House, and no other. He paid Norman, the young Wiltshire man, a substantial fee in advance. Jude told him the Lady would double it if he led her party back to them at this inn as speedily as possible. Jude described no further details of his master's condition, but his earnest manner, as well as the promise of bountiful payment, combined to urge the courier to start out immediately and ride hell bent for leather.

Twas not a fortune being offered him, but given the recent depression of opportunity this side of Salisbury, the courier wasted no time in saddling his horse and pounding the road for Exeter.

* * *

Apollonia was enjoying a lively supper in the hall with her sons. All three were at home, free from school, but each of them full of clerks' tattle from the Close. No one would have dared disturb her, but Nan had been called to the kitchen from her side. Soon the maid rushed back into the hall and whispered something into the Lady's ear. Expressing no change in mood or concern, Apollonia spoke quietly with Chaplain Anthony, who must remain in charge of the household with Mistress Periwinkle.

She was required to leave on a journey, Apollonia told her sons, and each of them would have to maintain his studies during the upcoming week. Raising one eyebrow in an expression each knew well, she told the boys she would offer her own examination of their accomplishments when she returned. It was very abrupt, but Thomas, the eldest of the three, was keenly aware that his mother could be called away for important matters needing attention from the family's farms and businesses.

"Come hither brothers," he said, assuming leadership of the evening. "Mistress Periwinkle has promised to begin a new tale by the fire this evening, and Mamam may be home again before we are able to hear it all!"

* * *

Nan and the Lady went directly to the stables to find Gareth. They carried cushions and blankets, while ordering the stablemaster to help them make ready a sturdy wagon, covered over in canvas to protect them all from the weather. Apollonia could not bring herself to tell the boys that their father was ill in Salisbury. She did not dare to tell them he was on his way to them, fearfully sickened. In spite of her happy balance of appearance when in the boys' presence, the Lady was fighting heart stopping panic since the moment the news of Edward's sickness had come to her. She must travel to his side straightaway. She must see his condition for herself, and she must be present to nurse him. Edward was her life, the beloved half of her eternal soul. She prayed God and all the saints to bless him by their healing presence, but most of all she begged God to strengthen her faith. Before the boys had gone to bed that evening, Apollonia, Gareth, and Nan were being led by Norman, on the road towards Salisbury.

* * *

Jude could see that his master, Edward, had seemed to rally slightly when they had gained a comfortable bed. Edward's body had slipped into deep sleep shortly after he had removed his travelling clothes and laid his aching body into the pre-warmed bed. His faithful yeoman had returned to their chamber after sending the hired courier off, on the road to Exeter. Jude was desperate for someone else to assume leadership, to direct his actions, to tell him what to do. But as the night continued to fall, he concluded at last that he could do no more. Jude banked their chamber fire and crawled into the trundle pulled from beneath Edward's great bed. Soon his prayers had murmured into snores.

* * *

In spite of their steady pace on the road, eating their meals in the wagon and stopping only at the end of each day, it was three days before Apollonia and her party were led by the courier into the courtyard of the inn where Edward lay. Apollonia did not wait for Gareth to help her from her seat in the wagon. She leaped from the wagon bed, immediately it had halted, and ran into the inn. Guided by the innkeeper, she hurried up the stairs. She burst into the chamber without hesitating to knock on the door, as Jude gawped in surprise. Apollonia rushed to his bedside and grasped Edward's hands into hers. "My dearest, I have been so worried for you."

"Lonia, be at peace, my love," Edward said, kissing her hands as he pulled her towards him. "Your presence brings healing and such good cheer. I know I shall conquer this malady."

Jude heaved a great sigh of release from his solitary sense of responsibility, slipped quietly from the chamber, and walked down the stairs, hoping to find other members of the Aust household below. He found Nan waiting in the alehouse, assuring the courier that her Lady should return shortly.

"Indeed, I will pay you the rest of your fee, Norman. We are eternally in your debt for your services as messenger, as well as your guidance to this place. But I must ask you to wait until we know truly that my Lady has no further requests of you." The courier assured Nan he would gladly remain to speak with the Lady. He walked out to the yard to refresh his horse before returning for some refreshment of his own choosing.

When Nan realised that Jude had entered the room with them, she turned to him immediately. Her hands clasped in an attitude of prayer, she rushed to his side. "Benedicite, Jude, how does our Master Edward?" They walked towards a small table where they could sit and speak quietly together. Gareth came into the alehouse from the stables and joined them. Everyone seemed desperate for news.

* * *

Apollonia had not been able to move from Edward's bedside. She could see that he had lost weight, he was pale and undernourished, but his blue eyes did seem to glow with welcome of her. They spoke together quietly, sometimes exchanging meaning in silent glances but always rejoicing to be together again. The Lady could see that her husband was not recovering. His illness, whatever it might be, still held him dangerously within its grasp. But she felt in her heart of hearts that he needed most of all to be home with her and their boys to find recovery. So, she described for him the wagon preparations she had made to transport him as comfortably as possible to Exeter. Edward did not hesitate. "You are such a clever woman, Lonia; let us away as soon as we may. I have indeed grown weary of this inn."

Nan very quietly entered the chamber where her master and mistress lay together, to offer any needed services. Apollonia kissed Edward and slipped from the bedside as Nan approached.

"Dear Nan, please remain here with Edward. I must go below to prepare for the morrow." As she moved to leave the chamber, she held Nan's arm, speaking quietly into her ear. "Urge him to drink, Nan, but in your silence allow him to continue to slip into sleep." The Lady went down the stairs quickly to find the men of her household and speak with the courier.

Apollonia walked down the stairs and entered the alehouse. Jude and Gareth rose to their feet in anticipation of her next requests of them. She approached Jude with both hands and begged him accept her heartfelt thanks. He had not only served his master well, he had maintained his health and well-being until she could reach them. "I shall never forget your service, Jude. What you have done has far outpaced loyalty to your master."

Turning to Gareth, she asked him to bring the courier to her. Once the men were gathered, and before they could all retire for the night, Apollonia announced her plans for the following morning. Jude was being sent off on a further errand to Lacock Abbey, with a special request of Abbess Clothilde. Gareth would prepare the wagon to receive Master Edward's ailing body, and all three men of the household must be on hand, first thing in the morning, to assist Edward from his chamber in the inn, down the stairs, and into his bed on wheels.

Then, Apollonia took time to personally address herself to the courier and ask if he would be willing to continue in their service. She told him she felt it would be too great a task for Gareth to drive the wagon and control the horses that would need to be led back to Exeter. It would be a long journey, she explained, but she would reward him with a steady place in her service if he could continue to assist them now.

The courier spent no length of time in consideration of her offer. "Gor m'Lady, Oi'll serve ye well!" he announced. "Bu cou'd Oi be lowed ta speak wit me mum an sis afore Oi leaves Salisbury?" He now knew the way to Exeter House, and he assured the Lady he would follow with their mounts, directly he had completed his errand.

"What is your name?" Apollonia asked him, "and where do you live?"

"Me name be Norman, m'Lady," he responded enthusiastically, "an Oi livs in cottage down th road wher we farms. Bu Oi'll take some shillins ta moi mum an tell er Oi gots me a job!"

* * *

Edward Aust was a sturdy man; still, Apollonia was endlessly concerned for the impact of fever and chill upon his weakened condition. Within the canvas covering of the wagon, she kept Edward swathed in furs, his head wrapped in wool upon the cushions, and when he complained of his feet being cold, she simply moved to the back of the wagon space and sat upon them, lending her body's heat to sustain his. She repeated to herself, she must not allow him to feel the chill of autumn air. Each night of the return journey, Apollonia saw to it that a room, well warmed and prepared for him, was at the ready. Edward ate little, but as he seemed so truly happy to be returning to Exeter House and his family, his hearty spirit sustained the struggle, as his body continued to weaken.

For Apollonia, the journey crawled endlessly, but Nan was always there to offer food or drink, to encourage their thoughts of their sons, to find any occasion to share a smile or a sweet family memory. When at last Gareth drove their wagon through the East Gate of Exeter's city wall and continued up the High Street, Apollonia was exhausted but filled with gratitude. They were home. They were together.

Chapter Ten

Pagan Patrimony

The barge moved slowly upriver, pushed along by the incoming tide. On board, with several other Devon men, was their employer, a dark, stalwart fellow with powerful shoulders, broad headed face, and flashing, dark eyes. He was a short figure, whose limbs completed in small hands and feet. Adam Braund would have described himself as a "Deb'm mann" who took a sense of strength and greatness from his ancient heritage. He had followed in his father's footsteps, transporting Beer stone from Exmouth up the River Exe to the building site of the Christians' cathedral in Exeter. That job was nearly come to an end, as this shipment of stone would complete the uppermost level of the west front screen, once carved, painted, and gilded.

Living now nearer the coast in Littleham Parish, Adam could tell you his family had first come south from Hembury, centuries before. He worried little of letters or numbers, but he knew from his father and his father's fathers that he descended from the great tribes of Dumnonia. The oral tradition of their family was preserved and treasured. Adam Braund could not read nor write, but could sing round the fire each evening the tales of warlike tribes who had come to this land at the time of the Druids. They were not only true "Deb'm menn;" they had ruled before the Romans, before the Saxons, and gods be praised, long before these womanish Normans.

Smirking to himself, Braund was constantly made aware of how pathetically members of the upper classes of Exeter attempted to disdain his person. He especially scorned the clergy with their anti-pagan pretence to follow the teachings of Christ. Their hypocrisy, he asserted, was sickened further by their refusal of women. Why was a gift of celibacy valued by their god? How could they possibly think of themselves as real men when the most they could produce was piss?

Braund's father had known many of the masons who had filled the interior of Exeter Cathedral with wonderful carvings of Christian saints. But deep in his Celtic soul, Adam treasured the knowledge that many carvings within this great, southwestern Christian cathedral celebrated Celtic worship of fertility and procreative life. Three generations of his family had served to bring stone to the masons working on the cathedral. When local carvers produced their marvelous roof bosses, corbels, and capitals with foliate, human faces, whose mouths, eyes, or ears produced stems and leaves, the priests would occasionally question their symbolic meaning. "Indeed, father, this face I have carved is the symbol of rebirth, the hope of new life found in Christ Jesus," a mason would respond. Then, while the priest walked away, nodding reassurance in his answer, the mason would silently chuckle that he and his fellows had created a greater number of images of the green man in Exeter Cathedral than they had carved crucifixes.

* * *

Once the barge had tied to the Quay and his men had been paid, Adam Braund made his way up from the port towards the West Gate of the city. He would remain in Exeter only long enough to gather a profitable load for the downriver journey, but he truly wished to visit briefly with his good friend, Eric Aunk. Adam had received no word from Eric in months and had begun to worry. It was not in his friend's nature to remain so distant. Passing through the West Gate of the city wall, the bargeman walked upward towards the heights of the town and finally through the gates of the Cathedral Close.

His childhood friend presently lived in a miserable hovel at the back garden of one of the canon's impressive dwellings near the Green. But Adam was proud of Eric, as he alone from their community, had risen to serve as squire to an important knight. During the recent wars with France, the knight's wealth had grown substantially. But the ignoble wretch had dismissed his squire with nothing, in spite of his having sustained dreadful, battlefield wounds in defence of his lord. Eric never specifically told Adam the cause but suggested that his lord, the knight, was nauseated by his disfigured aspect and unable to look upon his servant. Eric's young face had healed but remained horribly scarred, ravaged by sword's slashes between his eyes and across both cheeks, splitting his lips to a permanent growl of front teeth broken into jagged fangs.

Adam and Eric had grown up as village boys in Littleham Parish of Exmouth, one who was content to remain working with his father, the other pushed by his parent to "move on" in life by serving the great. "Well, ee shan't 'move on' past pitmaker now," Adam muttered to himself, "an ee kno's well, ee's fortunate ta ave dat ta sustain is mis'rable life." Both men were in their late twenties, mature but still vigorous and strong. Braund had a good wife, Telitha, whom he cherished as mistress of his household. Telitha was not only mother to his sons, she kept his family well fed, warmly clothed, and devoted to each other.

The only daughter of his old friend, Eric Aunk, had been put into a wealthy merchant's household here in Exeter, after the pitmaker's wife had run away. Eric said little about it, only that she had told him when he returned from the wars, she could not bear his ghastly face. And to complete the wounded and scarred nature of his life, she abandoned her family with no further word.

"So wha are ye about, Eric Aunk?" Braund muttered to himself. "An why ill ye nay send word ta me?"

As the bargeman walked through its paths, the Cathedral Close was, as usual, cluttered with living bodies who clamored about atop the graves of the dead. Some 'prentices' hiding from their masters were playing a rowdy game of bat the ball near the cathedral north porch and were being vigorously scolded away by the virgers, shouting that their villainy threatened the precious stained glass. Choir boys jostled each other, pushing from side to side, as they rushed out from school, inattentive to their masters' calls for order. Shopkeepers and merchants, gathered in small groups, argued amongst themselves as to the means they might employ to find adequate help. Since the plague years, fewer folk were available to work and were constantly demanding more pay! What profit could be found if wages continued to increase?

Adam walked into the garden behind the canon's house and came to the shabby hut, with its wooden door closed and shuttered window clamped against the chill autumn air. He knocked loudly upon the door, and as it included no strong latch, the rough wooden panels pushed open. Peering inside the light starved room, Adam could see little except the figure of a man suddenly lifting his head, beneath a large hood covering his face. There was little furnishing in the room, simply a raised pallet serving as a bed upon which Eric sat. Suddenly aware of the arrival of his long time friend, Eric pulled the hood across his lower face and stood up, heartily extending his hand.

"Oh Adam, God has sent you. How my heart has longed to see you. Dear friend, you are my only hope left in the world."

Grasping the extended hand and wrapping his other arm about his friend's shoulders, Braund briskly pushed the hood back and chided his friend for his gesture. "Wha do ye think yu'r doin?" he said with a great smile. "Dere be no need ta ide yer artful face, Eric Aunk. Oi ave told ye since boy'ood, ye be an ugly worm!"

Adam was shorter than his friend, so Eric bent to throw himself into his friend's strong arms. He had been beyond tears, beyond hope, with no idea of what he might do to save himself. But now, with the presence of his one true friend here in this desperate hovel, its wretched walls seemed filled with comfort. Eric forgot the hood and grasped his friend with both arms. "I am most heartily glad that you have come!"

They sat on the pallet and put their heads together, as they would have done years before when they were boys hiding from adult scrutiny. "Zo, moi errant friend," Adam taunted him gently, "as th plague returned, or wha keeps ye from us? As th cathedral's pitmaker ne time fur old friendships? Are ye still alive an well?"

"I fear you shall be disgusted with me when you learn what wickedness I have done," Eric said, while dropping his head. "I have stayed away from you and Telitha to avoid comparison with your honest goodness and honourable lives."

"Eric, ye kno Oi ave nay th slightest respect fur t'ese self-righteous, womanish churchmen an wou'd judge ye severely only if ye deigned ta join em," Adam laughed.

"I know you have no wish to share our faith, my friend, and at first I could see little seriously ill in stirring the clergy's unease. But I am being forced to move far past that which can be judged as mere irritant of the arrogant. The men of the vicar's choral, though they know not it is I who am their villain, are arming themselves against me during the night. Adam, I do not fear their clumsy attempts with weaponry, but I truly do not wish to cause harm to any one."

The bargeman sat back upon the pallet and looked directly into his friend's eyes. The tone of his voice dropped to that of very personal inquiry. "Eric, Oi belief ye mus begin at th beginnin. Wha precisely ave ye done, an who be forcin ye?"

"To make an honest beginning, I must remind you of my daughter, Ariana. When her mother left us, and I could offer her no proper home, I placed her in the household of a wealthy merchant of Exeter. He provides her room and board in his fine house on the High Street and pays for her to attend studies in a local nunnery. I am able to pay him a small amount towards her care, but he demands far more in service from me. In truth, Adam, he seems to require the sale of my soul."

"Thou art a strong man, Eric, a courageous squire an battle ardened soldier. Ow can dis tradesman presume ta control yer life in sech a manner?"

"I dread to seem weak, especially in the eyes of my greatest friend, but the merchant demands more of me, and I am in no position to refuse him for he controls the precious life of my Ariana. My only access to his house is allowed in the dark of night, and then I may only speak with him in his dank wine cellar. He tells me of Ariana's life within his household, but allows me no sight of her. He says my face would terrorize his servants; therefore, I must keep my distance as nearly to that of a leper."

"Dis be unthinkable, Eric; ow can ye be secure in anithin ee tells ye, if t'ere be ne occasion fur ye ta speak wit Ariana?"

"I am secure in nothing he says, and still his requirements of me grow daily."

The two friends continued to sit together, while Eric described his discovery of underground tunnels beneath the Cathedral Green. "I know not who built these underground passages, but they are obviously in place to bring water into the Cathedral Close. One tunnel can be exited here, Adam, next to the wall of this hovel. But I found its opening near to the cathedral, covered with an iron cap, now carpeted by weeds and grass of the Green. I discovered it when digging a pit for a recent burial, so I have carefully marked it to keep it hidden from all future digs. In the daytime or the darkness of night, I may wander freely but unseen around the Green or below ground. No one amongst the cathedral clergy can imagine how I gain entry, but then, no one amongst the clergy notes the insignificant presence of the pitmaker, unless they have need of me."

Eric went on to tell Adam of his theft of indulgences he had stolen from the walet of a young pardoner. "After I picked his walet, I sent him out to Dartmoor, telling him someone in Grimspound Village wished to sell a valuable relic from Hailes Abbey." Adam laughed out loud because every local knew Grimspound was a ruin. "It was a fool's journey onto Dartmoor," Eric said, "but it was his own avarice that drove him to pursue it." Eric explained that he wished the pardoner to be far away from Exeter before discovering his loss.

"Well, th gods ill truly bless ye fur destroyin evil, preyed pon th poor by t'ose oo call deyse'ves pardoners," Adam said with disgust.

"Oi can fin ne touch o honest pity or piety in ta lies an fraud dey sells ta simple folk."

"I did destroy the bishops' seals on the indulgences but reused them in a devilish way myself, Adam," Eric said smiling. "I changed them into documents of threat against the cathedral clergy, on orders from the merchant. I believe he seeks to stir bad feelings between the town and clergy to hide his own malevolent purpose. It seemed a perfect ploy for me to stir fear from our Celtic knowledge of the green men. The clergy feel they are threatened, but they can determine no source, no meaning. They have never truly understood the life giving truth of our Celtic spirits," Eric said with some sense of humour returning to his voice.

"Oi dare say tha mus ave been a bit o fun, bu Oi see ne great evil in it!"

"I never wished to go further, Adam, but the merchant's demands grew more deadly. He said I was to inspire fear in the Close. So I used a skull from the charnel house as bearer of one of the threats. But that, too, was not sufficient. So I employed the body of the dean's watch dog for the following threat. I felt dreadful about the dean's dog, but as the pup followed me, he fell into my secret pit and broke his neck."

"Well, ye cou'd be in danger from th local sheriff, if th dean decides ta press charges, bu be ye nay protected by canon law as pitmaker? Oi kno ye ave always been able ta speak Christ's prayer in Latin," Adam said somewhat scornfully.

"Adam, my friend, it is far worse. I fear he now wishes me to serve him as an assassin!"

* * *

Apollonia set her household into a frenzy of activity to assist her ailing husband from the wagon and into the hall of Exeter House. Servants raced to clear the way and stir the fires. The cook was informed of their return and told to speak with the Lady at first opportunity. Chaplain Anthony was summoned from his study carol to come to his master's side. Gareth and the courier, Norman of Salisbury, nearly carried Edward to a large armchair in the hall. Once there, Edward was breathless, insisting he must remain and rest, but with his usual good humour.

"I pray thee, good men," Edward said, "allow me to sit a moment and gaze at my hall. London has no glory to compare with being home. Oh, Chaplain Anthony, greetings, dear friend. Allow me to receive your welcoming blessings, but first let our prayers of praise and thanksgiving be offered to God, for I am home."

Apollonia could see that Edward was making light of his extraordinary weakness, but his heavy breathing betrayed the effort required just to sit in his chair in the hall. She desperately wanted him to remove to their chambers, but that would require his mounting a series of stairs, and he obviously had neither the strength nor the desire to achieve any further exertion. So she remained at his side, holding his hand and kissing his feverish cheek while ordering a beaker of ale brought to continue to slake his ongoing thirst. Father Anthony forbade him to kneel, but knelt at his side instead and offered prayers of thanks on behalf of the entire household for Master Edward's safe return to them.

Meanwhile, Nan came into the hall with Gareth and young Norman and drew Apollonia aside to speak quietly with her. "My Lady," Nan whispered to her, "Master Edward is so weakened by our journey. Gareth and Norman have devised a brilliant scheme to help him up into your chambers."

"Dear Nan, I have given little thought to what we must do next, but of course Edward needs to be in his bed. What have the lads devised, and how may we enable them?"

Nan simply took the lady to Gareth's side, and the stablemaster showed her the large beams he and Norman held. "Can ye fin two mor chaps ta elp us, m'Lady? We be able ta slip t'ese beams under Master Edward's chair. Den four o us shall carry im up ta yer chamber"

"Oh Gareth, you are brilliant. Stafford will bring two more of the stable lads, but will it be safe? Will the great chair not slide upon the beams?"

"Ne m'Lady, we shall tie th legs ta th beams and do o'r best ta keep im calm an level as th pond," Gareth assured her.

Within a matter of minutes, Edward was suspended aloft in his great hall chair. Then, slowly but carefully, four men of the household carried him up the stairs, two leading the way by bending low while powerful Gareth and his new friend, Norman of Salisbury, lifted the burden to their shoulders. It was a slow but steady climb, and Apollonia literally held her breath until the stairs had been accomplished. But then, it seemed no time at all, the lads had carried their master into his chamber, settled the chair, and were lifting him into his bed.

Apollonia's heart swelled with gratitude for their achievement. Edward was so very happy to be home in his own warm bed. She could feel his sense of exultation, even as he seemed to relax utterly. The lads moved to carry his chair back to the hall; Apollonia called Gareth to her side. "I shall stay here with Master Edward, Gareth, but see to it that you and the rest of the men go straight off to the kitchen for beakers of ale, warm bread, and cheese. Mary will see that you have whatever you desire. But, Gareth, you must accept my heartfelt thanks for all you have done for us these days. I shall never forget it."

He said nothing in response but nodded to her with a small smile on his face; Apollonia could see how grateful he, too, was to be home. Gareth's eyes held hers for a moment; then he slipped quietly from the chamber.

Edward soon sank into a deep sleep, his steady breathing granting to her worried soul the cherished rhythm of his presence. Apollonia lifted the fur bed coverings to his chin; as his body turned to one side, she pulled them up to his ears. She longed to crawl into the bed and grasp him to her breast. Instead, she turned to collapse upon her prie-dieu and prayed silently, passionately, searching her heart and mind for wisdom and guidance. "Lord, in your mercy send your healing angels to my dearest Edward. Sustain him always in your loving care. Help me to find your ways to restore him, and grant us your peace."

Chapter Eleven

The Doctor of Physic

Edward slept until late the following morning. When he wakened, Apollonia was sitting in a chair near his bedside. Opening his eyes, he simply looked at her in silence, as if he was unable to absorb enough of the view. At last he said, "Lonia my dearest love, I am unable to tell you how wonderful it is to be with you again."

Quickly looking up from her prayer book, she put it aside and rushed to his bed. "Dearheart, have you slept well? Indeed, my world seems whole again, just having you lying next to me through the night. Please do tell me how you fare?"

"There is so little to tell," Edward said with a sigh. "I am endlessly weak. I cannot enjoy my food, my innards seem always distressed, and I grow daily weaker."

"I have sent Jude to Lacock Abbey to speak with the Abbess Clothilde. It is my prayer that she will allow Sister Mary Redemptia to return to us with him, bringing her herbs and simples. Her skills are great and, I believe, divinely inspired. But until he returns, I shall keep you here in our bed where I can hover about you and fuss!"

"Precious wife, I am precisely where I wish to be, and I hope you will hover and fuss endlessly. It was not that our stay in London was difficult, and good Jude was sustaining company to me. But I have learned that there is great suffering in the land. Hundreds of villages lie abandoned after the last visitation of the plague. We have too few workers in the fields or taxpayers in the towns. The people are angered by the heavy costs of the unsuccessful war with France and the new poll tax, on the head of every subject, now levied to pay for it. Those of us working with the government have done nothing but add to the people's burdens, and I fear rebellion is in the air."

"Be calm, Edward, please set aside your fretting just now. You and I can do little but continue to help where we may, here in the Southwest. Past that, we shall pray for our young king and our country. But, I beg you; please address yourself to rest and growing strong again. When our sons return from school, they will want to race to your side and jump all about your bed, as is their usual habit. I have not yet told them of your illness, and I must help them to understand that they may not see you until we know from a proper healer the nature of your sickness."

Edward was crestfallen to think that he would have to hold himself distant from his boys, but he had no desire to share illness with them. He would remain in his chamber, and they would stay in their quarters with Mistress Periwinkle. Apollonia was correct to insist upon their protection first. Great bear hugs or father and son wrestling must wait until they knew the true nature of his body's distress.

* * *

Late in the afternoon, Jude returned from Lacock Abbey alone, but bearing a message from the Lady Abbess. She expressed her sincere concern for the welfare of Lady Apollonia's husband, but Abbess Clothilde said she could not allow Sister Mary Redemptia to leave their convent. The good sister had grown thin and aged within the past years, and although her healing arts were beyond compare for others, she seemed unable to find cure for herself. The abbess feared her precious nun would never be able to stand the rigours of the journey to Exeter. However, she wished her dear friend, the Lady Apollonia, to know that Exeter had, within its precincts, a well known surgeon who served the Cistercian monks of Dunkeswell, as well as the canons of the cathedral. His name was Nicholas of Tiverton, who had trained with the foremost surgeon of the land, John of Arderne. "Surely," the abbess continued in her message, "as a doctor of physic, he must serve the great families of Devon and will surely come to your aid."

Apollonia thanked Jude for his devoted service and suggested he return to his quarters for a well-deserved rest. She did require him to send their new courier, Norman, to her. He was then dispatched to the house of Canon Chulmleigh, requesting his help in locating the dwelling of Nicholas of Tiverton.

"When you are informed of the surgeon's whereabouts, Norman, please deliver this message to him in person." She placed a small missive into his hands. "Do not return until you are able to bring him with you."

* * *

It required another day and a half before Norman was able to return to Exeter House, bringing the physician in tow. Upon his entry into their home, Doctor Nicholas roughly informed Apollonia that he would first require a complete examination of the patient. Afterwards, he would wish to speak with the men who served him, as well as the cooks who prepared food for him. Further, he insisted, he would need to speak with the mistress of the laundry.

Apollonia thought the physician to be proud and aggressive, but she knew she would be eternally grateful to him if his methods found cure for Edward. She took him to Edward's chamber and attempted to introduce him to her husband. Doctor Nicholas ignored her efforts, as he seemed to have no interest in the name of the person he was to treat. He pulled back the covers of the bed and began to examine all parts of Edward's body in a lengthy and detailed way. He looked into his eyes, his mouth, and his nose. He felt his head, his arms, and pressed several areas of his abdomen. When he was told there was no example of his patient's urine or faeces available, he demanded that she bring the chamber pot.

Apollonia carried it to him and then stood back to one side of the chamber. Doctor Nicholas continued to move about the bed, endlessly examining and prodding, all the while urging Edward to relieve himself into the pot immediately. The Lady felt somewhat overwhelmed by this physician; he was like no other healer she had ever known. But in her heart, she was grateful that Dr. Nicholas did not immediately insist upon bleeding Edward. Her dear husband was so weakened and enfeebled; Apollonia could not bear to think of him being further drained of his body's sustaining fluid.

The Lady had sent Nan off to complete Dr. Nicholas's orders. Everyone whom he had requested must be gathered in the hall for his instructions later that evening. Nan rushed from kitchen to stables, insisting that all members of the household must stop what they were doing and wash their hands immediately. The Doctor of Physic required it.

As Apollonia continued to stand in the corner of their bedchamber, Doctor Nicholas suddenly spoke directly to her. "All used and dirty linen must be gone from this chamber. I require an obsession for cleanliness. No one in this household, not even you, my Lady, shall be allowed near my patient unless he has carefully washed himself. Is that understood?" Apollonia assured the physician that she was fully aware of his instruction, and she was seeing to it that his requirements for cleanliness were being made known to everyone.

When the Aust sons returned from school that afternoon, they found the household in a turbulence of activity, but before they could touch a morsel of food, each was sent to the pump to wash. Then they were told that although their father was home, he was in the care of a physician and would not be able to see them. Apollonia promised she would come to them after their evening meal to fully apprise them of their father's state, for she knew how each of them would fret and worry when they knew he was seriously ill.

It seemed the early evening hours passed painfully slowly, but at last Dr. Nicholas returned to the hall to interview the staff. After he had spoken with Jude, Gareth, Nan, and Mary, the cook, in her presence, Apollonia waited to speak with him. "A chamber has been prepared for you to rest with us this night, doctor, but may I share some moments of your time to learn of the true nature of my husband's illness?"

"My Lady of Aust, you have probably noticed my methods are unusual and my requirements may seem strange. But I received my training in the home and practice of the great English surgeon, John of Arderne, who lives in Nottinghamshire. He studied the achievements of the medical school of Salerno and perfected ancient Arabic methods of human healing. I possess a copy of his scholarly book and am devoted to his healing methods. That said; let me also inform you of my use of the 'zodiac man.'" Dr. Nicholas produced a parchment with a diagram of the human body, its various parts linked to their signs of the zodiac.

"Arderne utilizes this diagram, as a surgeon, to determine proper times for operations. I also employ it to determine causes of malady. I have conferred closely with your servant, Jude, upon the timing of your husband's increasing illness and its relation to the stars. I have come to the conclusion that your husband has developed a severe digestive ailment, first introduced through the foul food of London, but worsened through the advance of an intestinal distress, aggravated by evil signs. I have given him a purgative. After he is fully purged, we shall begin afresh to heal him."

Dr. Nicholas heaved a great sigh. It had obviously been a very long day for him, as well as for the Aust household, but seeing the Lady's obvious distress and fear, he continued to explain his approach to Edward's healing. "My Lady, I have instructed your cook to ply him with camomile tea and pomegranates. As there are no pomegranates in her kitchen, she will seek them out in Exeter's market first thing on the morrow. I shall remain with you this night. Pray accept my thanks for your hospitality. God's blessings upon this household as I retire," and with a great yawn, Dr. Nicholas prepared to leave the hall.

Stafford stood ready to escort the physician to his chamber, while Apollonia expressed her sincere thanks to him. He was barely gone before she ran up to the bedchamber where Edward lay. Her husband's hearty grin seemed somewhat diminished; still, Edward reached up to her, as she approached his bed, and kissed her hand. He was nearly ready to fall asleep once again, but as his eyes drooped, he also seemed to retain a naughty twinkle. "You know, Lonia, I do not believe I have ever in my life been so cleansed—inside and out!"

* * *

Early the following morning, Mistress Mathe returned to her kitchen from the market with a basket including three pomegranates. Muttering aloud, she was unaware that the rest of the kitchen staff kept beyond her notice until she could be seen to have calmed from the cause of her anger. Apollonia walked into the kitchen to bring an empty cup and request yet another one, refilled of camomile tea for Edward. Noticing the distress of the cook, she paused to speak with her. "This tea has been most beneficial for Master Edward, Mary. Did you have any luck in our search for pomegranates?"

"Oh aye, m'Lady, Oi ave returned wit three. Bu thee'll think me th worst o spendthrifts! Oi ad ta pay six shillins fur em!"

"Dear Mary," Apollonia said as she put her hand upon the cook's sturdy arm, "it will be a small price, indeed, if these fruits restore Master Edward. Kindly wash one thoroughly and cut it up for me, that I may take it to him directly."

* * *

"Dere is ne udder way, Eric; we mus remove yer daughter from th house o dis merchant!" Slapping his knee, Adam Braund stamped his foot on the floor of the hovel and stood to his full height.

"But even if we do, Adam, I can not bring her here. This hovel is little more than covering from the rain; I can offer her nothing! Beyond that, females are never allowed to remain within the Close after Compline. I had hoped that she might live in comfort in Wolfson's great house and receive an education to improve her station in life."

Adam scowled and took his friend by his shoulders. "Ye dimwitted worm, why ill ye nay turn ta yer friends? Oi ave a good ome, an moi wife, Tely, ill open er eart ta yer Ariana. O course, we can nay offer a grand ouse in th city nor schoolin in th nunnery, bu she ill be safe an well cared fur wit us in Littleham."

Eric dropped to his knees, grasping Adam's hand. "I could never ask for such goodness, but I confess to having prayed daily for deliverance. Do you believe it may be done? I can not go near the merchant's house except after dark, when bidden, and even then may not show my face to his servants."

"Wha be dis merchant's name, Eric?"

"He is called Raymond Wolfson, and he has grown mightily rich in the woollen trade. Ye can not miss his great house in the town. It is on the High Street."

"Ye mus see tha dis Wolfson as wicked designs, or ee shou'd nay be usin ye so, Eric. Ee presumes ta require dastardly deeds o ye, cause ee beliefs ye be friendless. An moi best loved worm, ye be ne'er witout friends."

* * *

In the darkness of the autumn evening, at the hour when great houses served their evening meal, the two friends walked together out of the Close and through the empty High Street. When they reached the Wolfson house, lights could be seen burning within its many rooms, but especially in the great hall. Servants were rushing into the house through the side doorway, carrying extra wood for the large fireplace. Eric stayed some distance away from that entrance, his hooded face hidden in the shadows of a space between buttressing of the nearby church.

"Oi mus git Ariana out o der afore curfew," Adam announced to him. And with that, he strode towards the house.

As Eric watched from his safe distance, he saw Adam pick up several logs in his arms and march into the house with the servants, as if he belonged to the household.

Eric held his breath. "What would Adam do if he were stopped by the owner? How would he explain his presence? Oh, why had he allowed his hotheaded friend to become involved?" Eric knew well that Adam had not, since their youths, acknowledged anyone to gainsay him.

Time passed slowly. Eric pulled his hooded cape more tightly round his shoulders and began to stamp his feet silently, so that they would not grow numb in the evening's chill. Eric's clothes were worn, and he had not been able for years to consider replacing his boots, now also worn with patched holes in the under soles. The noise from the Wolfson house continued to grow, he noticed, as many inside imbibed their way towards drunkenness. "What a crowd is gathered here," Eric thought to himself. "There must be some sort of celebration going on."

Then, from his side, a small voice spoke into the darkness, "Father, are you really here?"

His hood dropped to his shoulders as he reached down to scoop his little girl into his arms, holding her next to his heart.

"Ne, nay now, moi friend." Adam pulled him from the wall. "Old er close, bu we mus be away!"

Adam led the little group up the street and into an alleyway, as Eric carried Ariana, her arms clinging tightly round his neck. Staying within the dark, back alleys of Exeter, they quickly walked down towards the city wall, slipped through the West Gate, and turned towards the Quay. Throughout their journey on foot, neither friend said anything to the other, and Ariana, too, seemed to realise that her silence could only contribute to their safety from being discovered. Set at last upon the ground, Ariana held tightly to her father's hand and walked closely beside him. She pressed his hand to her cheek, telling him wordlessly how happy she was to be with him again.

When they reached the dock along the River Exe where Adam's barge was moored, they walked silently across the boarding plank and climbed onto its long deck. "Ey dere, oo go's?" came the call of Adam's watchmen, the last two remaining members of his crew from Exmouth.

Adam laughed aloud and shouted in return that he had come to test their watchfulness. But then, signaling the men to come to his side, he silently indicated to them the presence of his passengers, while holding a finger pressed across his lips. As they stood near, he ordered them to continue a keen watch throughout the night, to be certain he and his friends were ne'er followed. Then he and Eric, still clutching Ariana by her hand, walked into the low roofed cabin on the barge where Adam lit a small candle. For the first time in many months past, Eric was blessed with the sight of his daughter.

* * *

Edward was sitting up in his bed, supported and propped on all sides by great cushions. He was a sturdy man with great strong arms and powerful legs; yet on this day he had not the strength to hold up his own head. Still, his manner was cheerful, and he obviously sought to reassure his wife in every way he could imagine. "Lonia, I can not tell the pleasure you bring me by walking once again into my presence. Do you know I am ever surprised by your beauty and your willingness to accept my clumsy attempts to love you?"

"Oh yes, indeed, do add more compliments to my morning, Edward. You know how my vanity longs for them. Silly one! You are to open your mouth and allow me to feed you until this entire pomegranate is consumed!" Apollonia put a large napkin beneath his chin. "Mistress Mathe has washed this fruit until its skin has nearly smoothed, then cut it into pieces so that you may suck out all its best juice, eating its pulp and seeds as you go."

Edward was somewhat surprised at this choice of nourishment, but he offered no objection. As she offered each piece to him, he sucked its juices, filling his mouth with its interior pulp and seeds, chewing and swallowing everything edible from within its skin.

"What do you think of it, dearheart; can you enjoy this fruit?" Apollonia asked him.

"It has a strange sweetness, somewhat austere, difficult to tell if it is sweet or sour," he said as he continued to chew. "But yes, I do like it. Its seeds are strange but very edible, and I have always enjoyed fruits with a bit of tang to them."

"Well, my love, Doctor Nicholas has prescribed pomegranates for you to ease your stomach distress. He will be in to see you later in the morning, as he has gone to the Cathedral Close to make a call."

"Oh I say, this medical recipe is far more to my liking than any purgative," Edward said with a sigh, as he settled further into his cushions.

"Well, our dear cook has strained her parsimonious soul to achieve them for you." Apollonia noticed that Edward seemed to be slipping towards sleep once again. She wiped his chin, put the napkin aside, and held his hand in both of hers.

Edward seemed to drowse, so she remained with him. Gently holding his hand, Apollonia slipped to the floor to kneel beside his bed, praying silently. "God in Thy Mercy, bless my Edward with restorative rest. Gracious Father, bring back to his family the hale and hearty, loving father and husband he has always been to us."

She was still deep in prayer and meditation when Dr. Nicholas burst into their chamber. He was a tall man with a huge head and unkempt, dark hair, ill controlled by his liripipe, hooded head dress. His face was illumined by intense, dark eyes that seemed to possess the ability to peer into one's soul, Apollonia thought. The physician's first request of her was to be allowed to examine the morning faeces of his patient. Seeing it to be entirely liquid, he nodded his head, satisfied with the results of the earlier purgative.

Then, he turned to the Lady and said very distinctly, "I have employed a sedative to encourage your husband to sleep. But when the sun approaches its high noon, I would like for him to attempt to eat porridge of oats and honey. Your cook tells me that you have two more pomegranates. I should like you to encourage him to eat another pomegranate after his porridge. Again he should sup in the evening with yet another bowl of porridge and after that, yet one last pomegranate. By morning on the morrow, I shall return to examine his progress."

With those instructions, the physician looked to the Lady to see if she would require any further directives. She had only one question. "Will you allow our sons to visit their father during his convalescence? They are aware they must be well scrubbed and cleanly clothed before they may enter his presence."

"Not yet," Dr. Nicholas said forcefully, "he must be encouraged to rest. Please let us await his progress on the morrow."

* * *

Later that evening a quiet supper was prepared for the boys in the kitchen with Mistress Periwinkle and the chaplain, when Apollonia sought to explain to them their father's present condition. She took special care to describe the temporary nature of the physician's reasons for not allowing them to see him, making every effort in her tone of voice not to cause them alarm. Their sons were obviously disturbed to think of their father being ill. He was never ill, they thought, and said as much. To avoid further explanations of their father's condition and questions she could not answer, Apollonia was pleased this evening to address a very different distraction that David had managed to bring into their home, needing their care.

"I found him in the Close, Mamam," Davie explained. "Perhaps he fell from the trees, but he was lying on the grass, and naughty boys were beating upon him with their sticks."

David was speaking of the body of an emaciated squirrel, now lying upon a small nest of hay inside a falcon's cage in the barn.

"We know he is not dead, Mamam. Gareth told us he could still feel his heart beating, and Jude told me that squirrels are very sturdy creatures," Alban said.

"But he is so hungry, and one of his paws seems badly hurt. Can we not care for him until he is hearty once again?" David pleaded. "I will go everyday to the barn after school, so that Gareth will not feel overburdened by his care."

"First of all things I must ask you, Davie and Alban and Thomas as well, have you all washed your hands very carefully since you carried the squirrel home?" Apollonia questioned them sternly. "Dr. Nicholas has required everyone coming into our household to wash and wash again to protect your father in his weakened state."

"Oh yes, Mamam," Thomas said with his presumption of authority as the eldest, "I saw to it that Davie and Alb washed first; then I scrubbed my hands well. But Gareth also told us that the squirrel's damaged paw may heal if we can just find enough nuts to make his belly fat again."

"Hmmm," Apollonia mused, looking into the pleading eyes of her boys. She was, in her own heart, proud of their desire to care for God's creatures, but she knew she would have to enforce some conditions. Holding up her graceful left hand, she pointed to one long finger with her right hand. "First, we shall house your squirrel in the barn only. Secondly, you must all acknowledge to me that you understand that the little creature may die in spite of your loving care." Then ticking off another finger to emphasize her point, she said forcefully, "Thirdly, you may not ever bring the squirrel into our home, and lastly, if he should survive, you will release him once he is restored. Will you all agree to these conditions?"

With an enthusiastic, "Yes, Mamam!" the boys began to think out loud where they knew to search for some nuts or leaves the squirrel would enjoy eating. But Apollonia brought their attention back to the more important concern of the household. "You may see the squirrel tomorrow, but for this evening we shall all repair to the chapel while

Father Anthony leads our prayers for your dear father. He is so truly pleased to be home with us once again, but we need to thank God for his safe return while we pray for the continued blessings of healing."

As the little group prepared to leave the kitchen and walk towards the chapel, David pulled at his mother's long sleeve.

"And when the physician says it is allowed for us to be in father's chamber, I have a wonderful story to tell him," he said with sly wink at his mother.

* * *

Eric could see his daughter, Ariana, was utterly fatigued, but she offered no complaint and continued to hold tightly to his hand as if fearful of losing him again. "My dear child," Eric said, "I want you to know my greatest friend. This is Master Braund, whom I have known and loved since we were boys together in our home village of Littleham."

Ariana curtseyed to Adam and continued to say nothing but hold tightly to her father's hand. "She did'n esitate ta coom wit me when Oi tol er Oi wou'd take er ta er Daddy," Adam said. "Dere were sech a great doin goen on in th Wolfson ouse, Oi do'n think anione noticed o'r leavin!"

"Ariana," Eric said to his still frightened daughter, "I took you away from the Wolfson's great house to be certain that you are truly safe and well cared for. I now have reasons to distrust Master Wolfson's purposes." As they sat together, Eric continued unaware that while he spoke his hood fell, leaving his full face and head uncovered before his daughter and his friend. Ariana was not the least bit frightened by the twisted scars and lifted her small hand to his cheek, silently caressing it as he spoke.

"Father, I have so longed to see you; please do not make me return to that house. Master Wolfson is incapable of kindness to anyone in his household. May I not stay with you always? I shall clean for you, wash your clothes, and cook our meals."

Eric's eyes, so full of hope and welcome, became downcast. He knew he would be forced to tell her there was no way they could be together yet, until he could find a place for them to live outside the Cathedral Close. "But I shall find a small dwelling where we may live together, if you will agree to stay with Adam's family until it is possible."

It was then that Adam leaned towards the father and daughter, suggesting they could speak of these things in the morning. He had prepared a small bed in the corner of the cabin that he urged Eric to use. Ariana, he said, could sleep on the truckle pulled from beneath it. Father and daughter, both fully exhausted by the emotional demands of their reunion, nodded in agreement and lay upon their separate berths readily. But Adam noticed when he moved to blow out the candle that Ariana still clutched her father's hand while Eric's arm dropped from the side of his bed to continue to hold hers.

Chapter Twelve

The Account of the Aulnage

The days that followed Edward Aust's return to Exeter House were enlivened by an entire household, joyfully devoted to the restoration of their master, father, and husband. Everyone seemed to wait each day until Lady Apollonia would bring the physician's comments upon Edward's growing return to sound health. After sharing her news with the household each morning, Apollonia would smile to herself. Indeed, she knew that her husband was recovering, slowly but definitely, for he seemed unable to keep his hands from her whenever she moved to his bedside to wash or help to feed him. The touch of his hands always pleased her, but especially now when she wanted to believe that his private caresses betrayed an even greater improvement in his own body's sense of well-being. In so many ways, various appetites were returning to him. "Could we not try a bit more meat, Lonia? I have a real desire to find a good chop resting upon my plate."

But it was the first evening when their sons were allowed to enter Edward's chamber and greet their father that Lady Apollonia allowed herself to believe that soon all would be well. Thomas took Alban and David very sedately into the bedchamber and stood at some distance, as if waiting for their father's notice. Edward, sitting up in his bed, dropped his legs to the floor and threw his arms up into the air. All three rushed to crowd into his arms and be swallowed in their father's love. Thomas emerged from the squash first, straightening his clothes and urging his brothers to be gentle. "Me thinketh, Father, you need us to express our good wishes as gently as possible until you are returned to full strength."

Alban, too, wishing to display his masculine dignity, pulled away but only to stand near to his father's bed and hold his hand, while Davie remained curled into his father's other arm. Edward looked at his boys with infinite pride in his smile. "Tom, Alb, Davie, I must tell you all how proud I am. You have grown into young men, offering important help to your mother and assistance within the household during my illness. You have behaved dependably and honourably. I commend you: Thomas, for your leadership; you, Alban, for your strength; and you, little Davie, for your constancy. I thank each of you for your willingness to fill my place whilst I have been ill."

"Oh, Father, none of us could take your place," Thomas said with great feeling. "We just hoped to be good enough to help you grow better."

"And I found I could offer real help to Gareth with the horses, Father," Alban went on. "He showed me many ways to keep their stalls tidy and exercise them well!"

"Mamam has let us keep a sadly injured squirrel in the barn, father," David added. "Jude said he is growing stronger, too, but we shall have to turn him loose soon, cause we promised."

"All is well, my cherubs," Apollonia called to them from the opposite bedside, "but now you must allow your father to rest. Please kneel to receive his blessing, and return with Mistress Periwinkle to your supper."

When the boys left the room, Apollonia closed the chamber door and ran to take their place next to Edward. Without the slightest hesitation, she threw herself into his arms as their conjugal embrace fell back to engage the entire bedstead. Theirs was a glorious sense of reunion and healing, completing the physical and spiritual joy Edward and Apollonia knew best when their two bodies pressed firmly together as one.

* * *

Later in the week, as Edward had grown strong enough to sit in his great chair in the hall to oversee the growth of their woollen stores in Exeter, he and Apollonia received a surprise visit from one of Apollonia's new friends. They were going over accounts and carefully examining the stamps of the aulnage when Nan entered the hall, obviously pleased with her announcement. "My Lady, Master Edward, we have a caller. Mistress Phyllis of Bath has come."

"Oh, Edward, you will so enjoy meeting Phyllis. She is one true friend amongst many hospitable people here in Exeter, but she has also been most graciously helpful to me as a stranger, learning the ways of the local wool trade."

"I shall be delighted," Edward said. "Please, Nan, do show her in, and kindly bring us a bit of refreshment as we chat."

Phyllis of Bath seemed to enter the hall in a roar. Not only her voice but her boisterous good cheer seemed to fill the great room. "Mawster Aust! Oi ave eard o yer recovery, an Oi do add moi thanks an praise ta God fur Is blessins!"

"Mistress Phyllis," Edward said as he remained in his chair, "my greetings and heartfelt welcome to you. Kindly forgive my not rising, but do sit yourself in this chair next to mine that we may meet on equal terms. My dear wife has told me of your goodness and helpfulness to her as she struggled alone here in Exeter. You will always be regarded as our true friend, ever welcome in our home, and confidant in matters of business."

"Ye mus'n tire yerse'v, Mawster Edward, bu tis o matters o bus'ness tha Oi also coom ta speak wit ye." Phyllis of Bath settled her substantial body into the chair at his side but next spoke directly to Apollonia, "M'Lady, Oi ken see ye ave already received th stamp o th aulnage pon yer cloths. Ave ye met is onour, Moreton Molton?"

"Indeed I have, Mistress Phyllis," Apollonia said, "and I found him to be extremely competent and a truly honourable gentleman. He takes his role as the king's servant very seriously and assures for all of us in the trade the mark of quality upon our products." In truth, Apollonia had found the aulnage to be an extraordinary man, very quiet and unassuming, but so confident in his desire for excellence that everyone who received his stamp felt their woollen cloths increased in value.

"Well den, Oi mus tell ye both, Oi belief is onour, Moreton Molton, is bein threatened an requires o'r elp." Phyllis went on to share some troublous comments she had been hearing in the markets, specifically that some in the trade had attempted to bribe the aulnage and, when he proved beyond bribery, made suggestions of scheming to remove him. "Oi do'n wish ta charge ani person wit wrongdoin, bu th gossip says on merchant in Exeter, by name o Raymond Wolfson, is reglar gatherin wool merchants to is ouse ta see ow many o dem be disgruntled wit th aulnage."

"This is a serious charge, Mistress Phyllis," Edward said slowly. "And I thank you kindly for bringing it to our note, but we must have some proof of ill intent. Should we do so, we must inform the mayor."

"Aye, Mawster Aust, Oi be thinking as ye be, bu ow are we ta gain sech 'proof?'"

Apollonia looked at Stafford, their aged household steward, and acknowledged to herself that he would not be a good candidate for spying in the market place. As if in response to her glance, Stafford groaned quietly and put his head down, wishing to continue unnoticed. Then, she said, "But Edward, why can we not go directly to the aulnage and speak with him? We know him to be an honourable gentleman who may well have faced such threats before. Would we not be wise to share our concerns with him and put him on his guard, so to speak?"

"Oi wil coom wit ye," Phyllis said with enthusiasm. "If'n we tells im o'r worry, it'l at leas giv im time to protec imse'v."

"Indeed, I believe you are both correct," Edward said thoughtfully. "Yet, I fear we must also try to protect ourselves, simply by inviting him to come to us. It would not be unusual for the aulnage to be seen to examine our woollen cloths here, whereas it would be noticeable to others if we were to go to his home. What think you?"

Apollonia grasped his idea immediately. "Why not send an invitation to him to assist us on Thursday of this week? Phyllis, will you be free to return then?"

"Oi'll be certain ta be ere."

"Then we are agreed?" Edward held out his right hand, and each woman placed her own hand into his palm.

* * *

Ariana awoke to see her father moving about the barge, talking quietly with his friend, Master Braund. She stretched with enthusiasm. What a good night she had enjoyed, sleeping next to her father for the first time in nearly a year! Pulling her long, blonde hair into some semblance of tidiness, she rose from her truckle bed and bent to fold the blankets, before tucking all neatly beneath the larger bunk. Eric and Adam walked back into the cabin to find her risen for the new day and already busy. "Greetings my little love, did you sleep well?" Eric said, as he took her in his arms.

Adam brought out some bread and cheese, and they all ate heartily after their adventures the previous night. "Oi shall ave ta go inta th town dis mornin ta arrange a load fur transport back ta Exmouth," he said. "That'll give ye bot time ta consider yer choices. Ariana, child, Oi kno ye do'n kno me well, bu Oi can tell ye truly moi good wife, Telitha, wou'd love ta ave ye be wit us, jus til yer fadder can work thin's out." With that, Adam put his hat onto his head, firmly clasped Eric's shoulder, and walked onto the deck, leaving Eric and his daughter to speak together.

Ariana sat on a stool with her head down. "Father, why must I always stay in a stranger's home?"

"Ariana love, look at my face. You can see straightaway I am a vision of horror. People flee from me. But I have found a good way to support us through using my strength as pitmaker for the cathedral chapter." Eric kneeled by her side and took her shoulders into his hands. "I would love nothing more than to have you with me, but even if my hut at the back garden of the canon's house were warm enough and comfortable for you, I cannot have a female living with me in the Close. The cathedral clergy are all celibate, and every woman who comes into the Close during the day must be gone when its gates are closed for the night." He dropped his head as if in utter despair. Then he could feel her small hands touching both of his cheeks, lining his deep scars with a soft finger, and pulling his head up towards her face.

"I am looking at your face, and I shall never flee from you, Father. I see in your scars, wounds achieved through your strength and courage in the defence of your lord in battle. Your face does not frighten me; it is the face I love most in the world," Ariana said, as she lay her head upon his chest.

Eric wrapped her in his arms. "Forgive me, child, I have underestimated you in every way," he said as he held her. "I have also misjudged a dear friend and his desire to help us." With that, Eric tried to describe for her the magnitude of his lifelong friendship with Adam Braund. He continued filling her imagination with his warm memories from their shared childhood village of Littleham, their devotion to each other, and willingness to protect and defend each other against any threat. "Adam is the greatest of friends, and I am ashamed to admit that I sought to make something of myself better than him. My father endlessly urged me to serve the nobility, model my life upon theirs, and attempt to become a gentleman. As you may see, I can speak as the gentry, but I am and will ever only be a pitmaker."

"Father, you will always be my ideal of chivalry, and if I must have courage and strength, I promise I shall try to be like you."

Eric determined at that moment that he would never again cover his face from the world. If his precious daughter and his most faithful friend accepted him as he truly was, he would emerge from his shadow world and face the future with honesty.

* * *

Phyllis of Bath arrived early in the morning of the following Thursday, announced through her usual cloud of boisterous greeting. "Oi need no introduc'on to yer Mawster an is lady," she shouted to Nan, while being led into the great hall of Exeter House. "God give ye good day, m'Lady, Mawster Edward. Ave dere been ani word from is onour?"

"Blessings upon you, Mistress Phyllis, we have indeed received his willing response. Pray be seated with us as we await his coming," Edward said, when he rose to welcome her.

"Ye need'n stand fur me coomin, Mawster Edward, bu Oi dare swere, ye seemeth stronger as th days pass!"

"Indeed, having Edward at home has seen his recovery from malady, but now I am stressed to achieve all he requires," Apollonia said with a warm smile.

They sat together near the great fireplace, as the days of autumn brought more chill to the mornings. They had not been long in their visit when Nan entered the hall to announce that His Honour, Moreton Molton, the Royal Aulnage, had arrived in response to their invitation. They all rose together to greet and welcome him as he entered.

"God's blessing be upon this household, my Lady of Aust, Master Edward, Mistress Phyllis; I bring you greetings." The aulnage was a relatively small man but graceful in his movements, with generous sweeping of his hands when he spoke, as if to display his very elegant long fingers. He moved with a sense of self-awareness, unmistakably that of a servant of the King. "I thank you for your kind invitation and presume to be your guest this day, as I have already officially supervised all of your cloths' production full seemly."

"Our thanks willingly, Sir Moreton, pray be seated in the midst of our party, for we dare not deny a need to speak with you," Edward said, leading their guest to a large chair.

Nan entered the hall with a tray of wine goblets and began to serve the company as they were seated. Courtesy normally required that their conversation would progress slowly towards its real purpose, but Phyllis had no patience with such dithering. "Do ye nay kno o th gossip abou thee?"

Molton simply raised his eyebrows and said nothing, but Edward picked up her theme. "Mistress Phyllis has heard several voices in the market expressing some suggestion of growing threat against you, Sir Molton, largely because of your recognized honesty and rigorous refusal to take bribes. My lady wife, Apollonia, and I have agreed with Mistress Phyllis that such gossip may mean little, unless persons of influence be the sources of its spread."

The aulnage continued to listen patiently to everything they had to tell him. But once they had laid the extent of their concerns for his safety before him, he changed the subject completely and seemed only to wish to defend his activities.

"Since the days of our mighty sovereign, King Richard the first of that name, royalty has ordered an examination of all woollen cloths to assure they are of the same width and of the same goodness in the middle and sides. Latterly, our great King Edward, also the first of that name, appointed officials, the aulnagers, to enforce the royal order. As of late, the diversity of the wool and the importation of cloths from abroad have made it impossible to maintain standards of width, so that aspect of the law has been repealed, but I devote my life's duty to maintain the required standards of our Devon cloths," Sir Molton said with great dignity.

"By my troth, your honour, it is because of your maintenance of royal standards that our trade has achieved respect in all ports of Europe," Edward said earnestly. "But sir, we implore you to consider, there may be those who wish your replacement. They may seek to do you harm. Whether sayest you?"

The aulnage sat quietly for several moments and, having considered his words, responded very pointedly. "I am aware of the agitations of Master Wolfson amongst the merchant class in Exeter, and I do believe you are correct; he may be seeking my replacement. Gramercy, each of you; I shall be on my guard and should be grateful if you will share any further word of warning you may encounter. Most importantly, I am grateful for your gracious willingness to express your concerns to me. None other in our family of merchants has seen fit to do so. I am sincerely touched by your expressions of solicitation upon my account."

* * *

When Adam returned to his barge later in the afternoon, he seemed mightily pleased with his day's accomplishment. He had managed to acquire a sturdy load needing transport downriver to Exmouth on the morrow. As he approached Eric on the deck of the barge, he was happily surprised to find his friend walking about with his daughter, and amongst the remaining crewmen, with his face completely exposed; his hood was thrown back, his hair was combed to one side, and his twisted facial scars were browning in the sunlight. "Greetin's, moi ugly worm!" he shouted, "ow go's yer day?"

Eric strode towards his friend with Ariana walking at his side, her hand in his. "Adam, you find me renewed. My precious daughter is teaching her father important steps along the road to honest manhood. And she has an important request to seek from you."

Ariana seemed to shrink into shyness but then lifted her head and addressed her father's friend straightforwardly. "Master Braund, my father has told me of the great friendship you have shared since childhood. I truly thank thee for your kind invitation to live within your household, and I pledge to do all that I can to offer any service to your wife and family."

Adam grinned a great, broad smile and said to her with honest enthusiasm, "Den we be off ta Exmouth on th morrow. Moi dear Tely ill welcoom thee wit open arms. She did always wish dat one o o'r rowdy boys moight hav been a girlchild."

But Ariana had not finished her speech to her father's friend. Still looking up into his eyes, she continued to speak to Adam Braund. "May I ask, sir, why it is that you continue to call my father a 'worm?'"

Adam broke into a huge burst of laughter, while Eric, too, felt a need to smile at her earnest expression of protection of her father's image. But it was Eric who began to share their story. "Oh, pet, Adam and I share no expressions of discourtesy between us. Adam has always called me a worm, simply because I loved to dig holes in the sand when we used to play on the beach."

"Coom now, Eric, give th child th full story." Adam looked down upon Ariana and said in his straightforward manner, "Oi calls im a worm cause ee wer th worm oo saved me!"

As they sat together on the moored barge, Adam told Ariana how, on one occasion, when they were exploring along sandy cliffs looking for sea caves, a great portion of the cliff broke away, burying him beneath its suffocating weight. "Oi cou'd do nothin fur mese'v. Th weight o th sand pinned me arms an legs, bu yer daddy, ne mor'an a boy imse'v, dug me out o an early grave wit is bare ands. Oi calls im a worm, cause ee kno's is burrowin inta th earth saved moi life."

Ariana looked up proudly. "Oh father, I have always known you are a hero!"

"Oh aye, tha ee is." Adam agreed enthusiastically, "bu we mus'n let im grow a big ead abou it."

* * *

Eric said goodbye to his daughter the following afternoon but found it difficult to leave the dock where he had stood waving, shouting promises to be together soon, until the barge finally disappeared into the far distance downriver. At last, pulling himself to his full height, he reached for the hood of his cape as he normally would have done, to shield the greater part of his facial scars from public view. His hand stopped in mid-movement, and he said to himself, "I am who I am," and walked back to the lanes leading up from the river and eventually towards the West Gate of Exeter. He decided he would be worthy of his daughter's love. If Ariana loved him as he was, others must learn to accept him as well. He would no longer continue to serve as a creature of the underworld; he would no longer live in the shadows.

When he reached the High Street of Exeter, he continued walking to the great house of Merchant Wolfson. He approached the front entrance and pulled the bell. When the servant answered, he announced that he was Eric Aunk, pitmaker to the cathedral, who wished to speak with his master. He waited just inside the door, as the servant seemed unwilling to admit him further into the house but hurried off to announce to his master the apparition waiting at the entrance. The wool merchant steamed towards him from his chambers with arms raised in threatening ire. "Aunk, I have told you never to come here! You shall pay for your disobedience!"

Eric simply stood his ground and responded with courtesy and respect. "My daughter is no longer resident within your household, Master Wolfson, and I shall require nothing further of you in her behalf. Therefore, I shall no longer offer you my services."

He turned sharply from the hallway where he had stood and walked out through the front entrance onto the High Street, making his way back towards the Cathedral Close. He could not help but notice that some people, whom he passed on the street, did pause to stare at his disfigured face, but then each turned and went on. When he arrived at the entrance into the Close, the gatekeeper recognized him straightaway but did not stare. Eric was known within the Close.

As he walked along the lane leading to the canon's house, he turned into its back garden where his small hovel waited for him. One of the cathedral virgers was coming from knocking upon its door. As he saw Eric walking through the garden, he addressed him immediately. "Master Aunk, how fortunate I am to find you. We shall need your services this very afternoon. There have been two deaths in the parish of St Sidwell. Kindly come to prepare the pits by one of the clock."

Eric assured his prompt attention, and the virger, satisfied with his errand, walked away. What a glorious feeling of freedom he experienced. Eric could not help but lift his face to the sun. Its golden rays seemed to caress his scars and warm his cheeks. "Oh, my precious Ariana, your wise and innocent reasonings have saved me from terrors of my own making." Then, following the departing virger, Eric walked to the north side of the cathedral to the bread house to collect his daily allowance of bread.

Chapter Thirteen

With Malignity

The required graves were opened and ready when Eric entered the cathedral in search of the head virger. He was paid his usual fee, but this time the money seemed more than coins to him; it filled his heart with hope. He had begun to see that through careful savings from all of his fees, he could find a way to afford Ariana's return to Exeter. He required little to support himself, and with no more regular payments to Wolfson for her board, his wages could support a small flat in the town, perhaps down by the river, but outside the Close. The mere thought of finding a small accommodation, where he and his daughter would be able to live together, offered Eric exciting promise of a new life.

As he was walking through the graveyard, several of the young boys paused in their ballgame to exchange insulting remarks, behind their pointing fingers, in his direction. Normally he would have turned away. Instead, Eric walked directly to the place where they were playing and said quietly, "Lads, I have gained these scars in battle, serving my lord and my king. If you wish to continue in mockery, I shall speak with you singly, or together, in your masters' shops."

The boys were so taken aback to have him standing there, addressing them, they dropped their ball, and one or two doffed their caps. Each of them looked rapidly to the others and, finding little assurance of strength in their numbers, began to offer apologies. "Beg pardon, Master Aunk, we did'n mean ne arm," one especially bright eyed, young apprentice said earnestly.

Eric simply nodded to all the boys and grinned his broken tooth smile. "You are all good lads, but it is time you were back to work." The group of apprentices knew he was speaking truly, so dispersed in a variety of directions towards the gates of the Close. One of the boys, the bright eyed lad, remained behind and tentatively approached him, as if longing to speak with him. "Sir, did it be sword tha cut yer face zo terrible? Wou'd ye tell me o yer battles? Oi shou'd be glad ta carry yer pitmakin tools fur ye."

"What is your name, lad?" Eric asked him.

"Oi be Laston, sir, cause moi mum says she would'n ave ne more babies."

"Indeed, Laston, yours is the perfect name, then. But yes, the scars on my face and damage to my mouth are the result of several sword wounds. Where do you serve, Laston? Are you prenticed out?" Eric persisted.

"Fur th baker on th Southgate Street," the boy said. "Moi mum cou'd on'y ford ta put me a baker's boy, bu Oi do'n wish ta be a baker, Master Aunk! Oi wants ta le'rn ta shoot."

"Being a baker is a good trade, Laston. It can offer you employment in any town or village in the kingdom. So run back to your baker now, Laston, work hard, and when you truly find some free time, you know where to find me. I shall tell you battle stories, and you shall learn they are not all glorious. Now, be off with ye!"

"Can ye teach me ta shoot th long bow, Master Aunk? Oi'll elp ye wit anithin," Laston shouted as he ran off.

In the wake of the boys who had already gone, Laston made his way towards the Broad Gate. Eric, watching him hurry off, smiled to himself, suddenly aware that he had truly enjoyed the chance to chat with the boy, and he did hope he might return.

* * *

Two weeks later, when the last office of the cathedral before curfew was about to begin, hundreds of candles burned brightly in their many slotted candelabra, evenly spaced along north and south aisles of the nave, and surrounding the altars. The gathering of people moving forward to enter the cathedral nave included a darkly robed figure of towering stature. His voluminous, black cloak seemed to flow, from a great, high collar shadowing his face, nearly to the floor as he walked. Its folds were so generous, no one in the cathedral noticed he had entered sacred space, fully armed with sword and dagger. He stood proudly throughout the service, never kneeling or seeking to genuflect, and should anyone have been looking, he would not have been seen to make the sign of the cross nor bow his head in prayer. Instead, his dark eyes searched amongst the worshippers gathered, some seated, some kneeling, some standing throughout the service being sung in the quire.

In time he focused upon a pair of men, obviously worshipping together, one seated upon a small stool carried into the cathedral by his fellow. They were dressed very well but simply and moved with great courtesy amongst the gathered crowd, as if requiring no public acknowledgement of their presence. The darkly cloaked figure remained near the back until the hymns of the choir had ceased, and the priest began to intone the Latin benediction. But by the time the worshippers moved to disperse, walking towards the exit of the north portal of the cathedral, the tall, dark figure had positioned himself directly behind the two men whom he had carefully observed throughout the past hour. Everyone walked from the candlelit cathedral into the Close and the darkness of the new moon sky.

Chattering and exchanging hearty good nights began to enliven the people, as they emerged from the great church and hastened to rush home before the curfew bell had rung. The two very respectable fellows, one now carrying the stool in one hand and their lantern in his other, seemed engrossed in discussion, totally unaware of the tall, dark shadow walking behind them. In a matter of minutes, they became more isolated, as the larger group of worshippers broke away towards the Broad Gate whilst they walked past the conduit on a path through the Green towards St Martin's Gate. Suddenly from a small patch between several large trees upon the Green, the dark figure burst from the shadows ahead of the two men and plunged his sword into the shoulder of the man unburdened by the stool!

The second man immediately dropped the small seat he carried, placed their lantern upon the ground, and reached with both arms to support his fellow. He began to shout, "Assassin! Assassin!" The dark figure rapidly swung his sword back into the folds of his cloak and hastily threw something at the fallen man's side. In an instant, he had run from the place of the assault and disappeared into the darkness, leaving the Close through Bickleigh Gate. Silently as a footpad, he continued to stride within the familiar, dark space behind St Stephen's Church. All sight of him was lost by the time anyone had reached the injured man.

The assassin paused within the protective shadow of St Stephen's, threw off his huge cloak, and wrapped his bloody sword within its folds. In a matter of minutes, he emerged from the side of St Stephen's Church onto the High Street as a tall, booted gentleman, very fashionably dressed who walked with his great cloak nonchalantly thrown over his right arm. He strolled casually along the

High Street, and continued to amble past the front of the Guildhall. As the clamor of people screaming of a murder in the Close began to be heard from those leaving through the Broad Gate, he picked up his pace and joined a small group of bystanders hurrying back into the Cathedral Yard. Eventually he stood amongst a growing collection of folk, some weeping and some standing about in shock. One or two of the bystanders knelt on the ground, seeking to offer aid to the two brothers who had been so brutally attacked.

* * *

Early the following morning, Phyllis of Bath rushed into the hall of Exeter House, shouting to everyone within, "Ave ye eard th orrible news? Marshall Molton, th brudder o th aulnage, were attacked in th Cathedral Close!"

"Rest yourself, Mistress Phyllis," Edward said, taking her arm and leading her to one of the great chairs. "Take deep breaths to calm yourself, dear friend, and then, if you please, do tell us what dreadful thing has happened."

Phyllis was so full of agitation, she was nearly gasping. Following Edward's advice, she sat in the chair, forcing herself to breathe deeply. At last, a semblance of calmness returned to her words, and she shared with them the shocking gossip of the marketplace that morning.

"It appened lawrst evenin, jus afore curfew. Th aulnage an is brudder ad gone in ta worship in th cathedral. Bu it were awfter th benediction, as dey was walkin towards St Martin's Gate fro th Close. Th devil o attackers thrust a sword inta is shoulder an ran away, leavin im fur dead!"

"Are you absolutely certain of this, Phyllis?" Apollonia asked gently, while she took her friend's hand. "It is not to be believed, not within the sanctified space of the cathedral burial ground."

"Aye, m'Lady, it ain't ta be beliefed; still it appened!"

"Has the aulnage been mortally injured?"

"Bu it weren th aulnage, m'Lady! Ee be whole. Th brudder o th aulnage were taken inta th deanery, dreadful wounded ee were. Thanks be ta God, yet ee lives!" Phyllis's words seemed to pour unstoppably from her.

"Calm, pray be calm, Mistress Phyllis. The aulnage is unharmed, and his brother lives. We shall all thank God for His great mercies." Edward crossed himself, pausing to ponder her terrifying news.

Edward Aust was normally a very happy fellow, one content and grateful for the gifts of his life. But in times of shock or emergency, he grew silent and thoughtful, seeking first to bring order to his thoughts. At last he said to his wife, "Lonia, do you believe we may call upon your good friend, Canon Chulmleigh, for the most reliable word regarding the horrible events of the night passed?"

Apollonia was heartsick to learn Phyllis's news, but as was her habit, she had retreated into silence. She, too, sought some order to her frenzied thoughts. "My dearest heart, I dare suggest that everyone within the Close has been driven to their knees, trying to deal with an event of such brutality. But you are wise and to the point. Canon Chulmleigh will be best informed of the entire truth of the matter. First, however, we must express to Sir Moreton our prayerful concern for his brother's recovery. Let us call upon our yeomen, Jude and Norman, to take our messages and wait, if possible, for any response."

"My love, you are always a source of order in the midst of chaos," Edward agreed. "We shall send Norman to the home of the aulnage with our message of condolence and prayers. But let Jude approach the canon with our expressions of anxiety for the cathedral community. Jude has the grace and sensitivity needed for such an errand."

* * *

Norman was the first to return to Exeter House and carried his message from the aulnage into the hall. The day had passed to luncheon, and though no one felt hunger, the small group of Edward, Apollonia, and Phyllis sat together sharing a light repast. Edward jumped to his feet as Norman entered, taking his sealed message from the yeoman's hand and reading its contents aloud.

"The aulnage wishes us to know that his brother is holding his own at the moment and is under the care of a distinguished physician, Nicholas of Tiverton, recommended by the cathedral canons," Edward said fervently. Then he went on to read, "Sir Moreton says that he will call upon us at first opportunity, but at present can only be grateful for our friendship and continued prayers."

Apollonia inhaled a deep breath and, releasing it slowly, could be seen to acknowledge an obvious sense of relief. "Edward, this is good news. I am truly pleased to learn that they have called in Nicholas of Tiverton. He has proven a skilled healer for you, dearheart, and we shall continue to pray that his great gifts will be guided to restore the aulnage's brother as well."

Phyllis, too, heaved a great sigh of relief, then stood up from the table and placed both hands upon her hips. "Oi shall be goen naow, moi friends. Bes get back ta work. Bu Oi mus ask ye both, as ye ave become so dear ta me, please take ev'ry step ye may ta protec yerse'ves. T'ere be a murderer abou in Exeter town, an we, none o us, be safe."

"Gramercy, Mistress Phyllis," Edward said gently, "you are a dear friend to us as well. We are eternally grateful for your willingness to share your news. Apollonia and I will take every precaution, as I believe you are correct. No one can be safe whilst such an assailant is abroad. I shall ask Norman to accompany you home."

"Ne'er, Mawster Edward, Oi shall be foine. Ne'on ill touch me whilst Oi carry moi whip!" And with her small weapon in her sturdy right hand, she marched out towards the door. "Bu Oi shall be wantin ta ear ifn ye learn anithin from th canon."

* * *

It would not be until the following day when Nan could announce the arrival of Canon Chulmleigh. As Edward and Apollonia rose to receive him, both were stunned by his appearance. The clergyman seemed to have diminished, his body collapsed within his burdens of the moment, his pale face distressed by an immensity of inner turmoil. Apollonia, particularly concerned by the obvious strain of her friend's recent days, walked to his side and took his arm.

"Canon Chulmleigh, I am so grateful to be able, at last, to introduce you to my dear husband, Edward Aust. But as we are both seriously alarmed by the reports of the assault on the Green last evening, pray forgive us for lacking further courtesies. Kindly sit with us and inform us of anything we may offer as help to you, to the aulnage, or to the chapter."

As the canon sank into his chair, Edward offered him a cup of wine. "It is my pleasure to meet you at last, Canon Chumleigh, and express to you my sincere appreciation for your friendship and kindness to my wife and our household, whilst they have resided in Exeter during my absence."

The canon rose briefly, extending his hand to Edward, but with a shake of his head. "Indeed, Master Edward, I am pleased and grateful to make your acquaintance. Your Lady wife has brought intelligence and beauty to our companionship. But I do so wish we could have met in a more providential time. Even now, Dean Walkyngton prepares for the reconsecration of the Cathedral Green. After this criminal spilling of blood, there must be a reconsecration before we can allow any further burials to take place.

"Indeed, the events of recent days have been shocking, Canon Chumleigh. But allow us to offer our help in any manner within our power," Edward said. "Can you share with us the truth of all that has occurred?"

"Ah, Master Edward," the canon sighed deeply, "if only one could be certain of any truth in this matter! Pray forgive my wandering thoughts, but to offer the whole, I must take you back in time and describe an ongoing intimidation which has been haunting all of us within the Close for the past months. I can barely think where to begin, but the signs of threat were issued towards us first in the form of the Bishop of Exeter's own indulgences."

Edward and Apollonia listened intently, struggling to understand all they were hearing. The canon recalled for them a bizarre tale of repeated warnings, left in the form of mutilated indulgences discovered at different places within the cathedral.

"We thought at first it may have been the work of vandals, wishing to create damage or hatred in our cathedral church. There is much distress and misery within our kingdom, as you must know, Master Edward, having recently returned from London. We thought perhaps some demented mind sought to direct its anger or sense of injury against the clergy. The very first threat was worded, 'No Forgiveness Judgement is Mine.' More frightening yet, the mutilated indulgence was rolled into the eye of a skull left sitting upon the tomb of Bishop Grandisson of blessed memory."

"Great God in Heaven, Canon Chulmleigh, was there no further content? What could such a message mean?" Edward asked him.

"The far more confusing aspect of the words was in their form," the canon said, with another great sigh. "The words were inked upon an official indulgence, with the seal of the Bishop of Exeter ripped away, and in its place a foliate face was attached, angrily spewing forth the words of threat."

At this, Apollonia drew an audible breath. "Dear Canon, this has been troubling you for weeks, has it not? I know you to be a man of great scholarship, as well as a man of faith, but I could not help feeling that my impertinent questions regarding the green men of the cathedral were more troubling to you than I could understand. Pray forgive me; I truly meant no offense. But why should anyone, commons or gentry, use the face of a green man?"

"Dear Lady, you must pardon me. I did, indeed, put you off and avoid your reasonable questions during our tour of the cathedral and later, because I could not provide adequate answers. Past that, threats of the same nature occurred twice more, each growing in its murderous intent. The second hurled the threat, 'Beware the Ancient Revenge!' The third cruelly suggested, 'Norman Dogs Must Suffer!'"

"Why should anyone wish to threaten Normans? Who even speaks of himself as Norman any longer?" Edward asked incredulously. "Are we not all English subjects of our English King?"

"Of course, Edward, the threats seemed beyond comprehension, especially when delivered in such a bizarre manner. Those of us in chapter could make little sense of them. But as you have heard, far more lethal than threats, an assault was made last evening against one of the king's servants and his brother, as they began to walk home from our Cathedral Green. And this was found lying next to the injured gentleman." With that, Canon Chulmleigh lay before them a crumpled indulgence with the seal ripped away, and in its place, a foliate face angrily poured forth the words, "No Escape My Sword Speaks!"

It was Edward's turn to gasp aloud, "Dear God! The assassin left this message after stabbing the brother of the aulnage?"

"Verily, Master Edward, Sir Moreton himself saw the shrouded figure who assaulted his brother throw this to the ground near his wounded body, before he disappeared into the darkness."

The two men seemed reduced to thoughtful silence. Apollonia bent to look more closely at the battered and stained indulgence now lying upon their massive table. "Canon Chulmleigh, pray tell me, have you seen the earlier three threatening indulgences found in the cathedral?"

"Indeed, my Lady, I have examined each of them."

"I pray thee, forgive my persistence, but can you tell me if all of these were created by the same hand?"

* * *

It was late in the afternoon when Eric Aunk walked back to the Cathedral Green from his journey upriver upon one of the construction barges coming to Exeter. His heart was so full of joy that his badly scarred face could not help being seen to smile. Ariana had thrown herself into his arms and told him of the wonders she had discovered with Master and Mistress Braund and their family. They had taken her to the seaside and had helped her collect a wonderful group of shells which she brought for his examination. "Look, look father, do see these lovely pastel colours! Are they not beautiful?" She told him they were teaching her to fish, and Mistress Braund was teaching her how to cook the fish they caught.

"She'll soon be able ta cook all er father's meals," Telitha Braund had told him proudly. "Ariana learns quickly, Eric, an speaks on'y o when she'll be 'lowed ta manage yer home fur ye!"

His mind wandering throughout a collection of happy memories, Eric did not at first notice how very subdued everyone on the Close seemed to be this day. There were no noisy games, and groups who spoke seemed to stand closer to each other, as if to share their thoughts quietly amongst themselves. No one seemed to notice him, especially as his was a familiar face on the Green, but one young voice called out to him as he walked towards his familiar garden hut, "Master Aunk, wher ave ye been?"

"Greetings Laston," Eric responded. "I am very glad to see thee once again. I have been downriver to Exmouth."

"Den ye do'n kno abou th murder, sir?" The boy's eyes were round as saucers and his question full of a desire to share more information with him.

"Come now, Laston, why wilt thou tease? I promised I should share battle tales with ye."

"Ne, Master Aunk, Oi ne'er be teasen thee. T'ere be a turrble attempt ta murder on th Cathedral Green, an ne'on kno's oo done it!"

Eric was truly alarmed by Laston's words and felt responsible to speak with the boy privately to sort out his tale. "Come along inside, Laston, and sit with me for a time. My hut is not beautiful, but we can speak together, man to man here."

"Thankee sir, Oi can nay tell ye much, bu wha is bein said."

Seated upon Eric's simple bed that served as bench, table, and writing desk, Eric looked directly into Laston's eyes and asked him sincerely, "Now boy, do tell me what has been going on, but I want the truth, mind, not your prentice tattle.'"

"Master Aunk, do ye kno anithin abou a jack o th green?" Laston asked with wide-eyed wonder. "It be said dat th green man be cursin th Cathedral Close!"

* * *

The aulnage came into their hall. Edward moved to greet him and lead him to a chair. Moreton Molton's refined demeanor was subdued but gracious, and he began immediately to share his sincere appreciation for their expressions of support through these recent days of trial for his family. "Lady Apollonia, Master Edward, my dear brother has suffered several setbacks, as the wound went deep into his neck and shoulder. There is no doubt the attacker meant to murder him. Yet today, as I left his bedside, he seemed more assured than ever that, with God's help, he would recover! Marshall has been considered a weakling since childhood, but one with great intellect and courage. He could never have been a soldier, but no one would ever best him in strategy."

"God's name be praised, Sir Moreton, we are truly grateful for your welcome news." Edward spoke with honest sincerity, and the aulnage obviously noted it. "But I must tell you, sir, Apollonia and I have been equally concerned to learn the truth of your health after the dreadful assault. Forgive our intrusiveness, but we do wish to learn how you fare."

"I came through the entire attack without a scratch," the aulnage said, shaking his head. "I was carrying Marshall's stool upon which he had set himself through the evening's service. As I have said, dear friends, he is not strong enough to manage to carry such a thing but is most grateful to have it to be seated when necessary. It had been a beautiful office, and he and I were discussing some points of the priest's Latin pronunciation when, out of the darkness, a large figure leaped upon us!"

"Was it a thief's attack? Did he seek to steal from you?" Apollonia asked him gently.

"My Lady, that was my first assumption, but it was not so. The figure attacked my brother with mortal intent and, in the swiftness of his movements, threw a document at Marshall's side. He fled the scene of his crime instantly, taking nothing with him except his own sword, stained with the blood of my brother."

The aulnage put his head down, for it was truly painful for him to remember the event. Apollonia and Edward said nothing but continued to wait in silence to assist their guest struggling to compose his thoughts. "The document hurled at my brother's sinking body was an indulgence, badly mutilated with a horrific charge, 'No Escape My Sword Speaks.'"

"If this is too difficult for you, Sir Moreton, we shall speak of other things, to distress you no further," Apollonia said quietly. "But do you have any idea why anyone should wish to attempt to kill your brother, if this was not the action of a thief in the night? Have you been able to assist the sheriff with a suggestion of one holding a grudge, or bad feeling, in his search for the culprit?"

"Dear Lady, you do not know my brother and can, therefore, never see the impossibility of his being the truly intended victim. I can assure you the assassin was not seeking to rob and kill Marshall. The purpose of the assault was to murder me."

Edward was aghast and stood to emphasize his sense of outrage. "Sir Moreton, how could this be so? You are an official of the king; you serve to establish the quality of English woollen cloths, the staple of the king's income."

"It is precisely as you say, Master Edward, and my brother is a weak and helpless invalid who threatens no one. But it was I who carried his stool from the cathedral. It was I who played the role of servant to my well-dressed brother. Someone, not knowing either of us, may well have confused my brother for me, the despised aulnage."

"Holy Mother of God," Edward exclaimed, "have you shared these thoughts with the Sheriff of Devon? Have you adequately alarmed your entire household? If you fear the office of the aulnage has placed you in danger, can you not call in officers of the king to maintain your security?"

Apollonia leant forward in her chair, as if begging to offer assurance. "Sir Moreton, we shall all join the struggle to protect you."

"My Lady, your grace and good will flatter me, but I shall not be seen walking in fear. If I am so hated, my assassin will be required to confront me in the full light of day!"

Chapter Fourteen

Romaunce of the Rose

Laundry day was always Nan's favourite. Since her childhood, she had been personal lady's maid to her mistress, Lady Apollonia, who would never have asked her to assume the duties of a washer woman. Yet, everyone in the Aust household knew Nan Tanner was in charge of the laundry. She would be directing the process early in the morn, when the washing began, and she would be present when all of the linens had been dried, smoothed beneath the press, and finally stored away in a cloud of fragrance. Nan loved doing the household laundry.

She relished watching garments, sheets, and linens emerge, dripping clean from the basins, then hung to dry, whenever possible, within the sunlight of the outer garden. Dry linens were taken from the lines, returned to the laundry cell next to the kitchen, and hurried to the huge press in the laundry closet. There, they would be straightened by her small but mighty hands into the press, then flattened beneath the huge, weighted boards until they could be seen without a wrinkle.

Nan loved the reassuring sense that she had smoothed away life's wrinkles, had transformed them from knotty, sometimes nasty problems, to clean, sleek, smooth fabrics once again. Doing the laundry was such a sense of accomplishment. Nan always kept a store of dried flower petals from the garden every summer, so that she might mix her favourite aroma of herbs, spices, and dried flowers to scatter across the folded cloths and fill the household's storage chests with fragrances, sparkling clean and aromatically heavenly.

Nan was in the garden on this bright autumn morning, with sunlight pouring from the heavens, lighting and warming the chill of the early day. The back garden was not far from the barns, so Nan could not proceed with her work, unaware that Gareth was well into his morning routine with the stable lads, brushing down horses, and cleaning out their stalls.

Nan loved such days; she was precisely where she wished to be in life, hanging the washing. She could not help but begin to sing a favourite tune, usually begun as gentle humming but soon sung full voice in her light soprano, as crystalline clear as the morning air. Emily, the kitchen wench, was at the far side of the garden, also hanging clothes while Nan saw to the collection of fine linens left to her care. Suddenly as she walked around the line to take another garment from her basket, Gareth stepped into her path with his hat in his hands.

"Good morrow, Gareth, is it not a fine morning? It should be perfect for the airing and drying." Nan was so perfectly at home with Gareth that she saw nothing unusual in his presence before her. He, on the other hand, seemed surprisingly uneasy, more than ever tongue-tied and unable to speak. As they stood looking at each other, Nan did as she always would, simply enjoyed looking at him.

She regarded Gareth's tanned and blue-eyed face always handsomely desirable to her, his perfectly sculpted body the nearest to godlike proportions Nan could imagine. Without saying a word, he whisked away his hat and exposed a superbly deep red rose that he offered to her with downcast eyes. She gasped with delight! "What a glorious surprise, Gareth! This must be the last of the summer." She turned the blossom round in her hand, holding it near to her face to sniff with pleasure. It was now largely bloomed and opened to pour forth fragrance.

"Gramercy, dear friend, what an elegant gift to my day. I shall treasure it." But without saying a word, Gareth bashfully turned rapidly away and hurried back into the barn. Nan could not help but smile as he left, holding the moment preciously between them. She knew this was an extraordinary gesture from him. He was so painfully shy; he was completely unable to put into words any feelings of appreciation or respect towards her. But this lovely gesture said it all. Holding the rose close to her heart, she walked away from her laundry basket and into the kitchen, where she found a small vase and filled it with water. Saying nothing to anyone, she carried the beautifully shaped and brilliantly coloured rose to her bedroom, where she could place it near her bed.

Nan never expressed words to describe how she felt towards Gareth, but she knew he had the gift of making her feel exceptional, and on this precious morning, she would take a few moments alone in her room just to treasure those feelings.

* * *

As Gareth walked into the barn again, he felt such a lout! Why did he not speak to her? Why was he unable to say the words he wished to tell her? He was a grown man, likely past his twenty-fifth year, he told himself. If he were ever to speak with a woman, Nan would be the one. He felt comfort in her presence. She admired him; he knew it, and she never offered a sharp word to him. He put his hat square upon his head and turned to walk back to the garden. He would tell her; he would do it. But when he reached the garden, he could only find Emily hanging laundry. "Mornin, Gareth," she sang out to him, "can Oi elp thee? Are ye lookin for som'on?"

"Wher be Mistress Nan?" he asked her sharply.

"Ne doubt she be back in th laundry room. Shall Oi gets er fur ye?"

"Ne, Emily, tis nothin." And he left the garden once again.

* * *

Later in the morning, Nan was helping the Lady sort through the linens and undergarments for the Aust sons. "They are all three growing like weeds, Nan," Apollonia complained. "We must remain at our sewing, or we shall never clothe them properly. Just look at these? Even Davie is too large about the middle for these."

Nan nodded in agreement with her mistress, but suggested that perhaps they could be let out at the seams a bit. "Should give Master Davie nearly an inch yet."

The laundry was all hung to dry, and Emily came into the service chambers to report her return to work in the kitchen now. Nan thanked her for her help and asked that she would return at day's end to help fetch the last linens in. "Surely Oi shall, Mistress Nan. Bu Gareth were lookin fur ye in th garden. Did ee fin ye?"

Nan's face blushed brilliant crimson, and she put her head down towards the seams she was examining and said quietly, "Yes, Emily, he did. Gramercy."

Apollonia had been speaking with Nan and could not help but notice the startling change in her maid's complexion at the mention of Gareth's name. The Lady knew the friendship between Nan and Gareth went back to their earliest days in her service, but she thought to herself, "Perhaps I am missing something."

After Emily left the laundry room, Apollonia pulled the sewing basket between them on the table and began to pull out the seam in David's underdrawers. "Indeed, Nan, you are correct as always. We can gain at least an inch by loosening these." Then, noticing that Nan's composure had returned, she took a decidedly different direction to their conversation.

"Nan, you have been my devoted servant and dearest friend for many years. You have been with me from the worst days of my early married life through these very blessed years of my life spent with Edward. But I have been remiss. I have never paused to consider what hopes you may have for marriage."

The blush returned to Nan's face with a vengeance, but this time she lifted her face to respond directly to the Lady. "I have none, my Lady. I have no hope for anything, save to fill my days living in your household, working with you, serving you. Pray do not think to send me away!"

"Nan Tanner, how can you say such a thing? I have no desire except that you shall always continue in our household. You know you are precious to me, to Edward, and to the boys as well. We all love you. But you are a mature woman, and I must confess that I have been aware of your feelings for Gareth. Has he expressed affection to you?"

Nan put her sewing down onto her lap and lifted her face with eyes streaming tears. "My Lady, look at me. I am plain as a saucer and base born. You found me as an abandoned bastard and raised me to heights unimaginable for one in my station." Speaking quietly, as if in the confessional, she looked to Apollonia to reveal her innermost soul.

"In truth, I do dream of Gareth as the most handsome man in my world. I believe I do love him in many ways. But, my Lady Apollonia, I can love no one beyond you. I can serve no one other than you, and I shall live my life as your most devoted servant. Pray accept me as that."

Tears began to gather in Apollonia's eyes, and she reached for Nan's hands. "I thank God for you daily, sweet Nan, and will never imagine my life without your presence."

They would have fallen into each others arms for a good cry, but Edward crashed through the door into the laundry room, urgently seeking his wife. "Lonia, my love, we shall have an important guest this evening. Do we have any of those lovely pheasants in the larder?"

* * *

Their guest arrived fashionably late that evening, but swept into the hall when Stafford announced his presence with his usual ponderous intonation, "My Lady, Master Edward, Sir Edmund Falford."

Edward was on his feet and with hand extended in hearty welcome. "Sir Edmund, we are delighted to have you join us this evening. Allow me to present my dear wife, the Lady Apollonia of Aust."

"My Lady, your grace and intellect are the wonder of conversation within Exeter town. I am truly pleased to make your acquaintance." The gentleman continued to move towards Apollonia, then bow over her extended hand in a perfect expression of *noblesse oblige*.

"God give you good evening and welcome, Sir Edmund. Kindly join us by the fire that we may enliven our acquaintance whilst we seek to know you better. My husband tells me that you met in the wool market, seeking to inform yourself of its complexities." Apollonia always wished that she could share the ease of hospitality expressed by her husband, but her preference was to retreat into silence and allow the gentlemen to speak together, whilst she could quietly study their guest and note the characteristics of his person.

"Indeed, my Lady, Master Edward is a veritable wealth of information for me as I struggle to learn." As the gentleman walked to his chair, Apollonia noticed straightaway that their guest was unusually tall, nobly built, and carried himself with a courtly awareness that seemed to precede him. People often spoke of noble blood, as if some people had it whilst others had fluid of other kinds flowing through their veins. In Apollonia's estimation, Edmund Falford had probably been reared and educated within a noble family of means, regardless of the nature of blood in his veins.

Their dinner was brought forward and served. Sir Edmund seemed the perfect guest. He had travelled on the continent and shared wonderful tales of his adventures in Rome, Paris, Antwerp and the bustling cities of Flanders. His description of Rome was that of a derelict city in the clutches of neighborhood gangs.

"Mark my words," he told his captivated listeners, "Rome will not return to greatness until the Holy Father has reestablished control of the Romans by the Church. Whilst the papacy remains in Avignon, my Lady, Rome continues to decline to a lawless gang dominated town, infested with wolves!" But Falford reserved his special praise for the excellence of the urban construction and mercantile success of Bruges and Ghent. "These Flemish cities are truly opulent, my friends, where trade and commerce daily make men wealthy."

In easy conversation, the hours of the evening passed pleasantly. Sir Edmund seemed to find ways to praise their home, their food, their acknowledged reputation within the community of the guilds. He and Edward seemed to get on well with no presumption or expression of difference between them in class or station.

"Sir Edmund has a great gift for society," Apollonia told herself. But she could not discover, at any point in his discourse, precisely why he had sought out their company.

"You must know, my Lady, that I am the son of a landowner in Devon and Dorset, but though my bloodlines are ancient, my rank in birth order is well down on my family's list, succeeding as the seventh son. Therefore, it is my inheritance to earn my own way in the world."

"Come now, Sir, you seem to have achieved well as a very young man, but Lonia and I will always strive to offer our assistance to you within the market place or in any way that we can." Edward was sincere and straightforward in his encouragement; Apollonia also sought to wish their guest well, but she could see that Falford obviously meant to achieve in life no matter what.

The evening was nearly ended, and they found themselves near to expressing their good nights when Sir Edmund added, "If you please, accept my sincerest thanks for your gracious hospitality, and allow me to inquire if you should know the condition of the aulnage? I have heard that he was badly wounded on the Cathedral Green."

Before Edward could respond, Apollonia spoke to his point immediately. "It was not the aulnage who was wounded but his brother, Sir Marshall Molton. How have you learned this news, Sir Edmund?"

"How may I not, madam? Everyone in the town speaks of it, and the story is often confused and wandering in speculation. I was hoping that you may inform me truly."

"Thank God the aulnage's brother is recovering, but no one has been able to grasp the motive of the attack," Edward continued. "We all seek to gather information for the sheriff, but no one has been forthcoming as far as we know. Sir Edmund, if you should learn anything rumoured about the town that may assist the local investigation, please speak with the sheriff. I believe we must all seek to discover the villain and the cause of his assault. Surely we can not allow a murderous attack on an official of the king to go unpunished or unexplained."

* * *

As evening darkened, Eric paced about his tiny hut. He could find no rest. His thoughts were reeling. He found it more than he could contain to grasp the entirety of the attack on the Green as Laston had described it for him. Surely he knew the boy had repeated gossip, swirling about the town, of a murderous event that occurred whilst Eric had been south. But could Laston have heard correctly? The boy told Eric the assailant had thrown a defaced document at the victim, and the victim was none other than the brother of the aulnage.

Eric knew the merchant, Wolfson, hated the aulnage for his uncompromising standards and sought to have him removed by any means possible. Wolfson had driven Eric to increasing efforts to frighten and distract the cathedral clergy to focus clerical attention upon a perceived threat against them, whilst the real target of his malice dwelt on the High Street. Other citizens of Exeter would learn of the distress within the Close and become frightened and distracted by the ongoing mysterious menace there.

Eric held his head in his hands, struggling to remember all that Wolfson had muttered against the aulnage during their secret meetings in his wine cellar. Eric knew the merchant had his grudges, and he was seeking to gather influential support among the guildsmen in the city to remove him. But surely, he could not have attempted murder; Wolfson could never have considered cold-blooded murder.

And how much had Eric revealed to Wolfson of the nature of his green man threats against the clergy? "Think man," he insisted to himself. "What have I done to put myself in jeopardy?" Eric could not remember that he had ever mentioned using stolen indulgences to Wolfson. Surely he had never revealed his use of the green man as agent of his threats. "That would have meant nothing to Wolfson," he told himself, "but what was the purpose of the threat hurled at the brother of the aulnage after wounding him?"

Eric's heart dropped to his stomach. "Could anyone have learned of my secret tunnels beneath the Cathedral Green? Could someone have stolen from my cache of indulgences?" He had few left, but it seemed, if Laston were correct, the assailant had obviously attempted to copy the form and manner of his threats. Who wished to involve him? Worst of all, Eric knew the assault was not an act of mere intimidation; it had been an attempted murder. Laston had told him the dean of the cathedral had been forced to call in the Sheriff of Devon. If pressed, Wolfson would not hesitate to inform against him. Eric must find some way to protect himself. His foolish pranks against the clergy could now be seen as an attempted murder.

Eric decided, at last, to use the darkness of the night to return unseen into his underground retreat. He took his cloak and walked to the cathedral. Entering its candlelit interior, he was greeted as a familiar worshipper, and he remained through the last service of the evening, filing out of the cathedral behind the crowd, into the darkness of the cemetery, when the great doors were locked behind them. The evening worshippers made their ways out through the gates of the Close, while Eric made his way into the shadows of the north porch. There, Eric settled to the ground, covered himself with his cloak, and waited until he could be certain no one remained within the Close.

The lights of the cathedral were slowly extinguished. The room of the custor who lived above the north porch grew dark. The vicars and canons had all gone to their homes, and silence enshrouded the entire Close, sealed within darkness. Thus assured of his being unseen, Eric moved to the space on the Green where he knew to find the grass covered iron lid. He lifted it to one side and slipped his muscular body down into the tunnel, pulling the lid above him. Once he was safely inside the cave like tunnel, Eric lighted his candle and began to count the remaining indulgences. There were none missing! He looked carefully about his subterranean lair, examining every personal item he had hidden there, and could find no evidence of disturbance. He walked the full length of the tunnel, leading directly to the depths below his garden hut. In the candlelit darkness, he could see nothing in the length of the tunnel to betray its discovery by an outsider.

"Thank God," Eric muttered to himself, "at least, no one has found my secrets, but still someone copies my methods." The following thought paralyzed him. If someone was copying his methods, that same person may be scheming to press charges against him, and soon. Eric extinguished his candle and pushed his powerful arms upward to lift the second iron lid. He pulled himself from the tunnel and slipped back into his darkened hut in the canon's garden. He would find no rest this night.

* * *

Each morning as Edward and Apollonia walked into the family chapel for the celebration of Lauds, Apollonia could feel her heart swell with the growing beauty of their new construction. She noted to herself, very happily, that silence now reigned whenever the household began to gather within its walls. Everyone knelt upon entering, made the sign of the cross, physically preparing themselves for a time of worship. The Lady knew the chapel would, upon its completion, be dedicated to the Virgin in memory of her mother. Masons were hard at work preparing the saints' statues to fill the niches of the Virgin and Child and the family's patron saints, as well. The chapel's inner walls were now elegantly lined with painted stone pilasters, and their carved capitals upheld the series of wooden arches, now carved but still in process of being painted with vibrant colours. The aperture for the new stained glass rose window above the altar was prepared and waiting to receive its completed work of sacred art.

Apollonia grasped Edward's hand excitedly. He shared with her the renewed sense of worship and devotion their household found, coming together here, at the beginning and end of each day. But he also knew that Apollonia personally enjoyed the process of chapel building. Everyone of their acquaintance would have judged her enthusiasm as offensively unfeminine, but Edward knew it to be completely consistent with his wife's love of creating order and balance in life.

It was she who pressed their master mason to explain every detail of the construction, as well as the decoration. Her enthusiasm seemed to bubble over with her own visions of shimmering light that would fill the chapel, once the rose window finally assumed its central place, when saints' statues filled every niche surrounding the altar, and when the crucifix would be raised above the altar as focus of their Christian devotion. It was all coming along so beautifully, but they must speak with the master mason, William of Wedmore, after chapel every morning. Apollonia insisted!

She always carried a small bone or morsel in a parcel from the kitchen for William's beloved dog. The aggravating little pooch seemed a noisy nuisance to Nan, but Apollonia and Edward knew he simply required a bit of recognition with his treat. After a welcome series of patted greetings, he would take his food or bone happily to his blanket, while William would join them to bring the Lady and Master Edward up to the moment, describing their progress. The dog had no name that anyone could recall. He was simply referred to as "William's."

The young master mason of Wedmore had truly enjoyed building this chapel, its construction as well as its design. William's own joy of the creation of sacred space was a public expression of his personal faith. He had brought to Exeter the latest in design from France. He had been able to explore the great churches of the Isle de France, especially the construction within the royal Sainte-Chapelle.

Edward preferred to remain an enthusiastic observer. He would simply step back to watch Apollonia and William poring over sketches in the sand, debating over details of colour and symbol. He was the master of the household, but Edward knew Apollonia was building their chapel.

"I do wish you would reconsider this carving of St Alban, Master William," she said, as they examined the collection of saints' statues emerging from blocks of stone in the masons' work area. "It will be important to our son, Alban, that he sees his patron as a real Roman soldier and martyr, not merely a kneeling saint in Roman armour." She walked amongst the unfinished statues with her upper teeth pulling at her lower lip in concentration. "But this St Hugh is perfect, William. You have placed a lovely swan at his feet as his symbol, but more importantly, you have created a portrait of the bishop with a sense of humour."

"Indeed, my Lady, I shall grant your preferences for St Alban, but I have been asked by my carver to request your reconsideration of St Apollonia. No one is presenting her as an aged, toothless deaconess any longer. The carver wishes to create a beautiful, young maiden who holds the pincers with a tooth in her right hand," William insisted.

"That is unseemly, William," Apollonia said. "My patron saint was an aged, toothless deaconess."

"But, my Lady, consider the beauty of her space. Do not require my mason to sculpt a vision of age and sunken lips."

"All right, if you must, a youngish maiden is possible, but I shall allow no crowned princess. That, I am certain, is an alteration of her holy legend."

"Lonia, my love," Edward intervened, "I would prefer the saint to employ your likeness. Is it not desirable, Master William, that St Apollonia will grace our chapel with the brilliant smile of our own Lady Apollonia of Aust?"

"Indeed, Master Edward, you have bested our interests in creating a truly worshipful saint. I shall instruct the carvers to observe our Lady more closely, and I promise our very own St Apollonia will emerge."

"Mind how you speak, both of you," Apollonia said with lips slightly pursed to conceal her own desire to break into a smile. "You verge upon sacrilege with your foolish chatter. But, back to business, William; what of our rose window?" Apollonia pressed him. "When may we hope to see our own 'Rose without Thorns' complete this space with glowing colour?"

"I shall walk to the glaziers' shop this very morning, my Lady. I know they have been hard at work for several weeks, but they find my rayonnant tracery a bit of challenge," he said, slightly smugly. "Still, they are up to my requirements, and they will complete it to your expectation."

"Are you are able to set a date for its installation, Master William?" Edward asked. "The dedication of our family chapel must be a day of great celebration, and Canon Chumleigh will be the perfect priest to officiate with Chaplain Anthony. What say you, Lonia, shall we hope to celebrate the mass of dedication on All Saints' Day?"

* * *

The tall figure, concealed entirely behind a long, black cloak, spoke in a mocking voice to interrupt Wolfson's whining complaint. "Cease! Your whimpering disgusts me! You have created your own chaos, merchant!"

Raymond Wolfson looked up from his stooped posture, his hands stroking fingers together, as if in some attempt to display obeisance while obviously trembling. He could be seen to twist his head upward, seeking to peer behind the collar hiding the face of the man who was obviously enjoying his humiliation and fear. "But do you not see, sir, I need to employ your gang to cover for me. Several in the community are suggesting my responsibility for the recent attack upon the aulnage. I have done nothing. I am innocent. I must find some avenue of defence!"

"If you make an ass of yourself, you shall remain amongst asses."

"I thought your men would help us when we strove to unseat the aulnage. It was you who proposed his removal. I thought you meant to keep your word."

"Damn you, creeping reptile! How dare you accuse me? It was you who promised to achieve his removal whilst you and your craven confederates achieved nothing more than frightening choir boys and pissing yourselves."

"But I must not be insinuated against in this way. I have done nothing illegal."

"Be silent! I shall inform you of the manner of my assistance. You will gather all those merchants who resent the aulnage. Then you shall all flock to his home. Fall to your knees before Sir Moreton, offering your humblest apologies for stirring any possibility of misunderstanding. Express to him your heartfelt concern for the health of his brother. From thence, you and your confederates shall continue on to meet with the sheriff. Speak to him of your concerns that a violent miscreant is roaming the streets of our city, and you, as concerned citizens, intend to issue a reward for his capture. Having displayed yourselves publicly on the side of the law, suggest a possible villain as worthy of their suspicions."

"Who might that be, sir, the villain I mean?"

"The pitiful creature you paid to do your dirty work within the Cathedral Close. You must tell the sheriff of his evil, unwarranted threats against the good clergymen of Exeter Cathedral!"

"Eric Aunk is no longer in my employ, and good riddance! He dared to enter my home and somehow sneak away with his daughter." Wolfson paused, leaving his complaint incomplete. Then after a moment's thought, he suddenly caught on. "But of course, Aunk is known throughout the town as the cathedral pitmaker. And he is so grotesquely scarred and misshapen, he frightens children and adults. Indeed, he will be easily imagined as a dealer in death threats."

"You have the quick insight of lead for brains, Wolfson, but eventually you catch the drift. Of course, dolt, report Aunk to the sheriff as a likely suspect in the assault of the aulnage's brother, but first go directly to the dean and reveal Aunk to be the menace of the Close. Dean Walkyngton will be thrilled, at last, to realise the culprit is the cathedral's pitmaker who dwells within his own domain."

* * *

"Master Aunk," Laston had run so quickly from his deliveries to the dean's residence that his breath could not keep pace with his feet. "Master Aunk, dey be coomin ta git ye! I eard it at th deanery kitchen!" he shouted. "Ye mus flee."

Eric did not hesitate to press the boy with questions. As he had feared, there could be little doubt he had been betrayed by Wolfson, and Eric must not wait to learn the details.

"Laston, I shall need you to be my eyes and ears here about the Close. I shall not leave Exeter, but I shan't be far away. Do you know the Leper's Hospital of St Mary Magdalene? It is found when you bear to the left going outside the South Gate of the city wall. No one will think to look for me there, but will you be willing to come to find me?"

"Oh, sir, Oi shan't wish ta go inta sech a dreadful place, bu Oi'll send in a message ta ye." Laston was now terrified by the thought of his friend being amongst the lepers. He had heard frightening tales of how such creatures looked, with missing noses, fingers, even hands! Everyone he knew always told him to keep far away from the leprosarium; he must never even breathe the air in the vicinity of lepers. But Master Aunk was his friend, and he did earnestly wish to help him.

Eric took the boy into his arms and held him for an instant. "I shall always be thankful for your loyalty, Laston. You have the courage of a true warrior and the devotion every father cherishes. But do not come to find me unless you have some solid news. I shall try to hide there for the next few weeks." Eric took the lad's hand and pressed it firmly to his heart. "God bless you! Stay beyond the gate of St Mary Magdalene always, but if you learn something, send in a message, asking for Deadman. Until I can clear my name, I must remain amongst the living dead."

Pulling the hood of his cloak over his head, Eric left Laston and walked swiftly out from his garden hut onto the Green. With his cloak clinging round him, he ran through the boisterous games of the Close, through St Martin's Gate to disappear amongst the High Street beggars, totally unnoticed by the crowds of citizens living their important lives of commerce.

Chapter Fifteen

Sicknesse of Choice

Eric knew well the back alleys and paths of Exeter town. Staying within the shadows of the buildings whenever possible, he hurried into the narrow, filth filled sewers of the lanes where the poorest of the poor of Exeter lived, making his way towards the city wall. But as he ran, he told himself he must transform before he could seek entry into the leprosarium. He must create a disguise, at least enough of one, to present himself believably as a wandering leper seeking sanctuary and care with the Franciscans. He pulled his cloak from his shoulders and used his knife to cut away a large square of the lining within its hood, so that the fabric lining would fall, covering his face. Within that square of fabric, he pierced two holes, each large enough to allow his eyes to see through, whilst the cloth hid his face from public view.

He picked up a tall, abandoned tree branch from the lane. He stripped it with his knife to a single column, free from bark. Then, looking for a way to create a noise maker upon it, Eric pulled three leather ties from his jerkin and looped a collection of small stones along each length. He attached one end of the laden ties around the top of the branch. Then, when he pounded the stick to the ground, he twisted it, making a rattling, warning noise of his approach. He knew he must change his robust physical appearance, too, so he rounded his shoulders and bent his body into a stoop. Eric made himself appear shorter, infirm in his movements while leaning heavily upon his great stick. With each pounding step, the stones rattled their warning, and he shouted aloud, "Unclean! Unclean! Beware, keep away, leprosy walks with me."

People who approached him on the road would turn away immediately. Even the gatekeeper of the South Gate, hearing his warning, would not look out from his perch. Everyone who saw hooded Eric now assumed he was a leper, so they moved hurriedly away from his path, keeping their own faces covered. "Unclean!

Unclean, leprosy walks with me," he continued to shout as the rattling stones hung from his stick shook a crackling tattoo.

* * *

Eric approached the walls of St Mary Magdalene in his limping, hunched, and bent posture. There was absolutely no one in the street leading to the entrance, as no right thinking person would walk near the leprosarium if they could avoid it, but he continued to shout, "Unclean! Unclean," and pound his rattling stick. When he rang the entry bell, he was received immediately and pulled inside quickly as the door shut behind him. He could not help but feel as if its closure declared his departure from the world of the living.

"Well, brudder, wher be ye from, den?" the gateman said gently. His eyes stared into emptiness, betraying his lack of sight, but he moved about with a perfect awareness of himself within his space.

"I have come to this place for peace, brother," Eric answered, "but I once lived in Gunwalloe on the coast of Cornwall."

"Ye speak wit th polish o th gentry, brudder. Wer ye gentry?" the gateman persisted.

"Aye, brother, I served a gentleman once, but as with all else, the Mass of Separation was spoken against me. I have been cast out from all human community."

"Fin yer way ta th chapel, den. Seek amongst th gathered folk fur Friar Francis. Ye mus speak wit th friar."

Eric walked on towards the small, towered chapel with a framed porch over its door and across its entire front facing the inner courtyard. He could see, seated along the full width of the building, a group of humans in varying stages of disease, enjoying the sunshine and warmth of a perfect autumn day. Some were so ill as to be lying in makeshift beds. Other residents walking about had faces betraying spots and pustules of the developing disease. Still others extended arms with deadly, whitened skin, or arms with no hands, or hands with few fingers. He would speak with the friar as he had been directed, Eric told himself, but he must keep his distance from these pitiful creatures. He knew he could remain undiscovered here, but Eric struggled to keep from retching.

The happiest sight from the collection of human refuse before him was a group of children playing together, singing a song of "Ring around the Rosy." They twirled and sang, finally collapsed to the ground, giggling and rolling backwards together. The Grey Friar, holding the circle together with his hands, picked himself up from the ground and suggested they must do it again, until he realised Eric was approaching and seemed to be looking for him. He brushed off the dust of the ground from his hands and robe and looked towards Eric's hesitant, masked figure. "Greetings brother," he said warmly, "have you come to join us?"

Eric, with his head bent down, responded with a brief but doleful, "Yes, brother, I have no choice."

Friar Francis asked no further questions of him but directed the new arrival to a pair of stools in the shade of a tree and brought him a beaker of ale. "Drink this, friend, and be refreshed." Then he seated himself next to Eric. "May I know your name?"

"Please, Friar, call me only 'Deadman,' as I have been declared untouchable to all amongst the land of the living."

"If the Mass of Separation has been performed against you, friend Deadman, we can at least offer to share our portion of life with you, here within our community of St Mary Magdalene."

"I have travelled from Cornwall, Friar, and would be eternally grateful to you for some days of respite before I begin my journey to the North and the Benedictines of Shrewsbury."

"Then, I bid you welcome and offer all that we may, to your spiritual as well as physical comfort. You will find my compatriots here are determined to lay their petitions before the Lord, because we believe that He answers all those who stand at His door and knock."

"I shall be willing to offer my assistance where you have need of hands or strong shoulders, Friar, but I prefer to remain by myself in the shadows, if you will allow."

Friar Francis was more than accustomed to dealing with those who had lost everything to this incurable disease: their families, their lawful rights as persons, even their hope of entering a church. If this man, who seemed to speak the language of gentlemen, had recently been expelled from all that he treasured, he may well find himself in the throes of angry resentment. Francis also knew Deadman would require time to achieve any acceptance of the other residents as his compatriots. The friar would allow him to remain distant from the others, for now.

* * *

It was a disturbed Canon Chulmleigh who asked to be presented to the Lady of Aust and her husband, late in the afternoon. Upon entering Exeter House, he approached Nan and bent to speak quietly with her. "Pray tell Master Edward and his Lady that I desire to speak with them in strict confidentiality." So, after Nan had presented him to Apollonia and Edward, already working together in the hall, she and Stafford bowed to leave them with their guest and retreated to the kitchen.

"My dear Canon Chulmleigh," Edward said, with concern in his voice, "what has occurred? Have you further news from the Close? Pray do be seated and share with us. How may we be of service to you?"

The canon collapsed into the offered chair. Apollonia and Edward joined him, pulling their chairs near. "My friends, I feel eternally grateful that I may turn to you, employing your intellect and sound, good sense. Events within the Close have reached a distressing state, and I am personally unable to sort out their import or their meaning. Would you be willing to share information with me, whilst extending the confidentiality of the confessional to our conversation?"

"You have our solemn pledge, Canon Baldwin," Apollonia assured him, and to emphasize the solemnity of the moment, she took Edward's hand to add to hers, placed upon her heart.

"We willingly commit ourselves to complete confidentiality, dear Canon; we pledge ourselves to an oath of friendship. But pray," Edward urged him, "tell us what has happened?"

"Earlier, when we spoke of the series of mysterious threats received by the cathedral chapter," the canon reminded them, "we agreed there was no clear message in any of the first three. But the fourth indulgence, hurled at the fallen body of Sir Moreton's brother, betrayed a murderous intent."

"Indeed," Edward said to him, "I remember being astounded that the attempt on the aulnage's brother was accompanied by an obviously premeditated message. What was it, something such as, 'My sword speaks?'"

"It said, 'No Escape! My Sword Speaks!'" Apollonia completed the warning and then addressed the canon, "did it not, Canon Baldwin? The bloodied document that you displayed to us definitely meant to say that the intent was murder. But, the aulnage told us that he believed he was truly the intended victim. Therefore, his life remains under threat."

"You have remembered precisely, dear Lady, and yes, we must assume murderous threats against the aulnage continue. But a very strange development occurred in the Close this day. The Merchant Wolfson and several of his fellow guildsmen spoke with the dean, accusing our cathedral pitmaker, Eric Aunk, of having sent the earlier threats. Therefore, they say he must be the attempted murderer. Dean Walkyngton sent round two of our strong, young virgers to bring Eric to him for examination, but when they arrived, they discovered his hut was deserted, and he could not be found anywhere in the Close. So Master Wolfson has taken his accusations to the sheriff, and a general search of the town is in progress."

"What do you know of this pitmaker, Eric Aunk?" Edward asked him.

"Those of us in the chapter have always been well pleased by his services, but he keeps to himself, so we know little to say of his person." The canon paused for a moment. Then he added, "You see, my friends, Eric's face was badly scarred by wounds received in the wars with France. Eric was rejected by the knight whom he had served, as repugnant to look upon. His appearance is somewhat frightening when seen by the unsuspecting. The scars twist and disfigure his cheeks and nose, while lifting his mouth into a hideous, broken tooth grimace."

"But does he have cause to wish to threaten the clergy or the aulnage and his family?" Apollonia persisted. "Why would Eric Aunk wish to harm those of you living in the Close?"

"My Lady, I do not know. I, personally, have always found Eric to be a good man, dependable and thoughtful in the preparation of gravesites for families suffering loss. But perhaps we have made him resentful. Perhaps our tendency as clerics to keep from him, except when his services were required, may have exaggerated his feelings of ill usage. I must say," the canon nodded his head, "Eric, as pitmaker, would have had access to all of the chapels of the cathedral where threats were found. He would also have known in the cathedral charnel house where to find a skull in which one threat was found. And he is certainly powerful enough to have broken the neck of Dean Walkyngton's watchdog."

"But, Canon Baldwin, from whence does Eric come? What is his background? Would he have reason to resent our Norman heritage? Has he displayed any anger towards those who may pride themselves on being of Norman descent? Why would he use such language as 'Norman Dogs?' In these days, we would speak of them as French, would we not?" Apollonia continued to repeat words used in the earlier threats sent against the canons.

"Your memory of our discussion is wonderfully precise, my Lady. I truly do not know anything about his place of birth, but his surname, Aunk, is an ancient Celtic name here in Devon. On the other hand, I believe Eric actually served as squire to a knight of well known Norman heritage when he went to France. Perhaps a bad experience in service, or resentment resulting from his disfigurement, may have inspired hatred?" Then the canon turned to her husband, "Have you some opinion, Master Edward? Can we assume this otherwise excellent pitmaker to be our cathedral villain?"

"Canon Baldwin, you have laid out several bases for suspicion of his motives, but I think we must hold our judgement until the man has been brought for examination, do you not? He may have sound reasons for his present absence from the Close, and having a Celtic name does not convict him of Norman hatred."

Apollonia could not help but smile knowingly upon Edward. She knew he was always a man of justice and order, who took his own understanding of civil responsibility very seriously. Most of all, she always felt proud of his insistence that there must be no rush to judgement, an attitude rarely shared by his compatriots.

"Allow me to add my endorsement to Edward's suggestion that we first allow Eric to explain himself," Apollonia said quietly. "Wolfson has made a terrible charge against Eric and presumes to indict him for the attempted murder. But why should Eric hate the aulnage and his brother?"

"God's blessings upon you both," the canon said earnestly, "you have the ability to bring balance and reason to my seething mind. We shall wait until the sheriff has been able to help us find Eric Aunk, and then we shall seek his answers. But for the moment, my Lady, may I ask a further favour of you?"

"You know I will always grant such favour if I am able," Apollonia said with a smile. "But I begin to suspect some discomfort of the distaff side once again."

"Your insight is astounding, and as always, you are correct. It is your friend, Mistress Phyllis of Bath, my Lady. She has been in the Close, raising a clamor concerning the lack of assurances we have been able to share with the town. She says the cathedral chapter must not hide within our walls but must tell the citizens of Exeter the full truth of the assault upon the aulnage's brother. And, as you gave her my name as canon of the cathedral, she comes to my door seeking redress!" The canon wiped his forehead. "She is a formidable woman, my Lady, but I do believe you may assist me to curtail her enthusiasm."

"Perhaps we should redirect her enthusiasm, Canon Baldwin. I shall ask her to make further inquiries for us within the guild community," Apollonia said thoughtfully. "She is a brave woman and one who may be able to help us discover the real truth of Merchant Wolfson's motives behind his charges against Eric Aunk."

"A brilliant idea, my Lady," the canon heaved a great sigh of relief. "Why did I not think of it?"

"You have more to trouble your peace of mind than any of us," Edward said, placing his arm upon the canon's shoulder. "Apollonia will set Phyllis upon another course, but you must always allow us to help as circumstances change."

* * *

It had been a very long day's ride from North Devon to Exeter's city wall, but as Brandon Landow urged his horse, Absolution, to turn from Fore Street down the lane to the walls of the Benedictine Priory of St Nicholas, the pardoner knew he would soon find rest and recuperation. He had carefully elected not to return to the friary, where he had found accommodation on his earlier visits in Exeter. Landow was not certain he would be welcomed by the Grey Friars any longer, and past that, he knew the Benedictines did not regard the Grey Friars highly, so would have little contact with them. Better yet, the guest house of St Nicholas was exceedingly comfortable and maintained a reputable kitchen.

Landow wished to hide away for a matter of months, here in the far South of the kingdom, and cease to function as a pardoner for awhile. His pockets were filled with coin. He had made a mightily successful sale of his faked relic of the Holy Blood in the North Riding of Yorkshire, and he simply did not wish to be found. He would become a young man of the town. He knew nothing of London, and the capital intimidated him. But here in Exeter, he felt comfortable. He was familiar with many inns in the city where he could find congenial company, and few questions would be asked.

As he dismounted at St Nicholas, Absolution was taken by the stableman, and Landow put a large coin into his hand. "See that she is well tended and carefully groomed," he directed. "We have travelled far these past days, and I would that she be brought to her best appearance."

The stableman touched his hat in thanks and swiftly hurried the coin into his pocket, as he walked Absolution away to her stall. Landow took his saddlebags, a large carrier containing a locked chest, and several items of new clothes purchased from an elegant tailor's shop in Bath. He was smirking to himself as he walked to the priory entrance. He had achieved everything he had hoped to achieve in Yorkshire. He had made himself rich!

"Oh yes," he said to himself, "I shall find other wealthy men of the town. I shall see to it that they will come to know the elegant Brandon of Cirencester, but not a word of Landow, the pardoner."

Chapter Sixteen

Manliness Meene

Gareth had watched for the week past, tarrying outside the barn for any moment when he might encounter Nan alone in the garden. It seemed nearly impossible to find her by herself. Her days were filled from dawn to dusk, because her presence was required whenever the Lady was at home and to accompany the Lady when she was making social calls about the town. Gareth knew Nan's days were not her own, but he told himself he must bring her into the garden where he would summon the courage to say his words to her.

In his role as stablemaster, Gareth was unlettered. He could recognise many symbols of heraldry and some important numbers on the weighing scale in the barn, but he could not write words. He could not ask one of his stable lads to carry a message to Nan for him, nor could he tell Emily from the kitchen that he wished to speak with Nan. The mere thought of the endless snickering and gesturing he might be forced to endure, should any of them sense his feelings towards Nan, drove him ever further into empty solitude.

In the late afternoon of this day, when the Lady and Master Edward's son, Alban, was freed from school, Gareth was suddenly inspired to employ the boy's skills. Alban had come sauntering into the barn, as was his daily habit, where Gareth was working. Greeting the stablemaster, Alb inquired what he may do to be helpful. Alban Aust loved being with Gareth and the horses, and although Gareth was usually very brief in any verbal exchanges with the boy, Gareth enjoyed showing the master's son basic lessons in caring for the beasts through grooming, watering, and good feeding. Alban would normally retreat into silence when he entered Gareth's domain, for he understood the stablemaster's preferences, but on this afternoon, he was completely surprised when Gareth greeted him with a request. "Mawster Alban, wou'd ye write fur me?" At that, he extended a small piece of skin, well scraped and stretched.

"Surely, Gareth," Alban said, collecting his school bag and pulling out a small pen with ink. "What shall I say?"

"Jus say, 'Coom ta garden.' Now't else."

Alban lay the skin on a small bench, dipped his quill into the ink from his school bag, and wrote, "COME TO GARDEN," across its surface. "Will that do, Gareth?" he asked. "See, it says just what you said," and pointing to the words, he recited them, "Come to Garden."

"Oh aye, Mawster Alb, dat be it. Thankee!"

"You must wait a bit, just till the ink dries, Gareth. Then you may take it up and do with it as you like. Is there anything else I can add to it?"

"Ne, dis be it! Thankee again!" Then, Gareth gingerly held the scrap of skin from its upper edge in his hand, walked into his space at the far end of the barn, and laid it carefully upon his bed. Returning quickly to the place where Alban stood in a state of some wonder, Gareth seemed mightily relieved and said to him, "Ave Oi ever showed ye ow ta oil th arness, Mawster Alban? Keeps leather soft an well wearin."

* * *

When the evening meal in the hall was finished, Lady Apollonia dismissed the household to prepare for chapel. Gareth walked close to Nan and pressed his piece of folded skin into her hand. She moved to a corner behind the hall screens passage and, standing beneath a wall sconce, opened it privately to read its brief message. Gareth had risen from table and was walking slowly from the hall. Nan hurried to reach him before he left. "Gareth, do you mean for me to meet you in the garden?"

Continuing to look straight ahead, he simply said, "Aye!"

"Tonight?" She persisted.

"Aye!" And he walked through the corridor towards the back entrance from Exeter House.

Nan ceased to follow him and turned instead to walk up the stairwell to the Lady's solar. When she entered the chamber, Apollonia noticed her cheeks seemed somewhat flushed, but she sat immediately near the Lady and picked up her needlework, diligently lifting it towards the light of the fire, where she began stitching briskly.

"Nan dear, are you well?" Apollonia asked her.

"Oh, very well, my Lady, but I do hope to complete this embroidery soon as a gift for our new chapel." All the while she spoke, Apollonia could see that Nan kept her head bent over her work and did not look away from it.

"It will be a truly lovely altar cloth, Nan, but do you really feel you should strain your eyes so in the darkness of the night? Would it not be better to begin again in morning's light?"

With that, Nan put down her needle and yawned quietly behind her hand. "Truly, my Lady, I do feel somewhat fatigued. Would you allow me to excuse myself to an early bed after chapel this evening?"

"Of course, Nan, please feel free to seek your rest. I shall read my book of hours until Edward and Jude return from his meeting in the Guildhall." Apollonia placed her book on a small table near her chair and then rose from her seat, taking Nan's hand into her own. "Let us go to chapel, and from evening's service I shall command you to your bed," Apollonia said in mocking tones of authority.

When evening chapel was ended, Nan followed her Lady only into the Great Hall and then turned towards the door to the servants' wing where her own bedroom awaited her. She bid Apollonia and other members of the household good night; then she walked up the stairs and entered her tiny room. She closed the door to her chamber behind her but did not continue to prepare for bed. She sat quietly until she was certain the fires had been banked, and all of the staff were moving towards their beds. When at last the household quieted, she put her warm, woollen cape round her shoulders and walked quietly into the kitchen, silently continuing through its back door out into the garden.

It was a dark night with large, flowing clouds covering the moon in windswept procession. Nan was grateful for the darkness, but she could not think where to go next in the garden. She began to walk towards the back, nearer to the barns where the clothes lines hung till next laundry day. She was looking down to watch where her feet trod on the carefully laid stone path, when suddenly two strong, warm arms reached around her and pulled her from the path. She made no sound, for she recognised the sensuous body scent of Gareth, as he turned her to him and crushed her small body against his.

Nan had no wish to struggle or resist him. She willingly put her arms tightly around his neck and thrilled to the heat of their full body embrace. Gareth suddenly bent down and lifted her legs into his left arm. He hugged her body, already pressed against him, in his powerful right arm and carried her into the barn. Neither spoke a word, but both continued to share, through ceaseless touch, their urgent expression of mutual physical desire.

He carried Nan into his enclosed space at the end of the barn, farthest from the horses' stalls. There, Gareth laid her gently onto his bed. Then with controlled and careful bodily pressure, Gareth gently laid himself close to her. He leaned his head next to her ear and whispered, begging her, "Oi pray thee, Nan, ye mus giv me ease." He pressed her hand between his legs that she might know of his hardening, bulging hunger.

Nan's arms pushed him gently back and holding one finger to his lips, she begged him to grant her a few moments. She slipped her legs from his bed and stood to remove her garments. Standing undressed in the shadows, she gestured to him to remove his clothes. In the chill of the barn, they both tumbled swiftly into the narrow bed, pulling its blankets up to their ears.

Nan had experienced male sexuality only once, as brutal childhood abuse. But during the years of her service with the Lady Apollonia, she had grown aware of the possible joy and warmth of physical love that she knew was shared between her Lady and Master Edward. She had always been aware of her own physical desires, especially her passion for Gareth, but always from a distance. Now Nan's spirit rejoiced. Gareth had come to her that she might know how desperately he needed her.

He feared that his body's weight might press too heavily upon her slight figure, so Gareth purposely sought to hold himself slightly suspended with one arm. He was aware of his own strength, and he did fear to cause her pain, so he struggled to control his passionate thrust. But, as she lifted her hips in welcome response to his entry, Gareth's entire being thrilled within the warmth and moisture he discovered between her legs. He had never known such rhythmic passion, and his muscular torso seized in ever increasing drive. He soon forgot his desire to remain slightly suspended above her and his nude body collapsed upon hers in his passionate warmth. He stroked more deeply into her; he soon lost himself in driving lust to become one with Nan.

At first they had made little noise, past their heavy breathing and gasping sobs. Both of them wished that no one would know of their union. Nan's mouth exhaled silent screams of pleasure when Gareth responded to the growing fire from within her. Nan's early pain morphed into passion's ever greater urging, as she continued to open herself to receive him more fully. Their lower bodies eagerly sought union, while their arms pulled themselves into mutually giving and sharing bodily love.

Nan and Gareth lay together utterly exhausted but continued to savour their moments suspended in sweetest fulfillment. They both knew they must not fall asleep. They must not risk being found in bed together. Still, each held the other closely, just to extend their moments of bliss as long as possible, cheek pressed against cheek, breast against breast. From their hips to their toes, their legs stretched along the other's, rejoicing in the warm union of touch. Nan had never been so happy in her life. Gareth said nothing but pressed her body to his in one constant, clasping caress.

When at last, Nan told herself she must return to her own bed, she kissed him tenderly and slipped from his embrace. Silently she dressed, tidied her hair, and pulled her cape round her shoulders. Gareth rose from the bed, hurriedly hoisted his breeches, and covered his shoulders with a blanket. He took her hand and walked with her through the garden to the kitchen entrance of the house. As she began to move from him, he held her back and put his head down towards her face. "Thankee, Nan, Oi do thankee wit awl me eart." Reaching up to his cherished face, she stroked his cheek.

"Bless you dearest Gareth, you have made me whole." Then she kissed him gently on his lips and went quickly into the kitchen.

* * *

It was just before curfew, and Raymond Wolfson did not wish to be on the dark streets of Exeter without his bulky body servant. But for this meeting, he had been specifically directed to come alone. The concealed gentleman, who had earlier come to meet briefly in his wine cellar beneath his house, had refused to do so any longer. Wolfson had no clue to his identity, and he presumed that the gentleman was one of good Devon family who wished not to have his connections with the underworld known. He left messages for the merchant in notes, hidden for him in a secret location in his garden. Recently, the gentleman had said that he preferred to remain distant from any contact with him until the public furore over events on the Cathedral Green had quieted.

Wolfson was incensed at that which he regarded callous abandonment. He had jobs he wished done for him. If the gentleman's gang was to be of use to him, he needed access now. He, Wolfson, had followed all instructions, taken all the public risks, and now discovered he had become vilified. People on the High Street said aloud that he had been responsible for initiating public anger against the aulnage.

The concealed gentleman had done profitable business for Wolfson in the past several years, all of it secret and always beyond the requirements of the King's Law and royal taxation. Wolfson had used these connexions to threaten and batter some of his weavers who proved troublesome. He had even seen to it that a self-righteous miller found his fulling mill put to the torch.

Wolfson assumed the gentleman was a local landowner, who was probably also running a tidy business in smuggling somewhere along the Devon Coast. He had taken a major collection of rejected, woollen cloths off Wolfson's hands and had returned to him a number of barrels of fine French wine to sell at a tidy profit, while keeping much for his own wine cellar. The mysterious gentleman's costs were steep, but Wolfson had always managed to profit significantly from their exchange.

The merchant walked towards the river, having fortified himself with a series of cups of the tax free Bordeaux before leaving his home. To make his way safely in the darkness, he carried a small lantern in hand, out through the city gate and down towards the Shilhay. He knew where he was to meet the gentleman, and he also knew a fulling mill, not far from their meeting place, from whence he had secretly enlisted the services of a shifty, but powerfully built, miller to serve as his concealed weapon of protection. The miller had been instructed to slip into the shadows of the place of their meeting, to add hidden muscle to Wolfson's arguments when needed.

Wolfson reached the arranged place of meeting and put his small lantern on the ground. He had told the miller to remain hidden until he signaled, so he made no attempt to locate him. Time passed, and the gentleman did not come. Wolfson began to pace about, growing increasingly irritated that he was being kept waiting. He turned and stamped his foot when the voice suddenly came from the darkness, and a tall, dark robed shadow demanded, "What is it you want, Wolfson?"

"I need you to threaten the Aust enterprises, seriously and soon. They are cutting into my profits and taking some of my best weavers. And you must see to it that you protect me and my good name! Other merchants of Exeter continue to blame me for the attack on the aulnage. I did as you asked, and you promised to safeguard my position." Wolfson's voice had returned to its usual, nasal whining.

"Cease whimpering! Have you done all as I directed you?" The voice behind the collar gave no suggestion of being sympathetic.

"Yea, I have seen to it that the dean was informed of Eric Aunk's threats to the cathedral clergy. The Sheriff of Devon also knows Aunk is accused, and a reward for his capture has been offered. But what are you doing to protect me?"

"All has been done. You will now be patient and continue to put it about that Aunk is the evil threatening the city." With that, the tall gentleman turned as if to walk away.

"Stop, I say," and shouting thus, Wolfson rushed up to the robed figure and pulled hard on the garment that concealed his identity. One side of the dark cloak pulled open and the collar fell to its shoulders. The face of the tall gentleman was completely exposed to the light as Wolfson lifted up his small lantern. "Murphee Miller, come out, I command you!" he called into the darkness.

Wolfson presumed his body guard would now be emerging from his hiding place. With a sense of triumph, he began to gloat. "Of course, it is you," he said, shining his lantern's light upon the gentleman's face. "And now, sir, it is I in possession of power. I know who you are and have arms at my side. You will protect me, or I shall expose you!"

With that, the tall man's right arm thrust out from his cloak and swept a dagger's blade across the chest of Raymond Wolfson. "Go to Hell! I need you no longer, fool!" the voice growled.

The merchant halted suddenly, dropping his lantern to the ground. Both of his hands struggled to contain the wound in his chest. Blood began to seep from beneath his clothes as all his fingers pressed across his boney chest, frantically seeking to stop his massive bleeding. Raymond Wolfson's eyes glazed. He was totally unable to believe what was happening to him. The assailant's long right arm thrust the dagger into its victim again, deeply slicing down from his chest into the merchant's stomach. Wolfson's knees buckled and his head lolled backward, while his body collapsed to the ground. The assailant paused only long enough to throw a folded document on top of Wolfson's crumpled body. Then he slipped into the shadows beyond the lantern's light and sped away. The miller was nowhere to be seen.

* * *

The miller's wife had gone to bed. She had spent the earlier part of the evening scolding her husband for his drunkenness. He had told her to bugger off; he had things he must do this night. She insisted on watching him. He simply sat and continued to drink. "If ye ave things ta do, why do ye nay do em?" she had persisted.

At this, the miller stood up and raised his hand threateningly towards her. "Shut yer trap, woman; Oi shall do wha Oi mus when Oi'm ready!"

His wife had one response to his drunken stubbornness. She picked up her broom and brought its handle crashing upon his head. Now, both the miller's hands went straight to his skull, and he shouted a volley of curses towards her scampering exit. Then, staggering mightily in place, he collapsed backward towards his stool. But one of his arms reached out in his fall to pull his tankard to him. Crashing onto his seat, the miller drained the vessel of every last drop. He threw the tankard to the floor while slipping into senselessness. His head fell onto his arms bent upon the table.

She slept soundly in her bed. He snored off into the night, only to wake with the break of day. Murphee Miller lifted his head from his achingly stiff arms and neck, and a throbbing lump grew in the middle of his forehead.

* * *

Brandon Landow had eaten a lovely meal in the refectory of St Nicholas Priory. He was feeling affluent for the first time in his life. His purse was full, his hunger was well satisfied, but other appetites had begun to ache in his loins. Now that nighttime shadows were abroad, he told himself, there must be somewhere to find a naughty, sweet young thing. So he walked out from the priory onto the street and continued up the hill towards the High Street.

The highest class of drinking establishments sat not far from the Guildhall. Brandon knew he might find members of the wealthier classes of Exeter there, successful merchants or their sons and some members of the gentry. His coin filled purse was jingling; his locked chest, hidden in his priory room, contained plenty more; so, why not seek his frolic amongst the upper classes? He surely could afford it, he laughed to himself, possibly better than they could. Brandon drew himself up to his full height; knowing he was dressed in the latest of fashion, cap-a-pie, he walked into the tavern and called to the barman. "Your finest Bordeaux, my man," he shouted. Then he sat at a small table to await service.

It was a buxom female who brought his wine and placed it before him. She leaned her body against his and asked suggestively if she could offer him any further service. "I need nothing of your 'service,'" Brandon said in disgust, as he brushed her back from his shoulder.

"But I pray thee, lass," he said more kindly, while placing a small coin on the table, "can ye not tell me who of importance may be present this evening?"

Pulling her shoulders back and straightening the cap she wore atop her ragged curls, the barmaid smiled upon his gift, picked it up, and pushed it between her significant breasts, bulging from her barely adequate bodice. The up and coming merchants and their sons were seated round tables in the corner, she told him, with a nod in their direction. "Bu ifn ye looks tow'rds th fireplace, a fine gentl'man olds court t'ere, as ye might say. Ee be Sir Edmund Falford, younger son o an old Deb'm family."

Adding another coin to the table, Brandon looked to her eyes. "Ye are a very knowledgeable maid, my lass. Can ye tell me where his family's lands be in 'Deb'm?'" he asked, with slight mocking tone at her southwestern dialect.

"Oh aye, sir, jus ride down ta th coast, on tow'rds Beer way. Ee's fadder's got lands awl long th coast!" With that she installed yet another coin into her bodice and moved on.

Brandon sipped his wine while continuing to gaze about the interior of the public room. There was no one worth his attention, he thought, except the fine gentleman by the fireplace, and yet he surely did not wish to be seen as too eager to make the acquaintance of Sir Edmund Falford. Instead, he remained alone in his seat until he noticed Sir Edmund looking in his direction. Bowing his head to acknowledge the gentleman, he was pleased to receive a welcoming gesture, beckoning to him. Brandon slowly rose to his feet and walked towards the group gathered round the fireplace.

"Good evening, gentlemen. My name is Brandon of Cirencester, and I have recently arrived from York." Brandon continued to stand, because no one in the group moved to allow him a seat. "I am currently looking to find a quality saddlery here in Exeter. Can you share your best local recommendations with me? I have come into significant funds, thanks to my success in the Yorkshire markets, and do wish to reward my own triumph."

One or two of the men sitting by the fire began to speak of a saddler whom they knew and would recommend, but the person at the very centre of the group waved their words aside. "Enough, friend Brandon, if you truly wish to display yourself as saddled amongst the highest of the kingdom, allow me to help you. I can achieve for you the superb excellence of a Moorish saddle from North Africa, by way of Toledo in Spain."

The man who spoke rose from his chair and, pushing one of his fellows out from his seat, signaled Brandon to sit next to him. "I am Edmund Falford. Will you join me that we may pursue your quest, as gentlemen? Bring another cup of Bordeaux for my friend!"

Brandon noticed at once the impressive height of Falford, a full head taller, peering down upon him. He was a ruggedly handsome man, probably in his late twenties, with a face carved deeply in lines across his forehead and cheeks, suggesting a love of the outdoor life. He had lithesome hands with long fingers that gestured elegantly, displaying several large rings upon each hand. One very distinctive ring upon the middle finger of his right hand featured a silver eagle's head, profiled to display a large ruby eye.

"Sir Edmund, it is my pleasure to make your acquaintance. I have, of course, heard of your noble family. Do you not own lands along the coast, near the village of Beer? As Brandon moved to sit amidst Sir Edmund's group, his thoughts raced as he tried to note every aspect of the gentleman, his dress, and his manner.

"My father and brothers do, indeed, hold extensive lands along the East Devon Coast for grazing as well as hunting. But, as my father's seventh son, there is little left for my inheritance, save to make my own way in the world." Falford spoke as if somewhat bored, having his family occupy the main topic of conversation.

So, Brandon expressed further interest into the possibility of buying for himself a finely tooled, Moorish saddle. "I have seen such a work only once. It was uniquely done, and I should rejoice to possess such an exotic creation. But how, sir, is it that you have access to such rarities?"

"One has contacts, Brandon," Falford answered him casually, "but I must make arrangements to have such objects as Moorish saddlery obtained for me. Are you able to place a significant down payment with me, to assure shipment from Spain?"

When Brandon asked the amount required for the down payment, Falford sniffed in response, "I require two pounds."

Brandon could tell that Falford was testing him, seeking to know if he truly had funds enough to afford such luxury. But Brandon, while easily able to spend such a sizable amount, did not wish to seem unaware of the ways of the world. Finally, after some exchange of verbal struggle, Brandon gave Falford the first partial payment in front of the gathered gentlemen, in gold. He told Falford as he stacked the money upon the table, he would supply the rest, payable after he had examined every aspect of the array in person, to his satisfaction. Sir Edmund stood and extended his hand to Brandon, thus signifying their gentlemen's agreement had been achieved in the presence of witnesses. Then, announcing to his fellows that the hour was nearing curfew, and he would need to begin his journey home, Falford asked Landow to meet him after a fortnight's passage.

"Come to this place, Brandon. Find me here at this same tavern, with your money in hand to complete the price. You shall not be disappointed, my friend." Brandon understood the continued use of "my friend" to express Falford's public declaration of his familiarity with him. But before Brandon could inquire further regarding Falford's family home, his holdings, or his business, Falford announced, "Adieu, gentlemen," and, with a great flourish, returned his riding gloves to both elegant hands and walked into the night.

Brandon could hardly take his eyes from the departing Falford, whose black boots and long, dark cape seemed to sweep him along like the winds whipping clouds in a violent storm. He truly did look forward to their appointed meeting, not only because of his significant down payment being carried away, but also because Brandon wished to learn to imitate the manner of this grand gentleman of noble family. The pardoner was a good actor. He knew he could recreate the courtesy, as well as the arrogance, in the manners of the great. And who knows, perhaps Falford might display further interest in him.

After Falford's dramatic departure, Brandon made a purposeful attempt to acquaint himself with the rest of the fireplace group. Some of the gentlemen seemed more readily interested than others to build acquaintance with this *nouveau riche,* young man whom they thought was from Cirencester. Brandon, on the other hand, sought to learn more about Falford and his Devonshire roots.

"Sir Edmund will do well by ye, friend," one older man told him. "Whatever it is ye may want in the world, he seems able to procure it. May come at a dear cost, but he will find it!"

"But what can you tell me of his family?" Landow pressed them. "Have you met other Falfords?"

"He speaks of them regular, and the family name is well known in the shire. But they stay down river when they be at home. Most of the time, his elder brothers prefer to remain at the young King's Court."

"Are they knights?" Brandon pressed. "Have they been off to the wars in France?"

"One of the brothers has been on Crusade, and we know little of him. The others seem to prefer to spend their days in London, whilst their father is thought to have become a recluse in the family manor of Withycombe Raleigh." This comment came from another of the older members of the group, who looked encouragingly at Landow.

"God save you, Brandon. I am Clarence Milborne, and I am a knight of the shire."

The pardoner guessed Milborne must be in his late thirties. Though relatively short in stature, he displayed arms still powerful through the hand he offered Brandon. "If blood will speak for the Falfords," Milborne continued, "they do have noble currents coursing through them, even if planted from the awkward side of the blanket."

"It is my pleasure to meet you, Sir Clarence," Brandon smiled. "As you are so well informed of families here in Devon, may I assume that you also are of ancient Devon family?"

"Indeed ye may, but as a cadet branch of the Milborne family and second son at that, I am relatively landless, only holding my manor in service to and by the grace and favour of the Earl of Devon."

The barman began to walk through the tavern, reminding of the approach of curfew. The rest of the fireplace group began to bid their goodnights and hurry off onto the High Street. Soon Brandon noticed that he and his companion were nearly alone in the tavern.

"I shan't be ready to end this lovely evening so soon, Brandon, so may I invite you to my humble townhouse for a nightcap?" Milborne's eyes did seem to be encouraging him to accept.

"But your lady wife, my friend, will she not be distressed by such a late call?" the pardoner protested.

"I have no lady wife with me in town. I do not always fancy women, Brandon, but I do favour thee."

Chapter Seventeen

Morderour Expresse

Nan's light soprano voice seemed to fill the kitchen, laundry, storage closets, or wherever she walked, sprightly stepping through her daytime chores. Everyone in the household noticed her obvious high spirits, but no one below stairs dared inquire further. Lady Apollonia sensed an extra expression of joy in all of Nan's movements; even when she sat to pursue her needlework that afternoon, she seemed unable to keep from breaking into song.

"Dearest Nan, you seem so pleased with yourself this day. Have you any surprises to share with me?"

Nan looked up from her needle with great, wide eyes, as if her Lady had suggested some unusual event in the household, and said, "Why no, my Lady, all goes in good order, and that never fails to please me. But I do rejoice that Master Edward has recovered completely from his ague. God has truly blessed us, has He not?"

"Oh, Nan, you are the most gracious of friends to me. I have been thinking the very thing in my own heart this morning. If only I could sing so beautifully as you, surely I would add my thanks to God in the sweet melodies you share. But I shall rejoice in your song and add my thanks in prayer. Gramercy, dearheart, your kind thoughts increase my joy as well."

They were seated in Apollonia's solar near to the fire. The day had risen brightly but with wintry chill and sharp, slicing winds. The two women continued their needlework, sharing a wondrous sense of contentment, when suddenly Edward burst into the chamber.

"Lonia, Nan, please forgive my intrusion, but I must ask you to come with me to the hall. Canon Chulmleigh has called upon us, Lonia," Edward said directly to his wife, "and the news he brings must be calmly shared with our entire household."

Apollonia quickly put her needlework aside. "What is it, Edward? What has arisen? Is something amiss in the town?"

"Please come quickly, my dear; it is best if the canon tells us when we are all gathered together."

Edward was so unusually grave in his manner the women asked nothing further from him. They walked together into the hall where Baldwin Chulmleigh paced about, deeply distressed. Stafford, the household steward, moved next to his master's side, saying nothing but groaning in his deeply voiced moan.

"Dear friend," Apollonia said to the canon, "you are as always most welcome to our home, but what news have you brought us?"

The canon paused in his pacing, and Apollonia could see his eyes bore dark circles beneath them, as if he had spent a sleepless night. "My Lady, I have already spoken with your good husband, but I feel it necessary to warn everyone in your household."

Father Anthony entered the hall bringing with him: Jude, Norman, with Mary the cook and Gareth the stablemaster. Canon Chulmleigh wasted no words but spoke directly to his point. "There has been a murder in Exeter last night, and the victim was an important member of our city's guilds."

A collective gasp slipped from Mary and Nan, but the male members of the group seemed to steady themselves for revelations yet to come. Edward spoke first. "Canon Chulmleigh, please tell us all is well with our Mistress Phyllis of Bath."

"Indeed, I have not spoken carefully," the canon said sheepishly. "Mistress Phyllis is well. I sent a messenger to her cottage early this morning after the discovery. The victim was the merchant, Raymond Wolfson, whose body was found lying on the banks of the leat round the Shilhay, though God knows why he would have been there in the late hours of last night." Canon Chulmleigh took his scarf and placed it to his forehead. In spite of the chill of the day, he was dripping with perspiration.

"I come to share this horrible news with all of you, because we have no insight or understanding as to cause; yet, we know the murderer has acted with intent to kill Wolfson. I beg you, every one of our merchant community must remain on constant guard until the perpetrator has been apprehended."

Mary, the cook, began to weep hysterically. Apollonia could see she was beyond calming, so she spoke to Nan and asked her to take Mary to the kitchen for a beaker of strong ale. "Remain with her, Nan, until she can return to herself. Then, you and she will gather the household maids and kitchen wenches. Tell each of them, we must be on our guard, keep behind our locked doors, and never venture onto the streets unless we are in groups."

The women left the hall. Edward spoke very seriously with Father Anthony and then addressed himself to Gareth, Jude, and Norman. "Men, I shall see to it that Stafford and I continue to protect the Lady and Nan, while remaining alert to any threat within the household. But you, Gareth, and the stable lads must see to the defences of the barns and the kitchen. You, dear Chaplain, with Jude and Norman, must help to protect our sons when they walk between Exeter House and the Cathedral Green. We shall all increase our guard within our walls and add protection if any of us is required to be on the streets."

Edward felt suddenly fatigued and moved to sit in his great chair near the fire. He did not fear to defend himself, but he was apprehensive that their family and the entire Aust affinity must be protected against the possibility of any murderous assault, when they moved about the town. Apollonia dismissed Stafford and the other men of the household but asked them to tell everyone in their service that they must report any suspicion of threat, any time of day or night, to her or to their master.

Then, she took Chulmleigh's arm and urged him to sit together with her and Edward. "Come, Canon Baldwin, we must think carefully through all we can know of this dreadful occurrence. Reason will be our first shield of defence, especially if it can lead us to any understanding." Apollonia sought her own chair and urged the canon to share with them every detail known to him.

"Thank you both for your balance and poise," the canon said, heaving a great sigh. "I require your insight as there is more to tell. First of all, it is known that Master Wolfson was deliberately murdered. He was stabbed in two places. Secondly, we know the murderer was wearing a dark woollen cloak because the merchant had torn threads from it, perhaps when he fell to the ground, still clutching them in his hand. Finally, a mutilated indulgence was found thrown upon the body, and yes, my Lady, it had the face of a green man covering the bishop's seal, spewing forth the words, 'I destroy those who thwart me.'"

"Dear God," Edward exclaimed, "Canon Baldwin, will this never end? Can this long series of threats continue as the work of one demented mind? What is the motive? Why the clergy? Why the aulnage? Why in the world Raymond Wolfson? Nothing seems to follow."

"But, my dearest Edward," Apollonia insisted, "have we not been given some very important clues to the demented mind at work here? I pray thee, husband, chief amongst them is the collection of despoiled indulgences. Canon Baldwin, I believe they must be examined very carefully. Can you help us see them gathered all together? I should like to compare them, to determine if all were made by the same hand." The Lady paused, as if listing in her mind the ongoing steps in their study of the facts.

"Also, remember the threads of woollen cloth you mentioned, found in Wolfson's hand, dear Canon. These provide us with the possibility of a piece of the garment of the murderer. Can you help us to see those also? If we could match those threads with a pulled tear on someone's garment, we may have evidence against a particular suspect."

"But, my Lady," the canon interjected, "Master Edward confronts us with the endless confusion of motive. Why would the same villain threaten cathedral clergy, as well as the aulnage and his brother, and now destroy the life of an important wool merchant of the town?"

"These are valuable questions, but perhaps the motive we seek was not always the same; perhaps the indulgence threats have been reused to suit a variance in motive. I know from my inquiries that the image of the green man was rumoured in the town as being used against the cathedral clergy. Canon Baldwin, you must ask amongst your friends within the Close, has any member of the clergy described the corrupt indulgence warnings to someone outside of the Green, and if he did, with whom did he speak?"

* * *

A week had gone by, and Friar Francis noted that the newest resident of St Mary Magdalene's Leprosarium was slowly being drawn into their community. It was the group of St Mary's children who seemed to speak most joyfully to the spirit of Deadman. They were as children everywhere: always looking to play jokes upon each other, always seeking to take sides in a new game, always full of questions asked shyly of any newcomer who may be able to shed light on the world outside their walls.

Eric Aunk loved children, perhaps even more so, now that he was forced to remain away from his daughter, Ariana. When he had lived in the Close, he had hidden from the children playing there, because he assumed they would be frightened by his dreadful scars. But Ariana had encouraged her father to show his face freely. She insisted that good people of any age would respect him for the good man he was. The children of the leper colony saw horrors of disfigurement in people about them every day. They did not mind his mask. They thought nothing of it. They sat, spoke, and played with Deadman because they liked him.

Eric was showing the children how to play a game of "Jack be Nimble, Jack be Quick," forming a line running in a circle around him until they reached the words, "Jack Jumped Over the Candlestick!" At that point in the rhyme, he bent in half, while each child was to run up and leap over him. Most of the children were agile and found it easy to leapfrog over his back. One very little boy found the hurdle too great for him to surmount and simply said quietly, "Deadman, can you help me, please?"

Eric got down onto his hands and knees and sank into a very low crouch. "Now put your hands on to my back and jump over me, Willy. You can do it just as well as the big boys."

Willy backed away, then took a running start and somersaulted over Eric's lowered back. "Hoorah, Willy, well done," Eric shouted.

Friar Francis was seated with several inmates who enjoyed watching the children's games. It thrilled the friar to his innermost soul when his ears could rejoice in the sounds of children's laughter and cries of celebration. He was very pleased to see Deadman willing to play games with them, but especially grateful to God that Deadman was beginning to find ways to enjoy life, even the life of the living dead. It was clear to Francis that Deadman's posture grew more lively, more erect when he played with the children.

The friar had not found an occasion to speak at any length with Deadman. They exchanged greetings each day, but little more. Francis hoped to find some time when he might offer any slight ministry to this obviously troubled man. His mind continued to think of excuses to speak with Deadman. Then, he saw Willy ask the children's friend to bend lower so that he could jump over him. When Deadman bent into his crouched position on his knees, he seemed to forget his mask. It fell away from his face, and for a brief moment, Francis was able to see his fully exposed face. Deadman had no typical disfigurement of a leper's rotting facial features or skin. Instead, Francis could see his face had been badly scarred. God had not destroyed Deadman's face through disease; the weapons of mankind left these dreadful wounds. The friar was nearly certain of it.

* * *

Laston walked through South Gate, exiting the city wall and turning towards the walls of St Mary Magdalene. He knew where to find the leprosarium, but he had no idea what to expect there. Would he have to go inside? What dreadful things would he see? Oh, if there were only some other way to find his friend. Would Master Aunk be able to come out to speak with him? "Dear God, be pleased ta make it zo," Laston prayed silently.

He tentatively approached the main portal to the leprosarium and looked about for some way to rouse a gateman. Seeing a large bell hanging near to the door, he pulled it very carefully, as if he were frightened of touching anything having to do with this hospice. There being no response, Laston pulled the bell once again, and a small door opened within the larger portal.

"Wha be it ye want, lad?" an older man's voice spoke gently to him from behind a small screen.

"Oi be wantin ta speak wit Master Deadman, ifn ye please."

"Go ta th end o dis wall, lad. Dere be a small screened space in th wall wher ye may speak wit im alone. Grant me moment ta find im fur ye?"

"Yea, sir, Oi'll do it. Tell im Oi be Laston, ifn ye please, sir." Laston seemed relieved to walk away from the door, down towards the corner of the wall. He reached the area of the wall where he found the screen, but it was tightly blocked. So, Laston just stood there quietly, waiting and waiting, but no one came. He walked about in circles, wondering to himself, "Per'aps Master Aunk ain't ere. Per'aps Oi shou'd be goen." But then, Laston reminded himself that the pitmaker had told him he would remain here for weeks, until he could find a way to clear his name with the dean of the cathedral. Laston also reminded himself, he did have important news to share with Master Aunk. He continued to pace in a very small circle.

Then, with a loud, squeaking noise, the small door in the hospice wall began to creak open. It was behind the metal screen and higher on the wall than Laston was tall, but he waited until he heard a familiar voice speak quietly from behind the screen. "Laston, are you there, lad? Do you have any news for me, my good friend?"

With that, Laston ran up towards the wall and stood on his tip toes. "Aye, Master Aunk, Oi'm ere. Can ye ear me?"

"Quickly lad, I am very grateful for your visit, but you must not stay here long. Please tell me your news." Eric wished he could reach out to take Laston's hand but instead tried to include in his voice some sense of his gratitude for the boy's help.

"T'ers been anoder murder, Master Aunk!"

"Laston, tell me all, quickly as you can. What in God's name has happened?"

"Twer down on th Shilhay. A rich guildsman were stabbed an lef near th streams."

"Who was it, Laston? Who was the man; do you know?"

"Oi knew ye wou'd want me ta tell ye. Zo Oi foun out fur ye. It were a man called Wolfson!" Laston kept on speaking before Eric could press any further questions. "An tha ain't all, Master Aunk. Ee were found wit a document lyen on is body. Some is sayen ye are th villain. But Oi knows ye wou'd nay murder, an besides, ye ave been ere when th deed were done!"

"Laston, you are the most blessed of friends to me, but please do not linger here, son. If ye have told me all, run back into the town. But should ye hear anything more, please help me to learn of it. Away with ye lad, and know ye bear my heartfelt thanks until I can offer more."

* * *

"Sir Edmund Falford, my Lady, Master Edward." Stafford, standing to his full height as if demonstrating his rank in the Aust household, announced their guest and then stepped to one side as the gentleman entered the hall.

Apollonia and Edward had nearly finished their late day's summaries of the accounts. It had been a very good year for them. Although total expenditures were up, their profits had increased more significantly, and the extension of their woollen enterprise in Exeter had flourished. But they could not rejoice in any of it. Attack and murder had shadowed their accomplishment, and the entire household was maintaining an uneasy aura of self-defence. Edward and Apollonia had even discussed whether they should take their younger sons from school, just to be assured of their remaining within the protection of their own affinity.

"Sir Edmund," Edward rose and walked to greet their visitor, "how welcome you are. We have missed your good company, but now may hope to offer you some dinner this evening to forestall your departure."

"God give you greetings, my Lady, Edward. I have only just returned to Exeter from business travels in the East of Devon. Forgive me; I must refuse your gracious invitation because I am required to sup elsewhere this evening."

"Then you must share a cup of wine with us," Apollonia said to him gesturing to a vacant chair next to her. "Do you have news to share with us from East Devon?"

"Nay, dear Lady, it is the news I found awaiting me when I return to Exeter that continues to frighten and terrorize the commons of the town. What can you tell me of the most recent murder? Who was the victim, and why was he attacked? I understand he was not of the lowest classes." Sir Edmund sat back into his great chair and lifted his cup to Apollonia. "Gramercy, my lady, your presence offers life's most beautiful refreshment."

"Indeed, you have returned to a dreadful state of affairs here in Exeter, Sir Edmund," Edward said. "The man who was murdered was Raymond Wolfson, one of our successful wool merchants. But we have more questions than answers to share with you. His body was found on the Shilhay, alone and unaccompanied, as we understand. But, why he was there, and what were the murderer's motives? We have no further word."

"Thieves and footpads are always abroad in the darkness of night, Edward. Is it not possible that Merchant Wolfson was simply murdered for his purse?"

"But, Sir Edmund, his purse was not taken. Why would the merchant have been abroad in the night in such a strange place, unaccompanied by any of his henchmen? And there is more...," Edward began to speak, but Apollonia intervened.

"You see, Sir Edmund, the murderer left behind a threatening document, one of these dreadful indulgences with the bishop's seal torn away and a monkey's face placed to spew out intent."

"Oh, I thought it had been a foliate face of some sort?" Falford responded.

"Indeed, sir, I have misspoke. Beg pardon." Apollonia looked away, but noted to herself that Sir Edmund had been made aware of the odious usage of the green man.

"But," Edward said with a sigh, "you can see why the entire town is stirred to worry and fret. We have nowhere to look for the culprit and no motive."

"Was not some charge made against an angry Celtic pitmaker of the cathedral?"

Before Edward could speak, Apollonia responded again, "Indeed, Sir Edmund, we have heard nothing of that."

Finishing his wine, Sir Edmund put his cup upon the table and rose to take the Lady's hand. "I do thank you for your willingness to keep me abreast of the latest rumours. However, I am assured the dean and the sheriff already have a guilty party in their sights; once he has been captured, we shall all rest more comfortably in our beds."

Bowing to the Lady and replacing his hat upon his head, Sir Edmund swept from the hall. "What a grand, young gentleman he is," Edward said with honest admiration. "He is one with all classes and stands not at all upon the privileges of his station in life."

"Edward, you are generously balanced in your view of folk. I believe it is you who are the most wholesomely open and accepting towards all," Apollonia said. "I agree, Sir Edmund has been very accessible to us. I am grateful for his lack of pride, but we should also seek to portend his reasons."

* * *

Landow dressed himself with great care that evening. He was to return to the tavern where Sir Edmund had promised to bring the example of Moorish saddlery. If this new saddle would be the elegant Moorish craft promised, Landow knew he would possess the very best a gentleman of fashion could own. The pardoner had spent many, late evening rendezvous with his new friend, Clarence Milborne, and had recently become Clarence's houseguest as Brandon of Cirencester. They had established an intimacy of reward and pleasure between them, but one that included no honesty on Brandon's part. Brandon allowed Clarence to believe he was a young merchant, and while he accepted the elder man's hospitality and favours, he gave little more than simple thanks in return. The gentleman Brandon really sought to establish friendship with was Sir Edmund Falford.

Brandon walked into the hall where Sir Clarence waited for him by the fire. "Dear one, you will make a handsome appearance in the tavern this evening," the knight said insipidly.

Brandon seemed to disregard his friend's compliment and said with slight irritation in his voice, "I am hoping Falford will prove true to his word and deliver my Moorish saddle this evening. We shall see if it fulfills his promises. Do get up, Clarence. We should have been there an hour ago!"

Milborne stood while his manservant placed his cloak upon his shoulders and ignored the reality of his having been made to wait. "Falford will deliver, my boy. When you see what he brings, you will know you must have it."

Brandon pouted noticeably. "Well, he is charging me a knight's ransom for it!" he whined.

"If I could, I would buy it for you, precious boy, but I can not, and I also know you have the means to achieve it for yourself. Please save your wiles for our night chamber where I may offer other pleasures. Let us away!"

The two men walked through the dark streets of Exeter until they reached the High Street. People hurried about to complete their tasks and return to their homes, well before curfew. No one wished to be found alone in the darkness since the dreadful murder of Wolfson. Clarence attempted to place his hand upon Brandon's arm, but the pardoner pushed it away, saying gruffly, "Not in public, Milborne!"

They entered the tavern and walked to the fireplace where Falford already held court, displaying an exquisite saddle on a large table where everyone could observe it closely and admire it. "I have the only other saddle such as this in all of Devon," Falford was saying. "Ah, and here comes the young man who will soon possess the second of its kind. Welcome, Master Brandon, please do examine your prize."

Landow walked directly towards the table, circling slowly and looking closely into every aspect of the saddle and its richness. He was thrilled with its exquisite design, tooled elegantly into the deep, rich, darkness of the leather, but he carefully allowed no disclosure of his pleasure. Keeping his facial expression unmoved, he slid his fingers along the tooling and caressed the leather. "Does it fulfill your expectations, Brandon?" Falford asked him.

"I am satisfied, Sir Edmund," he said. Taking his purse from his belt, Brandon conspicuously counted out the balance of the payment, displaying the sizable sum upon the table. Witnesses' eyes widened to see this very young man arrogantly flaunt such wealth. His presumption surprised them even further when he added, "But I shall require the saddle delivered to me, if you please."

"As you wish, young master," Falford said with a smirk, scooping the pile of coins into his own purse. He was startled by the brazen impudence of the demand, but he simply added, "I shall have my man carry it round to you on the morrow."

"No, Sir Edmund, you have my payment this night; I shall require delivery tonight." Milborne could be heard drawing a deep breath.

"That can be arranged. But do let us acknowledge our transaction with a drink. Barkeep! Serve wine round our table. We have much to celebrate." Edmund Falford did find this aggressive, young man to be impertinent and annoying, but he sensed in him an impudence he might be able to employ. He would pursue that course at another time, when he knew more of the truth of Brandon and his significant funds. Falford had profited well this night and would remain this evening, long enough to enjoy some of the tavern's highly regarded French wine. He knew it to be a very fine wine, because he had supplied it.

* * *

Darkness of the night enshrouded Eric as he left his bed in the leprosarium and walked to the wall surrounding its courtyard. On the wall, where a small, screened opening had allowed him to speak with Laston, Eric had noticed a stout vine grew from the earth on the interior side of the wall and hung over its height outside, into the street below. The entire community was at rest; no one stirred. Waiting in the silent night to be certain no one could witness his actions, he grasped the thick, central stem, powerfully testing the strength of the vine; then, he climbed to its top. Sitting on top of the wall, he hefted his legs over it and hung full length from the vine, finally letting himself drop to the street level beneath the wall of St Mary Magdalene. Eric was now not only beyond the walls of the leprosarium but also the wall of the city. Thus freed from all enclosure, he began to run towards the bank of the River Exe. He knew where a small boat was always stored by his friend, Adam, whenever he had deliveries to make upstream in Exeter.

Eric found the coracle lying upside down, well hidden beneath brush next to the tree where Adam always left it. It was so lightweight that Eric could launch it by himself. Once it was floating near the bank, he climbed into it, paddled out to the deepest part of the river, and rowed with the natural flow of the Exe downstream. He knew he had to speak with his friend, Adam. Serious crimes were being committed in Exeter, and he was being blamed. Eric had to find some way to clear his name, and he needed the help of his childhood friend. He could not run away from these charges; he must fulfill his promises to Ariana. His precious daughter believed in him, and he could not betray her trust.

Chapter Eighteen

Corrupcioun Cave

Whenever Gareth wished to see Nan alone, he would silently and secretly display to her his small rolled message, kindly written out for him by young Alban: "COME TO GARDEN." The petite lady's maid would always find a way to slip out, after the household was asleep, into the garden and walk into Gareth's personal corner of the barn. He had found a way to stretch blankets and skins about the small cubicle, containing his bed and his meager belongings. He added a small table with candle and stools where they might be allowed to sit together to speak privately.

Some evenings would find them together in bed, sharing their bodies as gently and lovingly as an old married couple. Some evenings they would sit together, holding each other and talking for hours. As the weeks progressed, Gareth had grown wholly comfortable with Nan, not only in touching; he was able to speak freely with her. He described to Nan how he felt inadequate, because he could not read. He had a keen awareness of being born lower class, so that he was never able to speak in the presence of their betters. He even worried that he would never be able to look directly into the eyes of a gentleman he respected, or a woman he admired such as their Lady Apollonia.

In every case, Nan would require him to look into her eyes as she described, through a series of incidents in their lives, how he had displayed his intelligence. She enabled him to recognize a collection of words from her prayer book, and he found great pride in being able to read the words of the "Our Father" and "The Lord is My Shepherd." Nan would casually describe how universally admired he was by all the men of the household, for his significant strength and his great skill in dealing with the livestock. She helped him to see that such men as Master Edward, one whom they both regarded as the best of men, truly looked up to him, not merely as a man but especially as a man of admirable skill. And Nan never ceased to emphasize to Gareth how good looking and well built he was.

"Fur aught Oi woot, ye jest wit me, Nan," he would insist. "Oi can nay belief sech things!" Then, Nan would take him back to the days of their youth. Gareth would grudgingly acknowledge that their Lady Apollonia had always especially admired him for his courage on her behalf, and maintained a heartfelt gratitude to him for saving her after the death of her first husband.

After each of their long conversations together, Gareth would walk Nan back through the garden to reenter Exeter House by the kitchen door. Their friendship had grown into touching and beautiful intimacy, yet it remained totally unknown to anyone else within the Aust affinity.

This evening, when Nan walked out from the kitchen in response to one of his invitations, Gareth met her in the darkness and took her arm. They walked to a bench in the garden and sat quietly in the evening's darkness, sharing the sparkling beauty of the nighttime heavens and a brilliant moon. The evening's chill soon drove them into the warmth of the barn. Gareth pulled up a great fur to cover them both, as they sat on his bed in the candlelight. He told Nan he had something he must say to her. She waited quietly, as she knew he still found it difficult to speak directly to her, rather than respond to her inquiries. Finally, she put her hand in his and told him, "Pray, my dear Gareth, trust me, dearheart, for you know you will always have my love."

He lifted his eyes to her and, before stumbling through any introduction to his request, simply mumbled, "Dear Nan, ye mus be moi wife."

Complete silence filled the candlelit corner of the barn. They sat, arms, hands, and bodies pressed together but nothing was said. Eventually Gareth looked completely puzzled and then hurt, as his face began to reveal his sense of rejection. "If'n ye luv me, can ye nay be moi wife?"

Very quietly, Nan looked into his worried face and placed a hand upon his cheek. "I will always love you and only you, Gareth, for as long as I live. But my life is already given to my Lady." They continued to hold each other, as Nan told Gareth the grisly details of her earliest childhood memories. She described herself as a discarded infant, a bastard abandoned by unknown parents and reared as less than a dog amongst the kitchen wenches of the household of Sir

Geoffrey Montecute. "The hounds of the lord's kennels were valued far more highly than I," she told him.

She forced herself to continue to describe to him her brutal sexual abuse as a small child by Wilfrid de Guelf, liege man to Sir Geoffrey, who took his carnal pleasures with little girls or little boys he found available. Gareth had known the reputation of Sir Wilfrid while he was a very young stable lad. He had always despised him and avoided him. Now the knight's corruption became personally painful, and he dropped his head in hate filled disgust.

Nan lifted his face to hers once again. "Gareth, it was our Lady who saved me. It was she who transformed my life from barnyard animal into that of a whole and respected person. She dressed me, educated me, taught me the full meaning of loving kindness, and saw to it that I was baptised into the church. But most of all, it was Lady Apollonia who granted me a soul, dearheart. I know she requires nothing from me, but I can live for no one save her."

Gareth listened carefully. He was a simple man, but there could be no doubt in his mind that Nan loved him. He grasped immediately the great respect she felt for him by sharing such long hidden, inner secrets of her life. He looked into her eyes, kissed her gently, and simply said, "Oi be ye friend, Nan."

* * *

The rapid currents of the River Exe widened and deepened greatly, once past Topsham, as the river rushed to follow the descending tidal waters to the sea. Eric felt so wonderfully free, with his hood thrown back and his paddle effortlessly steering him within the currents flowing along towards Exmouth. Suddenly, ahead in the moonlight, he could see a single horseman riding along the river road in the same direction he was going. Startled to find anyone travelling at this late hour, Eric steered his flat bottomed coracle towards the shallower waters near the bank, where he might remain hidden behind grasses and riverside trees. The rider was obviously unaware of his presence on the river, and Eric did not wish to be seen. So, though he continued to drift downriver, he was careful to remain close to the bank, hidden from sight.

Eric could see that the horseman was alone, obviously untroubled by the possibility of footpads and thieves. He sat tall in his saddle with a great, dark cloak dropping from his shoulders to cover the hindquarters of his mount. His large hat seemed to reach down to an extended collar, completely covering his face from the chill of the evening's breezes while he trotted southward. It was slower going at this pace, but Eric decided he not only preferred to remain unseen, he was mightily curious about this lone horseman who felt so at ease, unaccompanied and unthreatened, upon the road at this hour.

* * *

The first streaks of dawn sheared across the sky when Eric could see the mysterious horseman turn away from the River Exe and take the road towards Withycombe Raleigh. Eric remained on the river until he could feel the waters increased rush towards the sea. Paddling the coracle up to the bank, he hid the light craft and walked on towards his friend Adam Braund's house in Littleham Parish. He knew his appearance there would be a surprise, but he also cherished the welcome he knew would be his. As he knocked gently on the door to the cottage, Eric's heart thrilled when Ariana opened it, shouting in welcome, "Father, you have come!" and threw herself into his arms.

"Dearest Ariana," Eric whispered into her ear, "I have missed you so. But speak quietly, child; we must not waken the household."

"Oh, father, everyone is up and about. Aunt Telitha is milking the cows, and Uncle Adam will soon be on his way to the barge."

"Ariana, I must speak with Adam," Eric said as he walked into the cottage.

"Well den, why do'n ye, Worm?" Adam's voice came from the large chair next to the fireplace. He stood up to greet his friend, and they crushed each other into the warm embrace of longstanding friendship.

The two men walked to the table where Ariana announced she had their porridge ready, and they all sat together. Eric was so pleased to be with them that he ate his porridge with relish and forgot all else. "Well, Worm, Oi be truly glad ta see ye, bu wha brings ye ta o'r door dis early mornin?" Adam asked. "We be takin good care o Ariana."

"Oh yes, father, I have so enjoyed working in the kitchen with Aunt Telitha, and Uncle Adam is indeed our very best friend, even if he does call you a worm."

Eric's face darkened and the lines of worry seemed to deepen as he looked to his daughter. He put his head down and said with great agony of confusion, "Dearest child, I have tried to work towards our being returned to life together. I had such great hopes for us, now dashed! Once again I am come to beg Adam's help. I am accused of murder and am wanted as murderer by the Sheriff of Devon."

"Wha be dis tomfoolery ye be sayin?" Adam asked in the tone of a village boy's jest. "Ave ye been in yer cups befor yer porridge dis mornin, Worm?"

"Dear God, I wish I were drunk, Adam, but I tell you this in all sobriety. I am a wanted felon, and I need your clear head to advise me. I do not wish to run away. I pray to God to help me clear my name."

Eric told them both the entire story of how he believed he had first been accused by Merchant Wolfson. The merchant had revealed to the dean of the cathedral Eric's guilt in sending the mutilated indulgence threats to the clergy. Then, when the same sort of indulgence was thrown at the time of the attack on the aulnage and his brother, the dean was made to assume that he, Eric, must be guilty of that attack.

"But most terrifying of all, Adam, Raymond Wolfson was murdered on the Shilhay two nights ago, and one of the indulgences was found upon his body. By extension, the sheriff is now looking to charge me with threat, assault, and murder." Eric's scarred face seemed completely crumpled. "My friend, I am undone and in dire straits."

"Father, I can not believe you guilty of any of these things, but never murder!"

"Please forgive me, Ariana, I must confess to you that in my service to Merchant Wolfson I did leave threatening messages against the clergy of the cathedral. But they were very general threats in tone and never designed against a person. Wolfson told me I was to distract the clergy whilst he gathered ill feeling against the aulnage."

"Ye tol me o yer silly green man indulgences," Adam said. "The womanish priests ne'er did unnerstand th tru meanin o th green mann, bu why was dey fearful o'em?"

"I believe they were startled and surprised, but none of them, dean nor chapter, felt the need to bring in the sheriff," Eric said. "Although Wolfson accused me to the dean of making the threats, I know he never knew the design of them. Whoever is using indulgences, sealed with green men's faces, is some other person, someone who arranged to kill Wolfson and make it look to be my crime," Eric sighed. "But how will I ever be able to confess that of which I have done, while proving my innocence of the greater charges?"

Adam Braund had been leaning his chin into his hands, thinking with a great scowl upon his face. "Ye ave indeed got yerse'v inta a real muddle dis time, Worm. Bu ye be nay guilty o murder an we mus prove yer innocence."

Ariana came to her father's defence immediately. "We must be ready to prove where you were when the attacks happened, father."

"Well, I only learned of the attack on the aulnage when I returned from visiting you here, in Littleham Parish. And, I was in Exeter when Wolfson was murdered, but I was hiding inside St Mary Magdalene Leprosarium," Eric said.

"Den ye ave witnesses ta support ye, Worm. Oi'll gladly speak wit th sheriff fur ye. Oo do ye kno in Exeter's St Mary Magdalene ye may trus?"

"Oh, father, you must not live with lepers. Please do not go back to that place." Ariana looked as if she might begin to weep.

"Ariana, love, you must understand that no one will ever think to look for me in St Mary Magdalene. I have a fine, young lad who faithfully brings me news from the town. He waits for me outside the walls. There is also one living there whom I believe will speak for me. He is a friar, and although I know him little, I do believe I may trust him with my life."

* * *

There was extraordinary activity in the great cave, once the line of men had walked through a dark hole in the limestone rock face, hidden from view. They entered into a kind of antechamber whose arcing ceilings still bore the tool marks of Roman slaves. They had been the first to extract glorious, white Beer stone for their public buildings and villas. But these men, on this night, knew nothing of the Romans or their villas. They were seamen who, by any definition of their skills, gained a significant amount of profit from piracy and smuggling. A major shipment of goods from France had been landed on the beach at Beer earlier in the evening. The furious labour of the moment was to haul all of it from the shingle beach up into the quarry cave, for secret storage and eventual distribution of the spoils.

The cave was not of natural formation but one created as part of an underground quarry. It was three quarters of a mile west of the fishing village of Beer, on the south coast of Devon, facing the English Channel. The smugglers always posted watchmen when such shipments landed: on the pebble beach, along the transport route to the quarry, and especially around the entrance to the cave. In these years of the reign of the boy King Richard, there was erratic royal control over the major ports of England, but even less threat of the appearance of royal tax collectors in the tiny village of Beer, its small bay sheltered by the great chalk cliffs of Beer Head. But one needed to take care. Smuggling was a hanging offense, even though frequently practiced by members of the upper classes whose lands offered coastal access.

The collection of seamen deposited their burdens, carried up from Beer beach, in assigned areas of the cave. Their entry was lighted through and into the larger interior by a series of torches in hangers on the walls. After his delivery, each man then reported to a small table, where two well-dressed men sat, making lists of all that had been delivered. The seamen stood in line until each had received his payment for this evening's work, and then every one of them walked back through the opening, out from the cave, and disappeared into the night.

"This has been a rich shipment," his deep voice seemed quite pleased with himself. "We shall have buyers for everything," he said gleefully to his companion. "Huge profits will be ours from these Cordoban silks. The Spanish swords always sell well, and I know a local merchant, building his new hall, who will lust for the Carrara marble tiles and the Lowland tapestries. And, of course, we can not forget the French wine."

An impressive figure and the obvious leader, he continued his instructions to the other men. "I will need you to remain here on guard in the cave through the night until we can return with carts from Exmouth on the morrow."

The leader stood, folding his lists, made from the cargo received, into a pouch hanging from his belt. His gentleman companion continued to sit, drumming his fingers upon the table. "I keep with me the lists of all we received this night," the leader said to their henchmen. "As is our custom, you may freely help yourselves to the cask of wine set out for refreshment. Your payment will be made to you when we return tomorrow. But," he added in a menacing tone, "my partner and I shall be aware of any items missing. There will be honour amongst thieves. We tolerate nothing less."

* * *

Eric prepared to return to Exeter on the next barge shipment north. He had spent precious time head to head with Ariana. "Dear lass, you must know that I will do anything in my power for you. But first and foremost, I must regain my name and position within the Close. Being cathedral pitmaker is an honourable job and earns well, especially as most burials in the city are required to be made in the Cathedral Yard. If I can overcome these charges against me, I know I shall be able to support a home for us. Please have faith that it may happen."

Ariana was a sturdy girl. She had grown visibly in the months spent with the Braund Family. Eric could see she stood taller, asserted herself with confidence whilst her blonde hair brightened and fair skin blushed in the rays of the coastal sunlight. But she made it clear to Eric that she wished for no other goal in life than to finally be allowed to live with her father.

"I shall remain here happily waiting for you, father, but I know we shall be together because I believe in you. Take your truth to the dean. Surely he will understand the falseness of the accusations against you when he will know you have witnesses to your innocence. He is reputed to be an honourable cleric. The truth will set us free, father; I know it." Eric hesitated, moved by her words and still longing to remain with her, but a voice called to him from the road.

"Coom long, Worm, or we shall miss th tide," Adam shouted.

Eric shared one last embrace and then ran through the door, waving goodbye to his daughter as he joined Adam. The two friends walked together along the road towards the dock in Exmouth.

"Adam," Eric said, "who of the nobility lives uphill in Withycombe Raleigh?"

Adam shook his head and said he had no interest in the gentry, but he could find out. "Why is it ye be so curious o em, Eric? Do dey owes ye sommat?"

"Nay, my friend, but in the dark of last night, I was accompanied down the Exe by an unknown horseman on the road along the river's bank. He rode all the way from Exeter to Exmouth, where we parted. I did not wish to be seen, so I remained on the river in the shadows, but I was surprised to see a single rider continue so fearlessly into the night. He was obviously a gentleman in dress and mount, but unaccompanied by servant or henchman.

Adam assured his friend that he would make his way up hill and discover who or how many important folk live that way; then he changed the subject of their conversation dramatically.

"Oi did'n wish ta frighten yer Ariana ani furder, Eric, bu Oi think she be roight! Tis ne good fur ye ta be livin wit th lepers. Can ye nay stay ere wit us?"

"I must bring this disastrous episode in my life to an end, Adam, and I must do it with Friar Francis's help. I have come to know the lepers of St Mary Magdalene's. Their children are as any other children, but dreadfully afflicted and dreadfully outcast. The residents of St Mary's are good people and deserving of our compassion. You are right, and I shall try to move from there as soon as I can. I am terrified that I risk exposure to their disease, but I must stay with them for now. If you have news or need to find me there, just come to the entrance and ask to speak with Deadman."

* * *

Eric remained within the small cabin on Adam's barge throughout the rest of the day after they had docked in Exeter. In his solitude, he savoured the memories of his visit with Adam's family and especially the true contentment he felt in the loving company of his daughter. Late in the evening of that day, when darkness could hide all notice of him, he left the barge, pulled the hood's lining over his face, and walked up from the river towards the city wall and the leprosarium.

In the continuing silence of the night, he leaped up to seize the vine growing over St Mary Magdalene's wall. Using its strength to pull himself to its top, he sat for awhile observing both sides. Once he was certain no one was about to notice him, he climbed down the vine. When his feet touched the grounds of St Mary's interior courtyard, Eric's heart sank. Once again, he knew he had been interred. He shook his head as if to assert the correctness of his actions.

"I will do this," he whispered to himself, "I will do this for us, Ariana. We shall have a family life together." But Eric added to these thoughts a new commitment, burning in his heart. If he was allowed to return to his role as pitmaker for the cathedral, he would remember this sensation of being declared one of the living dead. "Those who have died must be remembered by those who loved them," he told himself. "But surely those who are declared dead, while still amongst the living, must not be forgotten either."

Chapter Nineteen

Deformity's Descant

The great hall of the moated manor house of Withycombe Raleigh was served by a select number of servants. All were male, and all knew they must remain suspicious of any new face daring to ring the great bell, demanding a lowering of the drawbridge. They were a grudging lot, each hating to give way to another in any instance, but all knew Rauf was in control. Rauf was a giant of a man, from somewhere in the North of England, whose muscular power was regularly seen when he carried his master into the hall. Every member of the household bore bruises and wounds from the back of his huge hands. He had served their lord for many years and was never seen to leave his presence. As their lord's voice had grown more coarsely croaking during the past two years, Rauf frequently spoke for him, turning the simplest of requirements into a booming, instantaneous command.

This evening, Rauf had carried his master into the great hall and placed him upon his especially constructed couch. Its leaning frame had been thickly covered with sheepskins and wool, so that its surface would gently receive the wasted body of the Baron Brutwald Falford. The couch was kept in the midst of the forty by twenty-four foot expanse of tiled floor, near the fire that roared in the centre of the hall upon raised flagstones. The lord of the manor constantly trembled with cold; he could not warm himself adequately and called to Rauf to add more wood to the fire.

"My hands and feet are numb. Do you intend me to die of the chill?" he croaked to Rauf. "Give me heat or I shall freeze. When I am gone, who then shall champion you for the rest of your miserable life?"

Rauf offered no response to the baron's distemper. He was accustomed to his lord's daily complaints, accepting them as his needs to be fulfilled. Baron Falford was covered from head to foot in layers of woollen cloth, with a great woollen turban wrapped about his bald head. As he leaned back upon his couch near the fire, Rauf placed yet another robe of fur over his feet and lower body. The lord's hands reached eagerly for the robe, and from his exaggerated sleeves, his palms could be seen to be bleeding. One of his fingers was missing from his right hand. Beneath the woollen turban, Rauf knew the hair on his lord's head had fallen out years ago. His eyes blinked repeatedly, their brows could be seen to be long gone, and his eyelids were also barren, without lashes.

Still the baron continued to press Rauf. "That is better, better, but where is he, my Rauf? Why has he not come? When will he come?" his voice croaked. "I must speak with him!"

"Soon, my Lord," Rauf said calmly. "The young master said he would return to you when the shipments were hidden away and properly stored at Beer." Rauf attempted to offer a beaker of ale to slake the baron's thirst but also to ease his agitation. The stump of an angry fist, covered in overlong sleeve, pushed it away.

It was then that the large entry bell began to toll its demands from the gate. Rauf remained with their master while two other servants ran to the entrance to peer through the peek hole. If it were the lord's son, they would lower the drawbridge. If not, the summons of the bell would be disregarded. No one was allowed to enter Withycombe Raleigh Manor unless he and his motives were well known and welcome. The baron was a widower who had borne seven sons upon his lady wife, but only one member of the family came regularly to the side of his ailing father.

From the entrance to the manor house, a groaning rattle of the chains of the drawbridge being lowered could be heard, and shortly thereafter, a younger servant rushed into the hall. "Sir Edmund has come, my Lord!"

"Show him in! Show him in now, you fool!" The croaking voice shouted, while he gestured to Rauf to bring another stool closer to the fire.

Edmund Falford walked into the great hall, throwing his cloak and gloves into the hands of the waiting servant and walked with great strides towards the fire. "The nights grow colder, father," he said rubbing his hands together briskly.

"Do not speak to me of the cold! I am martyr to its blasts daily, and winter is not yet fully come." The older man whined, then coughed, which soon became a choked gasp. Rauf moved to the couch and lifted his master's shoulders and upper body in an effort to relieve his strangled breathing. Slowly the hacking cough eased, calm returned to the old man's chest, and Rauf leant him gently back upon the cushions.

As if unaware of his father's struggle, Edmund said haughtily, "We have received a worthy shipment this day! It will prove a fortune for us, father, even after paying the guards who remain in the cave. I shall return to Beer with carts on the morrow to collect most of our luxury goods, as I have immediate buyers for them in Exeter."

"I told you I should make you rich, you disreputable boy, but you must be attentive to my instruction. I can not change the succession. Your pampered, eldest brother will inherit the barony and lands, but I am determined to leave you with wealth enough to destroy his pretensions."

"I say, father, must we cast aspersions upon my rank? Twas you who were born on the wrong side of the blanket, was it not?"

"Mind your tongue," the old man smiled, with lips crumpled into a smirk. "We have noble blood, just as pure as the Beaufort bastards of John of Gaunt.

"Oh aye, my Lord father, but it gains us little," Edmund said moodily.

"I have bought a knighthood for you, sent you abroad to gain acknowledgement in the courts of the great, and I have enabled you to become independently rich! Dare not forget it!" The ancient creature bent into a rage of coughing once again, and Rauf immediately came to his aid.

"Yes, yes, father! Indeed, I owe my access to fortune to you. But why is it you have summoned me this night? I am tired after a long evening's labour and travel. Could our conversation not have waited for the morning?"

"I am near to dying, you young fool. Can you not see?" Throwing open his woollen robes, the baron exposed his lower body, where even his intimate male member appeared to be rotting. Edmund grimaced openly and placed both hands over his nose and mouth in disgust. "As you can see, dear son, this disease has even begun to putrefy my penis." The old baron's voice croaked into wily softness as he covered himself again. "Your brothers have long wished to cast me out! My 'beloved heir' sought to have the Mass of Separation preached against me! You alone have remained faithful, Edmund, not from your undying affection, but because you are as driven as I. Even your stupid mother recognized you as being truly my son in all things."

The baron took the ale from Rauf's hand and sipped, swallowing tentatively. He could see Edmund pull a kerchief to his face to cover his nose from the stinking, foul smell of his body. Only Rauf never made such a gesture. "Faithful Rauf," the baron thought. "My Rauf, who holds me, carries me, and serves me with endless respect." The Baron knew that if Rauf could smell, if he could see, or hear, he granted his lord the grace of never being repulsed by him.

"When your eldest brother returns to collect his title upon my death, you shall have no more access to Beer Quarry and the cave. How shall you live?"

"I now have land, father, along the southern coast of Cornwall. Smuggling is alive and well in Cornwall, and I have my own access to the sea there. Sadly, I shall have no equal to Beer Cave for the storage of goods. But what ho! A little bay inlet will serve my ongoing needs. And, father, thanks to you, I have well-established contacts on both sides of the Channel."

Edmund turned his face from the baron. He seemed to be searching for any space where he could take a deep breath, free from the dreadful odour of the room. He put the handkerchief back to his nose. "When my manor house is built in Cornwall, I shall take a wife and breed. For now, my investments are solid, but I shan't ever be 'in trade'—eventually I shall buy a title of my own."

"Your future prospects are tidily arranged, Edmund. I commend you, though I shan't live to see any of it." At this point the baron leaned forward on his great couch and reached out a long sleeved arm, exposing his claw like hand. "I have but two requirements of you, my son, and you must promise me, on your very soul, that you will accomplish these for me, Edmund."

Edmund looked on with disgust in his eyes, as his father again collapsed into his racking cough. "Your elder brother will wish for me to disappear into Hell with no hope of remembrance," he gasped. "None of your brothers wish to have the truth of my disease known, so I shall be thrown into the earth and forgotten post haste. Therefore, you alone must see to it that I am buried with honour."

At this point, Rauf brought a small chest to the baron. "These are the Boterlegh family jewels, brought to our family by your mother. I give them to you now for your solemn promise. You will see to it that I am buried inside the parish church of Withycombe Raleigh. I wish to have a handsome tomb, with an effigy of a Knight of the Garter, to proclaim my noble family heritage. Do you swear you will do it?"

Edmund opened the chest and began to lift out golden chains, great lengths of pearls, and filigree broaches covered in jewels. "Indeed, father, these will bring a pretty price." His eyes sparkled at the wealth gathered in his mother's jewel box. "And yes, I do promise, I shall use their value to bury you well."

"But that is not all," the baron's voice croaked between gasps for breath. "You must buy indulgences for me. Buy me time from purgatory. Buy me pardon in every way that you can, do you hear?" The old man's voice broke. Edmund thought he might be sobbing. Rauf rushed to his side on the couch as the rattling and gasping from his throat continued, and the baron's head fell forward in exhaustion. Rauf fell to his knees and lifted the baron, holding him gently in his arms.

"The Baron suffers greatly, Sir Edmund. He has grown far worse." Rauf's deep voice trembled, and his head bowed in painful anticipation of loss. For the first time in anyone's presence, tears could be seen falling from Rauf's eyes.

Edmund kept his mouth and nose covered, but his eyes seemed to be mentally calculating the value of his unexpected treasure.

* * *

Friar Francis was pleased to see Deadman had returned. He did not know precisely how he had escaped nor when, but the friar was aware of the presence of every one of his residents at St Mary Magdalene. He knew Deadman had been gone for several days. Deadman was the strongest, most able of all in his community. Francis did not sense that he must feel sorry for Deadman physically, as he seemed so vital. Most of his adult lepers had numbness in their hands and feet; some were limited to crutches if they were still able to walk. Francis visited with each of them daily, prayed with them, read to them, and enjoyed their company just as he truly enjoyed playing with their children. But this morning, as he walked from the church, he could see Willy, the littlest of the residents, holding fast to Deadman's hand, pulling his favourite playmate into the court yard.

"Let us do it again, Master Deadman; let us play Jack be Nimble. I have been practicing, and I can jump as high as the moon!"

The rest of the children in the courtyard ran to join him at Deadman's side, adding their cries to Willy's, "Yes, let us play Jack be Nimble! You be the candlestick, Master Deadman, and we shall jump!"

Friar Francis moved to sit on the ground with one of his friends, and they both raised their faces to the sky, exchanging their thoughts on the warm sunlight's blessing, in spite of such a chilly day. "Shan't be long an winter will be ere, Friar," one of the more able of his flock said. Francis nodded his agreement, and suddenly everyone in the courtyard turned to watch the object of the children's cheers. Willy powered his little legs into a running start, ran towards Deadman, and sailed over his back!

The game continued until Deadman collapsed from his knees onto the ground. "I must sit awhile and rest," he insisted.

"Tell us a story, Master Deadman," Willy shouted, "please tell us a story." The rest of the children immediately sat round him, hoping to join in the telling. Eric was thrilled. He loved children, and these enthusiastic young lives, abandoned by the world into hopelessness, still seemed so beautifully charged with life. He simply could not refuse them.

"Then you must all close your eyes and imagine we have travelled to a beautiful, sun filled land far, far away. A loathsome, slimy, green dragon dwells there in a dark, evil cave," Eric's rich voice called his images into existence. The children sat together expectantly. He could see that their eyes were closed; each of them was prepared to slip into another world, created only in their thoughts. He continued his story, describing a gallant knight who came to this land to rescue a very fair, young maiden from being sacrificed to the jaws of the dragon. "Charging upon his war horse, the knight drove his lance into the heart of the great beast!" Eric brought his young audience to a thrilling gasp of recognition.

"It is St George!" Willy said enthusiastically. "Did he marry the maiden? Was she a princess?"

"Indeed, you have found me out, Willy, but the moral of the story is not that St George married the maiden. Instead, he saved her, killed the dragon, and spread the word of Christ amongst her people so that they need no longer be fearful. Even to this day, St George wants you to know that if you believe, you too will be protected from evil." Eric looked about him and found general agreement amongst the children. It moved him intensely to see these children choosing to believe.

The story ended; Deadman announced to his young friends that he must speak with the friar. The children withdrew straightaway to other pastimes, some continuing to expand the tale amongst themselves. But everyone in St Mary Magdalene's Hospital esteemed the friar. If Deadman needed to speak with him, the children knew their games and stories must wait. They waved goodbye to their friend, and Deadman walked to the place where the friar sat. He asked simply, but very sincerely, "May I seek confession with you, Friar Francis?"

The friar was surprised by Deadman's request but rose immediately and gestured towards the church. "Of course, brother," Francis responded, and the two walked into the cool darkness of St Mary Magdalene's Church, where the friar led Eric towards the confessional.

But Eric delayed him, laying his hand upon his arm. "In truth, Friar Francis, I have much to speak of with you. My sins are great, and I am in sore need of absolution, but just now may we find somewhere to speak very privately, man to man?"

Friar Francis knew at once that Deadman was extending to him a gesture of personal confidence. He laid his hand upon that of Deadman's and said with earnest feeling, "Brother, I am aware of some of your falsehoods with us, but all God's children may come to Him in true repentance. Please do come with me to my cell. It is very simple but as private as the confessional." The friar led Eric into his tiny cell, built onto the back of the church, where two woollen blankets lay neatly folded upon the floor. Francis moved to sit upon one of them and motioned Eric to join him. "Please tell me what I may do to ease your pain, brother. I know you are not a leper."

With that, Eric threw back the mask of lining and the hood of his cloak, revealing his full face, horribly scarred and twisted, but with dark blue eyes, fully expressing his complete faith in the friar's good will.

"My name is Eric Aunk, Friar Francis, and I am pitmaker to the Cathedral Church of St Peter. I am not a leper, as you have discovered, but I am wanted by the Sheriff of Devon for assault and murder. Although I shall willingly confess all of my sins to you, I am not guilty of either charge."

Francis sat back against the wall of the cell and inhaled deeply. He had known all along that Deadman must be in trouble, to seek refuge in a leper hospital, but he had never suspected anything as horrible as this. "Who is it you are alleged to have murdered, brother?"

"I am charged with the assault upon the aulnage and his brother on the Cathedral Green, and I am presumed to be the murderer of the wool merchant, Raymond Wolfson, on the Shilhay last week."

Friar Frances inhaled deeply once again. "Do you have anyone to speak for you against these charges?"

"I can bring witnesses from Littleham Parish to prove that I was with them at the time of the assault on the aulnage's brother. And, Friar Francis, I do beg you to be my witness, as I was here in St Mary Magdalene's on the night when Raymond Wolfson was murdered. I confess, I kept my distance from your personal inquiries of me at that time, but you know I was here, playing with the children, eating my evening meal, and singing the mass through the evening offices in the church. You even complimented me on my voice." Eric looked into Francis's eyes for any kind of reassurance.

Francis knew at once there was truth in what Eric was telling him, but the friar also knew there must still be guilt in this man for some misdeeds. Why should he have come to St Mary Magdalene, except to hide? Why did he not simply run away from Exeter? What did he hope to prove by remaining close to the city wall of Exeter?

Looking directly into Eric's eyes, Francis told of his ongoing doubts. "Eric, I must believe that you came here to hide, as you presumed no one, county sheriff nor guard, would search for you here within this leprosarium. I can, of course, vouch for your presence on the night Wolfson was murdered, but why did you come to us in the first place? Was it not then to hide from the law?"

"I do beg your pardon, Friar Francis," Eric began at the beginning. "I must share a portion of my life's story with you." He began with his injuries in France, his rejection by the knight whom he served, his desertion by his wife, and his being left to care for their only daughter. "I took my daughter, Ariana, to the home of Raymond Wolfson, who pledged to house and educate her. I could not keep her with me in my position as pitmaker within the Close. Wolfson promised me that he would care for Ariana, if I would pay him a small fee and accomplish various services he required of me. I confess I did serve him in many ways that were less than honourable."

Their conversation lasted well into the afternoon. Francis continued to question Eric, pressing him on his actions as well as his motives. "Why would you allow yourself to be used in this manner?" he insisted. "Why would you wish to threaten the cathedral clergy?"

"I threatened no one directly. I swear, Friar Francis, everything I wrote on the indulgences was indefinite, generalized, implying threat but specifying no man. I only intended to make the clergy fear the unknown. I used the image of the green man, because the clerics have no grasp of its true meaning, even though the green man's face peers down upon them from many places throughout their own cathedral."

Eric put his head down. "I am not proud of what I did, Friar Francis, but you must believe me. I only did it because Wolfson insisted I must stir up suspicion between the clergy and the town."

"But why, Eric? What were his reasons?"

"Perhaps Master Wolfson wished to reawaken old grudges or create some new basis of suspicion between the clergy and town," Eric told him. "I believe he wished to cause distraction, as there was some other evil purpose he intended. But I was never privy to his real purpose."

"What in heaven's name is a green man, Eric?"

"You will find them carved into the decorations of many churches in Exeter, Friar Francis, but especially in the Cathedral of St Peter. There is no evil in them; they symbolize assurance of the regular renewal of life through season to season, year after year. I simply employed a suggestion of a menacing foliate face to create threat, as Master Wolfson required of me. In truth, Friar, green men are spirits of the earth, the trees, and all that grows. Most of all, they are guardians, benign spirits of our Celtic world."

* * *

The pardoner was growing tired of his recent confidant, Milborne. Approaching his fortieth birthday, Clarence was a good and loyal friend, but he was no longer the handsome knight of his youth. Now, he seemed to Brandon an ageing collection of demands for constant displays of affection. Brandon, as Milborne knew him, continued to accept and share the benefits of living in Milborne House. He especially enjoyed his introduction to important members of the gentry in Milborne's hall, as well as Milborne's presentation of him into the homes of other gentry families residing in Exeter. But Brandon did not speak truthfully of anything with Milborne and began to push him away. Still, Clarence did love "his beautiful boy" and continued to excuse Brandon's peevish behaviour, while lavishing upon him any favour he could manage.

The two men had enjoyed a beautiful day, riding out from Exeter's city wall along the fringes of Dartmoor. It was a bright, early winter day, and Dartmoor seemed beckoning. Milborne, however, assumed an authoritative, almost fatherly tone, warning Brandon of the dangers of Dartmoor and how he must never venture upon it unattended.

The pardoner laughed out loud. "Oh, Clarence, you are such an ass. I have already been there. I have, indeed, done that by myself.

Alone on the moor, I ventured all the way to Lustleigh." He was feeling quite superior this day. Wherever they rode, his extravagant, new saddle never failed to gain him notice, and his still plentiful chest of coin, locked safely away, tended to make him feel disdainful.

They returned to the stables of Milborne House late in the afternoon. Brandon said, in a voice suggesting a new idea, "I say, Clarence, why do we not visit the High Street alehouse? I have a great thirst for that Bordeaux they always have on offer."

"Of course, my dear, we shall. Let us change, and we shall be off."

* * *

It was dark and cold by the time they ventured out towards the High Street. Clarence's manservant carried the lantern to light their way, as they each held their cloaks close round their arms. The tavern was busy as ever, full of the better classes of Exeter town. Already, music flowed from its interior when the doors opened and closed upon numbers of gentlemen entering. Brandon went directly towards the fireplace corner which citizens of wealth and class in Exeter reserved to themselves. One or two of the younger men looked haughtily at that which they deigned Brandon's presumption to sit amongst them, but as his name was called from the corner, Brandon knew the person whose company he sought most was present this evening.

"Sir Edmund," he responded, "how now? The Moorish saddle you procured for me is, indeed, the height of excellence and always gathers regard and admiration, wherever I may be seen mounted upon it." Purposely walking away from the place where his friend, Milborne, sat, Brandon went directly to Falford's space in the room and helped himself to a stool next to him.

"Ah yes, welcome, my aggressive, young Brandon. How you do put yourself forward! But, I am very glad to see you. Take a glass of wine with me. I have something I need to discuss with you."

"My pleasure, Sir Edmund, but surely you can not concern yourself with the town gossip of threats abroad in the Cathedral Green? Do you also fear the superstitious nonsense being put about of threats of an evil jack of the green?"

Falford grimaced and waved away Brandon's attempt to belittle the concerns of the moment. He hailed the barkeep, and when their drinks were served, he leaned towards Brandon to speak very privately into his hearing alone.

"I am not a man of the church, Brandon, and I care not a tuppence for perceived threats against the church. But my family will soon face a mortal loss, and I must find a member of the clergy who is willing to serve our needs. The priest must be willing to bury a leper, while being trusted to mind his tongue. Further, I need to acquire a significant number of reliable indulgences. I have discovered that you are a successful, young man of business with connexions in the clerical community. I need you to recommend to me an affordable way to acquire both, as a pardoner might do, shall we say?"

Brandon smiled to himself, while putting forward an expression of condescending assurance towards Falford. "At last," he thought to himself, "he knows that I have access to something he needs. I shall use this connexion profitably."

"It is a relatively simply request; Brandon, can you help me or no?" Falford pressed.

"Sir Edmund, I am able to fulfill all your needs full seemly. When shall you require the clergyman and the indulgences? I, too, have my sources," Brandon smirked.

Recognizing his own words being used in a shameless display of disrespect towards him, Falford did not miss noting the sheer cheek of this young man. He chose to disregard his growing irritation with Brandon and simply said, "I should like to have both available as soon as possible."

"Then, you must meet me by the South Gate at ten of the clock, tomorrow evening."

"Indulgences to the amount of twenty thousand years, more if possible, can you provide them?" Falford insisted.

"The very best of the Treasury of Merit shall be yours, Sir Edmund, signed and sealed by the Bishop of Rome."

For the first time since this return to Exeter, he had become, once again, Brandon Landow, the pardoner. No one else in the fireplace corner took notice, but Falford's eyes gleamed wickedly. He recognized immediately the twisted insight Brandon displayed, and Falford decided he would discover and exploit the truth of Brandon's arrogant riches.

Chapter Twenty

Confession and Return

The long awaited day had finally come. Edward and Apollonia were being escorted into their new chapel by William of Wedmore, their master mason, and several of his fellow craftsmen. Theirs was a devout but joyous mood of celebration on this wintry day and one of great anticipation. The processes of building, carving, decorating, and gilding had been observed throughout the passing months by every member of the Aust household. Everyone had taken time to peer into the work area and share his opinions of its progress with the others. But no one in the household had invested more daily time and personal fealty to building the chapel than Apollonia. Now, at last, she and Edward were about to see it in its complete, pristine, and glowing finality. Their master mason, William, drew open the double chapel doors and invited them to enter. Apollonia gasped, pulling her hands together in a speechless gesture of wonder.

"William," Edward said, marveling at all he saw, "you have created a vision. Our chapel is truly worthy of honouring the Virgin Mary and her Holy Child. But, dear friend, you will also bring us daily to worship at the feet of our name saints. Our family will always be grateful to you."

Apollonia seemed arrested in silence. The sun had risen behind the radiant rose window, illuminating the chapel with a shimmering blue light. Its rays pierced the smaller jewels of stained glass, splashing multicoloured streams of light, falling from above the altar onto the tiled floor.

William of Wedmore beamed, obviously thrilled by the reaction of his sponsors. "I do thank thee, Master Edward. My fellow craftsmen and I, we all thank thee. Your praise warms our hearts and endorses our work as builders of God's house. Creating your chapel has allowed us to share in your family's spiritual blessing."

The master mason could see that Lady Apollonia stood transfixed, her eyes craving to absorb every detail of colour and carving. He knew she was pleased by their handiwork, and her silent wonder thrilled his soul. Hers was not a distant appreciation of decoration; she fully understood the meaning of each symbol, every carefully selected colour, and all liturgical features now lifting their eyes upwards in worshipful admiration.

"I am without adequate words of praise, William," Apollonia said at last. "Edward and I will thank you in our hearts whenever we enter this glorious chapel. You have fulfilled our dreams of a place of worship within our home, inspired by and dedicated to the love of God and the Blessed Virgin. Will you and your fellows please join us in the hall? We shall raise a tankard of our best ale to mark this day."

There was an enthusiastic response from all the workmen to her invitation. She turned to lead the way to the hall, and William winked a "well done" at his mates as they all followed. They were ready to celebrate!

Apollonia had taken her husband's arm and pulled him to walk at her side. She looked into his eyes with a radiant smile. Each knew the other's pleasure in their new chapel, especially on this day of its completion.

"Now, my love," she whispered into his ear, "we shall call on Canon Chulmleigh to establish the date for our special service of dedication. We could not finish by All Saints' Day, as we had first hoped. But now that we are well into the Advent Season, we may plan the dedication of the chapel on the day of the second of Christ's masses."

"An excellent idea, Lonia!" Edward enthused. She knew he could hardly wait. "We shall employ musicians, players, and carollers and fill the day with celebration!"

* * *

All of the members of the household were invited to leave their daily tasks, stroll through the new chapel, and then bring their compliments to the masons and carpenters, now celebrating in the hall. Edward, restored to his hearty sociability, walked from one to another of his household, encouraging everyone to lift a cup of commemoration as they gathered. He introduced each carver to them and expressed his personal delight in the excellence of the man's work.

Apollonia, smiling upon them all, stood quietly next to William of Wedmore to grant a special sign of grace and favour for their master mason. More than that, she welcomed a chance to remain a quiet observer of the festivities. This morning had grown from a brilliantly sunny, new day into a most welcome time of rejoicing. The Lady always enjoyed watching happiness flourish, especially when there had been too many days of distress and tragedy in recent weeks. She felt they were all entitled to an unexpected holiday.

Apollonia turned to William to express her special love of his design for the rayonnant rose window. It was unique amongst the tracery designs she had ever seen. The master mason beamed at the heights of her praise. But the Lady wished to assure him that he had succeeded in all her hopes for the chapel. As she was speaking with William, Nan quietly slipped next to her and whispered into her ear, "My Lady, you have guests who require your presence in private."

"Who is it, Nan? Can this meeting not wait for another time?"

"It is Friar Francis of St Mary Magdalene's, my Lady. He and his companion have expressed an urgent need to speak with you now."

"Well then, please tell them to await us in Edward's office. Stafford will make room for them."

"If you please, my Lady, Friar Francis especially asks you to meet them in the garden. They have come from the leprosarium."

Apollonia shuddered involuntarily. She had never been able to overcome her innate terror of leprosy. But the Lady reminded herself, she had encouraged the young friar to return and tell her more of his ministry amongst those tragically afflicted people. Her next thought was of Edward's recent recovery. He must not be exposed to any of the air around these people.

"Nan, please take Francis and his fellow to the pump," she said very calmly. "Ask them to do me the kindness of washing their hands and faces, and I shall meet them in the garden. We may sit together amongst the herbs, whilst you keep all other members of the household here, in the hall. Edward is at his best when host. Remain with him, please, and encourage everyone to continue to enjoy this day's celebration of the completion of our new chapel."

Nan went off straightaway to follow the Lady's instructions. Apollonia walked slowly through the hall, nodding to each member of the gathered party while she moved towards the kitchen. When Nan found her near the garden exit, the maid stood on her tiptoes to place the Lady's cloak about her shoulders. "The friar and his companion await you in the back garden by the wall, my Lady. I shall keep everyone else, even Gareth, in the hall until you return."

"Thank you, Nan. Please say nothing to Master Edward just yet. I will speak with Francis and discover the nature of his 'urgent need.' I know not what to expect, but I too shall wash carefully before I next speak with Edward, or anyone."

* * *

Lady Apollonia walked to the back of the garden. She could see the two men standing in the warm sunlight near the garden wall, waiting for her. She recognized Francis immediately and could see that he had grown in stature and confidence since their last meeting. His companion was an even larger, almost military man in height, posture, and bodily strength. But his face was tragically scarred across his nose, creating a twisted, gaping mouth and exposing broken teeth. He bowed deeply as she approached, while Francis fell to his knees in obvious supplication.

"My Lady of Aust, I have come to you once again as my only hope. Gracious Lady, we have washed carefully at the pump. But please believe me, neither of us suffers from the dread malady that you fear."

"Gramercy, for that assurance, Friar Francis. I am truly pleased to see you once again, dear friend. My husband has been seriously ill, and his physician requires everyone in our household to wash regularly in his defence. Pray rise from your knees, accept my welcome, and introduce me to your companion. Then, we may walk to the herb garden where we may sit together privately."

"Allow me to present Eric Aunk, former squire to a knight of our realm, more recently pitmaker to the Cathedral Church of the Virgin Mary, St Peter, and St Paul in Exeter."

Apollonia seated herself on a bench and gestured to the men to join her. She recognized the companion's name immediately. "Master Aunk, your name and position are known to me, and I am fully grateful to you for your appearance here. Mystery and evil crimes have afflicted Exeter during these recent months, and I believe you may provide us access to the truth."

* * *

Throughout their time spent together, Apollonia could not help admiring this pitmaker. His face was dreadfully disfigured, but his goodness poured forth in his words. He had the ability to look directly into her eyes as he spoke, and his desperate honesty to clear his name in behalf of his daughter drew the Lady to share with him a parent's selfless love of one's child.

"Master Aunk, my husband and I have been convinced that the truth of these dreadful attacks will never be revealed until it can be heard from your lips. But I see now, the truth is far more complicated than your story alone. If you are not the attacker on the Cathedral Green or the murderer of Wolfson, then pray tell, how may we discover who is?"

"My Lady, I know not. But I promise I shall dedicate my life to seek out the villain and restore my good name," Eric promised.

"I have dared to bring Eric to you, Lady Apollonia," Francis explained, "because I know of your miraculous ability to speak with people of consequence and clear those who have been wrongly accused. I willingly stand witness that Eric Aunk is a good man, who will fully confess all he has done to the dean and chapter, and accept his punishment as proscribed by canon law. But can you help us to find a way to save him from the dreadful imputations made by merchant Wolfson against him to the sheriff?"

Apollonia did not respond immediately. She sat with them for a matter of moments, organising her thoughts, until at last she spoke very deliberately. "I can promise little, except to speak in your behalf, Pitmaker Aunk. On the other hand, you, Francis, will be beyond charge, since Eric came to you in disguise. But I must ask you both to gather your witnesses and be prepared to bring the truth of your story, when next I summon you. I will share all you have told me, Master Aunk, with my husband and to that extent, I must beg your confidence and trust. Edward joins me in an earnest desire to protect those unjustly accused, and together we shall do our best." She stood up from her garden bench and extended her hand to each of the men. "Let this remain our meeting place. We may speak freely and privately here."

"My Lady, if you require a dependable messenger from your household to St Mary Magdalene's, please seek a good lad of the town who has always served me well. His name is Laston, and he is prenticed to the baker on Southgate Street," Eric said. Then he knelt at her feet. "I shall be forever in your debt, gracious Lady. May God's presence guide and protect you."

* * *

Brandon arrived outside the South Gate of the city slightly before ten of the clock that evening. He had bribed the city watchmen to enable him to arrange this private meeting well after curfew. He was mounted, carried a small lantern, and was warmly robed against the deepening chill of the night. Absolution, his faithful mare, was not saddled in her elegant new Moorish array this evening. Returned to her role as mount of the pardoner, the horse bore a walet of indulgences about her neck, and Brandon rode, seated upon his workaday saddle. The pardoner presumed that this would be a workaday errand for him, but a profitable one. Sir Edmund was not waiting at the designated place near the South Gate, so Brandon dismounted, tied Absolution to a nearby tree, and took the walet from her neck.

The pardoner waited in the shadows of the city wall until, within a short time, he could hear the approaching hooves of another rider. At this hour, there were none about, but Brandon remained in the shadows till he was certain the approaching rider was truly Edmund Falford. He lifted the cover from his lantern to announce his presence.

"Ah, Master Brandon, I see you have come. Have you been able to supply my requests?" Falford spoke while mounted, looking down upon him as Brandon emerged from the shadows.

"Indeed, Sir Edmund, I have the indulgence with me that you requested, and I shall be able to supply you with an appropriate priest when your day for the funeral has arrived."

"Excellent," Falford said, obviously pleased that his needs should be so easily supplied. "I shall wish to take the indulgence with me this night, and I shall require you to bring your priest to my father's manor at Withycombe Raleigh, whither I shall call upon you after he has died. That day will not be long in coming. But be informed; I shall allow no discussion of the nature of his disease at the time of his burial or any time thereafter, and I can enforce my will. Is that understood?"

"It shall be done according to your instruction, Sir Edmund. And, in return for your alms, I have procured for you this indulgence, authorized by the pope, securing freedom from purgatory for twenty thousand years." Brandon lifted the resplendent Latin document, containing the papal seal, to Falford for his examination. "It will be yours upon my receipt of your gift to Holy Church of five pounds."

Falford lifted one eyebrow and drew in a great breath. "God's death, Brandon, your price is more than twice the annual salary of my reeve! Surely, you can not believe I carry about with me so vast a sum?"

"Truly sir, as I trusted you when my order was placed for a new saddle, I shall present this precious document into your care for two pounds now, the balance to be paid at the time of the funeral. Shall we be agreed as gentlemen?" Brandon could see that Falford was angry but eager to have the indulgence, even though he knew Brandon's price was excessive.

"As you wish, Brandon," Falford replied, with an underlying tone of threat in his voice. "Here are the instructions for your journey to Withycombe Raleigh Manor, and I shall expect you to respond promptly to my call." He dropped a purse of coins into the pardoner's hand.

Brandon coolly attached the purse to his own belt and proceeded to complete their transaction. "For whom shall I ascribe this forgiveness of sin?"

The voice of Edmund Falford had by now lost all of its former cordiality. "See that it is granted to Brutwald Falford, Baron of Exmouth and Lord of Withycombe Raleigh, Knight of the Garter."

"As our circumstances are so limited here, I must beg your leave to be allowed to make the inscription upon the document, leaning upon your back, Sir Edmund." Brandon seemed to be enjoying his sense of power over this member of the nobility.

Falford dismounted and bent upon his horse's stirrup, while Brandon took pen and ink to complete the inscription, leaning upon Falford's back. When it was written in an elegant hand, Edmund stood to his full height once again and took the indulgence from Brandon. Carefully examining its every word in the pardoner's lantern light, he gently blotted and rolled the document, placed it into his saddle bag, and mounted once again.

Restored to the superior height of his horse's saddle, Falford looked down upon Brandon once more. "Remember to come promptly, whence you are summoned," he said brusquely and rode off into the night.

* * *

Edmund Falford rode his horse over the drawbridge and into the courtyard of Withycombe Raleigh Manor near to the midnight hour. His return was expected by the household, and a stableman appeared to hold his horse as he dismounted. Sir Edmund said nothing to anyone in the courtyard but walked slowly towards the main entrance. He dreaded all that he knew he would find within, not only the bodily disfigurement of his father and the loathsome rattle of his voice, but the revolting stench that infused every chamber. As if in preparation for his reception, he raised his scarf from his neck to his cheeks, ready to cover his nose.

"Thank God you have come, Sir Edmund," the servant said, as he took his cloak, "your father suffers greatly." Ushering him into the hall, the servant left and Edmund found Rauf sitting upon the couch, holding his master, as a mother would nurse an infant in her arms.

Edmund stood his usual distance from the couch where his father always laid to receive him and announced quietly, "I am here, Father, and I have brought to you this mighty indulgence."

He unrolled a large document, displaying the papal seal, and read aloud in Latin its assurances. "See you, Father, I have achieved all that you asked," he said with triumph.

The Baron could no longer lift his head but leant it heavily upon Rauf's shoulder. His eyes did respond with gleaming trust in the assurances of the papal indulgence Edmund displayed before him, but his words struggled to express his further request. "You must see to it that I shall have the burial of a Knight of the Garter," he whispered his utterances with no strength of voice. "Adorn my tomb with a Knight, angels at my head and lion at my feet. Will you do it?" he demanded weakly.

"Of course, Father, I shall complete your every wish. You know I have been the most faithful of your sons." Edmund seemed to express some petulance at his father's nagging questions.

"You are my son, Edmund, and I have rewarded you well. I also know you long for great wealth but will do only that which benefits you to attain it. I command you to see that I am buried appropriately to my rank!"

"Father, I have already arranged for a clergyman to come from Exeter to preside at your services, the funeral mass, and the graveside committal."

"I want the effigy; see to it the effigy lies upon my tomb. Will you do it?" The Baron began to choke once again while Rauf raised him to ease its violence. "My tomb, Edmund, have it made as I commanded you. My tomb!" The old Baron seemed to hiss his last words.

A husky, gasping whisper began to rattle in the back of the Baron's throat. He continued to cough racking, choking coughs. Rauf elevated his master's upper body in hope of easing his breathing, but could find no position of relief. Rauf's desperate efforts to ease his Lord achieved nothing. The Baron's breath came forth in rattling exhalation, but when he sought to inhale, he choked into a massive spasm and collapsed, his desiccated body suddenly limp.

"My Lord, speak!" As if dictating to his master, Rauf's voice progressed to a shout, "Speak, Lord! Do not leave me!" He stood up from the couch, lifting the emaciated body within his arms, hoping the elevation would allow the Baron to rejoin his departing soul.

Edmund responded with disgust, his own voice assuming a tone of command; he shouted at the servant, "Cease this display, Rauf! Put him down!"

The powerful servant seemed to wilt. His shoulders fell, his arms lowered the precious body to the couch once again, and he fell to his knees at his lord's side.

Edmund walked to his father's couch and held his hand tightly upon his immotive heart. "It is over! He is dead, you fool! Order the servants to take this disgusting carcass to the chapel. Tomorrow the village carpenters must be required to assemble his coffin, do you hear me?" Edmund wiped his hand, that had touched his father's body, upon a towel and began to walk from the hall.

Tears flowed from Rauf's eyes, his voice trembled, and yet he felt he could not allow his young master to leave. "Stay, Sir Edmund, grant me leave to carry him to the chapel. He must be laid out in proper estate."

"Do as you wish. I will arrange for the funeral." Edmund kept the scarf covering his nose. He walked rapidly, as if he were sprung out of the hall, away from the lower level of the manor house, rushing up the circling stairs to his private chambers in the south tower.

Chapter Twenty-one

Meschaunce Grave

When the pardoner received the summons from Withycombe
Raleigh Manor, he announced to Clarence that he would be
leaving Milborne House. He planned to move on from Exeter within
the week; he told Clarence, "I need to return to Cirencester. Will you
see to it that my things are packed and ready for my departure when I
return from Withycombe?"

Clarence Milborne was startled, then angered by Brandon's
abrupt announcement, but even more by his cool, distant, ungrateful
attitude towards him.

"Why is it you wait till this instant to tell me you are leaving? Is
it because you wish to move up in class, Brandon? I am no longer able
to offer you adequate standing in society? Moving in with Falford, are
you? Trying to pretend you are noble? You are a nobody, and only I
have provided you access to gentility. Falford will not be fooled by
your pretence."

"Stop being an ass, Clarence. I go to Withycombe Raleigh
Manor on business, and when it is completed, I must move on to
Wiltshire."

"But why not return to me, dear boy? You know I have supported
your every desire." Milborne's whining only served to agitate Brandon
further.

"If truth be known, I have had enough of you, disgusting old
man. I thank you kindly for your hospitality, if that is what you
offered, but needs must be on my way." The pardoner stomped out
of the chamber. "See to it all my belongings are packed when I
return."

One thing Brandon knew he must do, before leaving Milborne
House, was to transfer his valuables and precious new saddle on to the
Priory of St Nicholas. The monks there would safeguard his treasures,
and Clarence would not be able to help himself to any kind of

payment. As he had much to accomplish, Brandon wasted no further words on Clarence who sat by the fire, near to weeping.

* * *

Brandon had arrived at Milborne House, representing himself as a wealthy, young merchant and man about town. When he returned to St Nicholas Priory on this day, he had become Brandon Landow, the pardoner, once again. He was remembered, and it took relatively little time to make the transfer of his elegant saddle and chest of valuables. The monks of St Nicholas were glad to hold them for him, for a small daily fee. They would never charge interest, but did expect to be paid for their services. He did not know precisely when he should return to Exeter, but when he did, they would settle the charges incurred, and he should require their best guest chamber.

The pardoner had now made all necessary arrangements. It was time for him to collect Friar Francis, the clergyman he wished to accompany him to Exmouth. He borrowed a donkey from the monks and rode off on Absolution's workaday saddle, leading the gentle beast behind him towards St Mary Magdalene's Leper Hospital.

* * *

Friar Francis and Deadman were returned to the leprosarium, and Deadman, with his face covered once again, was enjoying the friendship and playfulness of the hospital's children. They had played "Ring around the Rosy" so many times that Eric could do no more circling. To gain some moments of recovery from their dizziness, they were all sitting upon the grass of the courtyard whilst he told them a story. The doorman came to Friar Francis with a message that there was a man beyond the gate who sought to speak with him.

Friar Francis rose from his stool and walked across the courtyard, leaving the grounds of St Mary's at its main gate, opening to the street. He recognized the visitor at once and only consented to speak with him out of his strong sense of Christian charity. This was the same pardoner who had accused him of robbing the poor box of his order's church.

"Greetings, gentle friar, I am Brandon Landow, Pardoner of Holy Church," Landow said, extending a warm smile.

"God's blessings upon you, Master Brandon. I remember well who you are, pardoner. What is it that you require of me?"

"I say, brother friar, be never so suspicious of a fellow servant of Christ. I have apologised sincerely to the head of your order for my earlier error," Landow said with well-rehearsed humility. "On this day, I have been sent to take you to the side of a worthy Christian, recently died, who needs your compassionate services in burial. You see, I have even brought with me a donkey for your comfort. The journey is long, all the way to Exmouth."

"Has this Christian confessed and been shriven?"

"Certain he has, but the priest who attended him was called away," Landow lied grossly. Sir Edmund had said nothing to him of confession. "The deceased was a noble gentleman, Sir Brutwald Falford, renowned here in Devon. He suffered from a disease well known and understood by you. So the family has asked me to take you to perform the services of funeral and burial, while never revealing the cause of death. Theirs is a worthy plea, friar. Do say you will come to bless and comfort them."

"I am a priest as well as a friar, so I shall come with you. But first I must make arrangements that I may be gone for more than one day. I shall have to return to my flock here at St Mary Magdalene's." The friar could not help but retain some suspicion of this pardoner, but he knew his life and ministry compelled him to go to those in need when he was summoned. "Allow me to make preparations, and I shall accompany you."

"You shall have done so fair a grace this day, friar. I will serve as your guide to Exmouth when you are ready," the pardoner said with a slight smirk.

Francis hurried back into St Mary Magdalene's courtyard and drew Eric to his side. "Dear friend, Eric, I am being called away to Exmouth by a man in whom I can place no trust. I shall speak with Brother Phillip to cover services here, whilst we are gone, but may I ask you to follow us by the river? The pardoner who awaits me has brought a donkey for me to ride, and we shall take the river road to Exmouth. I should be ever grateful to you if you will watch our journey from afar. Did you not say you knew of a small boat near the river?"

"Aye, Friar Francis, I shall be more than grateful to observe your progress from the river and will wait until I can see you are prepared to return. I know well the area surrounding Exmouth and can find many places to hide myself. But do you really believe what this man says? If you have no trust in him, how can you have faith in his request for your ministry?"

"I have faith in God, Eric, and I know He will be with me. But someone here in St Mary Magdalene's must know where I have been taken, just in case I do not return, and I wish that person to be you."

Eric placed his hand upon the friar's shoulder to show his willingness. "You have extended your good fellowship and trust for me, friar. I can offer no less to you, as my priest and my friend."

Francis longed to be able to tell him how sincerely grateful he was; instead, he uttered a quiet, "Thank you, Eric, you are indeed a good friend." Then moving off to speak with Friar Phillip, he noticed Eric had already moved towards the portal exit to the street, once again with rattling stick in his hand.

"Wher be ye off ta, den, Mawster Deadman?" the doorman asked.

"I must do an errand for Friar Francis, but I shall give warning to any whom I may encounter on the road. Please, let me pass."

With that, the doorman opened the main portal of the gates of St Mary Magdalene, and Deadman left its confines shouting, "Unclean! Unclean, leprosy walks with me!" He strode, returned to his bent and leaning posture, towards the River Exe, where he knew the road to Exmouth began to turn south. "Unclean! Unclean, leprosy walks with me," he continued to shout, and slowly his voice began to fade into the distance.

Friar Francis hurried to place a few belongings into a small carrier, said his goodbyes to friends, and walked across the courtyard. When he passed the doorman, he said quietly to him, "Brother, I should be returned in a day or two, perhaps not till late in the evening. If I am held up in any way, I have instructed Deadman to bring you word of me."

Francis walked quickly out to the street, through the main entrance, towards the place where the pardoner awaited him. He climbed onto the waiting donkey and began to follow the pardoner who had already moved some distance away from the walls of St Mary Magdalene's Leper Hospital.

"I have just witnessed one of your inmates walking out from your doors, friar. Of course, I sped away immediately, but I can not believe you allow such creatures to reenter human society after they have been declared dead from all human contact." Landow made no effort to conceal his loathing, not only of the disease, but also of the person.

"Even the living dead must be fed, pardoner. Deadman goes out daily to pick up baskets of food left for us down by the River Exe. He gives regular warning to any passersby that they may turn from his path."

Landow said nothing in response, but could be seen to be shaking his head and muttering words of the dreadful threat posed to Christians by those diseased and expelled.

Francis said no more to his companion but continued to follow his guide towards the road to Exmouth, loudly singing songs of praise.

* * *

When Eric reached the place along the river bank where he knew Adam's coracle was hidden, he pulled the mask away from his face, lay his rattling walking stick upon the same ground, covered it in leaves, and let his hood fall to his shoulders. The coracle was very light, and he launched it quickly. Climbing into it, he had soon skillfully moved near to bushes growing along the river bank next to the Exmouth road. From this vantage, he could hold his position, whilst awaiting the pardoner and Friar Francis to ride past him.

He was fortunate in his location. No one would be able to see him from the road, yet he could see anyone passing on the way. Not long after he had hidden himself, he could hear the voice of Francis, singing one his favourite hymns. "Oh you clever friar," Eric said to himself. "Do keep singing that I may have your voice to follow, whilst never having to come too near the bank and be noticed."

The journey downriver went smoothly for Eric. Even as the road moved farther from the river, through Topsham, the pitmaker could hear Francis begin another hymn and know he was still following their progress. When, at last, Eric could see them turning away from the river road, he paddled to the bank and pulled the coracle ashore. Hurrying up to the road, he quickly ducked behind a tree, as he saw Francis dismounted and stretching his back, while the pardoner remained in his saddle complaining of the time lost.

"Come now, friar, you are delaying us needlessly," the pardoner complained.

"Grant me mercy from this bony ass's back. I am not accustomed to riding, certainly not such distances," the friar replied, while he continued to delay them.

Slowly he remounted his donkey, hopeful that Eric had seen them in process of turning away towards Withycombe Raleigh, and the two men rode on with Eric following them at a distance.

When they approached the Manor of Withycombe, Eric, now on foot and exposed to public notice, was not certain just where to hide. He could not enter the manor's gate, but he knew he must remain in a place where he might continue to observe it. At last he found a cluster of trees not far away. He settled there to watch and wait, as the pardoner led Francis across the lowered drawbridge, over the moat, and into the bailey. There were not many people about, but soon Eric saw three village men walk across the drawbridge, coming out from the manor. Two of them carried shovels, and one was dressed as a carpenter. Eric could not believe his eyes. One member of the group was his friend, Adam.

Eric emerged from his hiding place when the men turned to walk back to their village. Coming from behind, he placed his hand on Adam's shoulder. "Out with it," he said quietly, "what have you been up to?"

Adam spun round immediately when he heard the familiar voice. "Oi've been diggin a grave. Bu wha can ye say fur yerse'v, Worm?"

With that exchange, Adam bid his village friends farewell and walked back to the cluster of trees with Eric. When they could be seated out of sight, Eric asked his friend why he had been in Withycombe Raleigh Manor. "I thought you had no interest in the pretensions of the nobility," he chided.

"Oi did it fur ye," Adam said with some irritation in his voice. "It wer ye oo asked me ta look inta th greats oo live ere. When th call came ta th village fur grave diggers, I tells mese'v, Oi shall do it fur Eric. Ye bloody Worm, no on e'er gits inta dat place til naow, when th Baron be daid, an is sons wants im buried quick."

"I do thank thee for your efforts, Adam. Were you able to learn anything about the man who died?"

"Oh, ee wer baron somebodee oo's lost is wife, an is two sons was inside, grabbin up as much as dey can afore th res o th fam'ly cooms. Dey be younger sons oo do'n inherit, Oi belief."

"Well, I must remain here to be certain that my friend, Friar Francis, is finished with the burial, and then we shall go back to Exeter. Is there any chance you could come back to Exeter with us? I have told Francis everything and will need you as a witness to my whereabouts when the aulnage was assaulted."

"Oi shall tell Telitha wher Oi be goen; den Oi be back, Worm. It be abou time ye gits dis mess sorted."

Adam clapped Eric on his broad back and started off towards Littleham. "Oi'll be back afore th tide turns, an we can take th barge up river when ee cooms."

* * *

Friar Francis was taken directly into the family chapel of Withycombe Raleigh Manor, but he recognized immediately the distinct odour of the place. It was a small but beautiful old chapel. The body of the Baron had been elegantly dressed and wore the emblem of the Order of the Garter below the knee of its left leg. The dark blue ribbon, edged in gold bearing the motto of the Order, had to be pinned to the stocking of the emaciated shin. An emblem of St George, patron saint of the Order, hung from a blue ribbon round his collar. The body rested inside a newly made coffin. In spite of its noble array, Francis could see, from the decay of his facial features and especially the fingers missing from his folded hands, the Baron had suffered from leprosy as completely and painfully as the poorest of the poor.

The friar began the funeral while noting that he, the pardoner, four men of the household, and Sir Edmund Falford served as the only mourners. Only Rauf, the baron's personal servant, endured the odour to stand near the coffin, plaintively grieving. For everyone else, the attitude was one of impatient craving to be done with it and bring this delusive, religious mockery to an end. Perhaps motivated by that perceived spirit of mockery and amoral aggression that he felt in this house, Francis threw himself into the readings of the funeral mass most fervently. When at last he came to the final prayer, he spoke the words from the depths of his own soul.

"Remember thy servant, Brutwald, oh Lord, according to the favour which thou bearest unto thy people, and grant that, increasing in knowledge and love of thee, he may go from strength to strength, in the life of perfect service in thy heavenly kingdom . . ."

When he read the final "Amen," Francis stepped back to allow the men of the household to act as pallbearers. They surrounded the coffin, closed its lid, and lifted it from its place near the altar. They walked, carrying the coffin from the chapel door towards a small cemetery. There, at the sight of a newly opened grave, Francis continued to read the service. "Come, ye blessed of my Father, inherit

the kingdom prepared for you from the foundation of the world . . ."
The men of the household used ropes to lower the closed coffin into
the ground. Sir Edmund grasped a handful of dirt from the graveside
and tossed it onto the coffin lid, then turned and walked away.

Before Francis left the graveside, he walked to Rauf and placed
his hand upon the huge man's trembling shoulder. "May I pray with
you, Brother Rauf? I can see this death has proven a great loss in your
life."

"Far more, friar, my Lord Falford saved me from the gallows. I
owe my life to him."

"But he will join his Lord in heaven, Rauf. Time will help to ease
your grief, and you may now feel your spirit to be free, as truly as his
soul has been freed from the disease of his body."

"But what am I free to do, friar; can you tell me that? Let me be. I
have no purpose, but one left to me." Rauf remained at the gravesite
until the men of the household had completed the burial. Everyone else
walked back into the manor. But Rauf was on his knees, no longer
weeping but limp in body and soul, totally given over to grief."

As Francis left him and walked back into the hall of the manor,
he approached the baron's son who, the pardoner had told him, wished
for him to do the services. "It would be a great kindness if you could
send someone to stay by Rauf's side, Sir Edmund. He is desolate in his
loss and abandoned to grief."

"You need not presume to instruct me in handling my own
servants, young friar," he said coldly. "Gramercy for your services this
day. We have no further need of you; good day."

"God's blessings upon you, Sir Edmund, especially at this time of
your loss," Francis said as he bowed to walk away.

Edmund Falford gave out a loud guffaw, and Francis could hear
that it was echoed by another, very similar voice from the back of the
chamber. Francis was shocked. He thought Edmund Falford had been
laughing as he walked from the hall. But when Francis turned to look
back, he thought he could see Edmund Falford still at the rear of the
hall. He pressed his hands into his eyes. The voice from the far wall of
the room moved towards him.

"You have been told, friar, we have no further need of you;
begone!"

Francis left the hall and exited the manor through the main entry.
From there he hurried across to the still lowered drawbridge over the
moat, feeling as if he wished he could run all the way to Exeter. The

spirit alive in this manor of Withycombe Raleigh was not only one of disease and death, but also one of vicious hostility.

When Francis walked back to the road, his spirit rejoiced. On the far side of the drawbridge, he found friends waiting for him. Eric hailed him from their little wooded hideaway on the far side of the road and triumphantly introduced him to his childhood mate.

"Friar Francis, come join us; I am so thankful to see you are free from that place. I want you to meet my dearest friend, Adam Braund. He will stand witness to my character and whereabouts to the sheriff, and he has a barge that will take us all upriver to Exeter as soon as the tide turns!"

* * *

Brandon Landow did not worry in the least over what happened to the friar. He had remained seated in the hall, silent witness to the friar's curt dismissal by Falford. The pardoner's only concern was to collect the sum still owed him and return to Exeter. So, after the friar had departed, Landow stood up from his bench and walked towards Falford.

"I shall delay you no further, Sir Edmund. I only wish to have from you the balance due to me in our business transaction.

Falford looked at him as if he were mad. "And who in the hell are you?"

"I shall tell you who he really is, brother. This is Brandon Landow, the pardoner, who is wanted for the sale of fraudulent relics in Yorkshire. Is it not so, Brandon? Or do you now call yourself Pardoner Landow? I have contacts in Yorkshire, pardoner, and they have described for me your vicious felony committed there. It seems you sold a fake relic of the Holy Blood to an aged countess, cheating her out of a fortune." As Landow stood stunned into silence, the second voice began to approach him from the entry to the hall.

"Dear Sir, surely you are mistaken. I am indeed Brandon Landow but truly am no felon. I merely wish to collect from you the balance due from the papal indulgence and the priestly services I provided at your request." Brandon began to shift from foot to foot, growing more nervous as he watched two men walking towards him, menacingly. "I say, Sir Edmund, which is you?" he whined, seeing before him two Falfords, identical in every detail of their persons.

The first speaker simply said, "I loath pardoners, do you not, brother?"

"Indeed, brother, I think we should tie him to the hindquarters of his donkey and send him home to Exeter, ass upon ass. What say you?"

"Gentlemen, please, let us be men of reason. I, I can forgive the remaining portion of your debt. As you are both now struggling with grief and the loss of a beloved father, I say we shall call the matter to a close. Blessings be upon you; I bid you good evening." Brandon began to walk towards the door leading out of the hall and into the courtyard. He could see the drawbridge was still down, and he instantly decided he would leave his animals behind if necessary. Suddenly, the pardoner bolted from the manor and ran towards the drawbridge.

Out of the darkening evening, several of the men of the Falford household sprang after him, pushed him to his knees, and held him in place until the brothers could appear and determine his fate. Landow kept shouting, "I have done nothing wrong. I delivered all that you asked of me. How can you treat me thus?"

Eventually a gag was placed into his mouth to quiet him, and the brothers ordered him stripped and tied over the backside of the donkey. The Falfords did not remain to witness any of the following proceedings, but the men of their household tied the donkey's reins to Absolution, Landow's mare, and slapped her haunches hard enough to send her galloping over the drawbridge, pulling along the donkey with a pardoner splayed over her backside, a raging, thrashing, spectacle of a naked man.

* * *

Absolution did not stop until she had galloped to Lympstone, on the Exeter road. Some farmers, walking home along the road from the tavern, found the nude rider tied to a donkey and a horse, grazing by the side of the road. They untied the pardoner, stood him onto the ground, laughing all the while.

"Out fur an evenin ride, be ye?" joked the first.

"Nay, y'uve been lookin ta git a early bit o sunshine on yer arse!" replied the second.

Once Landow's hands were untied, he pulled the gag from his mouth and began to shout, "Rubes, simple fools, get clothes to cover me this instant. Do you not know who I am? I am Brandon Landow, Pardoner of Holy Church by the appointment of the pope!"

"Well, o corse, fur a fine churchman like yerse'v, Oi gots a tunic ere. But it'l cost ye," said the first.

"Oi shall fin some ose fur ye, but dey do ave oles in em," said the second.

In order to obtain any garments adequate to cover his nakedness, Landow had to wait, holding his body as closely to Absolution as he could to share her warmth, waiting for the farmers to return with the shabby items they had promised. He put them on rapidly as he had begun to shiver violently from the cold and exposure. He could not pay for anything, so the farmers insisted that they would hold Absolution until the morrow, when he should return with their money.

It was late evening when Landow finally rode through the gates of St Nicholas Priory, barefoot, foul smelling, and shabby as a beggar, mounted on a donkey.

Chapter Twenty-two

Confession and Penance

Apollonia and Edward were seated in their solar. The rest of the household had been dismissed to their chores, for the Lady wished to speak with the master alone. It was late afternoon and already darkening into night out of doors, but it had been a wondrous day of celebration for the Aust household. By this time of the day, everyone was grateful to be free to complete his daily tasks before evening chapel.

Edward stood to stir the fire against the chill, creeping into their upper chamber from increasing winds out of doors. He and his wife looked forward to evenings spent together, not only to share matters of concern, but because they cherished their togetherness. This evening, however, Apollonia had important news to share with her husband.

"I departed from our celebration of the new chapel early, dearheart, because we had important visitors who requested a securely private interview. Forgive me for not calling you to be at my side, but I felt I could not expose you to any possibility of further illness," Apollonia confessed.

"I am always aware of your absence, Lonia, and I noted that you were not long gone," Edward smiled. "I also know you will share the true cause for it with me. Who was it, my love, and why did he require such privacy?"

"It was Friar Francis from St Mary Magdalene's Hospital. He came to seek advice from me, as he knew I had saved him from a blatant injustice."

"Ah yes, I remember you telling me. It was an incident caused by that wretched young man, Landow, was it not? I have always regretted that we were unable to correct his many flaws whilst he remained within our household."

"Oh, Edward, I too regard Brandon as a tragic failure. He seemed to possess such promise as a young lad. But he has now become a very successful *quaestores*, with his appointment by the pope. His manner

of pilfering has now literally been granted protection by the church."
Apollonia sighed deeply.

"What sort of help did your young friar require this time?
Presumably it was something that he could not achieve without an
advocate?" Edward was obviously troubled by the behaviour of the
young pardoner but urged his wife to get to the heart of the friar's
matter.

"Indeed, husband, but he did not come seeking advocacy for
himself. Francis arrived with a companion, and it is for him that he
seeks our help. Do you remember all our conversations with Canon
Chulmleigh about the charges against the cathedral pitmaker, Eric
Aunk? It was he."

"Lonia, my love, we must inform the sheriff of his whereabouts.
What did you tell him?"

"I did not tell anything, Edward; I listened. Eric Aunk is, I
believe, a good man, who will bring witnesses to prove his
whereabouts when the brother of the aulnage was attacked and when
merchant Wolfson was murdered. He said he has proof that he was not
the perpetrator of those evil attacks, but he also confessed to me that it
was he who sent the green man threats to the cathedral chapter."

"Dear God! Apollonia, did he tell you his purpose?"

"Yes, Edward, he said he was forced to send threats to the dean
and chapter by merchant Wolfson, who held his only daughter captive
from him."

"But what did the threats mean? Why speak of such things as
Norman dogs and ancient revenge?"

"Eric said he worded them so generally they would be mere
puzzles, meaningless to any person within the Close. Wolfson never
told him why he must send threats, only that he must stir up the
clergy's suspicions against the town."

Apollonia could see that Edward was seriously taken aback by
her desire to protect the pitmaker. But then she told him that she
suspected the real murderer duplicated Eric's green man threats to
implicate him. "The mutilated indulgences thrown onto the fallen, both
the aulnage's brother and Wolfson, were probably copies meant to
incriminate him, Eric believes. Wolfson accused Eric openly to the
dean and the sheriff, after he no longer controlled the life of Eric's
daughter."

Edward sat back in his chair, trying to assimilate in his thoughts
where truth could be found amidst this confusion of events. "But my

darling wife, how can you be so certain of the innocence of the pitmaker in the latter half of the story, whilst he openly confesses to being the perpetrator of mischief in the former half?"

"I am moved by Eric's honesty, Edward, his willingness to acknowledge his wrongdoing, and his desire to prove his innocence in order to protect his daughter. If he and his actions are being unjustly used by the real murderer, should we not at least attempt to protect the innocent?" Apollonia allowed her husband time to consider. She knew there were very serious charges against Eric. It would be wrong for her or anybody to knowingly conceal a criminal from justice.

There was silence in their chamber for a time, as each searched his own mind and heart for answers. Finally, Edward said to her, "Lonia, I do not know where to begin in this matter. To whom shall we go for counsel, and how may we proceed?"

The Lady began, as was her pattern, to list the points of their actions upon her fingers. "To begin," she said as her right hand pointed to her left index finger, "we shall call in Canon Chulmleigh and ask if we may examine the collection of green man threats. I believe we will see a difference between those sent by Eric and those thrown later.

"Secondly, I believe we must ask Eric to take his confession to the dean of the cathedral after he has produced his witnesses to the sheriff, proving his presence elsewhere at the time of the assault and the time of the Wolfson murder."

Apollonia paused and then ticked her middle finger, "Finally, you and I must look more seriously into defining motive. Who were the persons who would gain most by causing the death of the aulnage. What think you, Edward? Shall we proceed thus?"

"'Tis clear you have already made up your mind, Lonia. But I do agree, we must do all we can to seek justice, especially to protect the innocent."

Then Apollonia really surprised her husband. "I shall invite Phyllis of Bath to come to our aid. She is the perfect sleuth amongst local gossips. If anyone will have insight into those wishing the demise of the aulnage, it will be she."

* * *

After morning chapel, Edward sent his yeoman, Jude Dennish, to call upon Mistress Phyllis and beg her to accompany him back to Exeter House, where his Lady and master would greatly welcome her assistance. The ride to Phyllis's Reliant Cottage was not a lengthy one, but it required Jude to exit the city at its West Gate and ride across the river to St Thomas Parish. Within a matter of two hours, Jude returned to Exeter House. Although he had been sent to accompany her, it was Mistress Phyllis who led the way on their return.

Phyllis's arrival required no fanfare. Her voice could be heard by her hosts from the moment she dismounted. Walking directly into the hall, she sang out her greetings to her dear friends and joyously proclaimed her pleasure to see them again.

Apollonia and Edward rose immediately to receive her and encouraged her to take her favourite chair by the fire, that they might share a private chat.

"Oh, aye, Oi ope ye ave some elpful news ta share," she said enthusiastically, but with her voice lowered significantly. She presumed it was to be shared only by the three of them.

"Mistress Phyllis, dear friend," Edward began, "we do welcome you on any occasion you may wish to grace us by your company. But we believe revelations may soon be in the offing, and we require your help to balance our understanding of them."

Phyllis's interest was immediately pricked by his words, but she remained silent to capture the full import of them. "You see, Phyllis, you have the best contacts amongst the merchant community in the town and always have your ear to the ground, so to speak," Apollonia said, with a sly wink at her friend. "If I were to ask you who, in all of Exeter, would benefit most from the removal of the aulnage, who would you propose?"

Phyllis thought quietly for a few moments, and then she replied, "Ye kno, m'Lady, Oi wou'd ave said it be Merchant Wolfson, bu ee be dead! Naow it be mor a mystree. Bu Oi ave eard som rumblins bout Wolfson's connexions. Do ye wish fur me ta look inta it, fur ye?"

"If you could ask a few well chosen questions in the right places, Phyllis, it would be helpful. We are all aware that the aulnage is disliked and resented by some, just for doing his job so well. But what we need to know is, who would truly gain most should he be removed?"

"Well, m'Lady, Oi shall try me best. Bu in th meanwhile, Oi ear aulnage's brudder be doin mighty well. Sir Morton's been seen bout th town, walkin wit is brudder, even goen back ta Cathedral Close wher it all appened."

"Indeed, Mistress Phyllis, we too have received good news from the aulnage, but I suggest we will best discuss it over a hearty dinner. I have heard we shall be treated to some of Mary's delicious eel pies. May I take you to the table?" Edward asked as he extended his arm.

* * *

The following morning, Norman was sent to the house of Canon Chulmleigh with a letter. In it, Edward asked the canon if it would be possible to examine the defaced indulgences that had been used as threats against the cathedral chapter, also those found at the sites of the assault and the murder. It was, Edward continued, his Lady wife's desire to examine them, if that may be allowed, due to her peculiar interest in the use of the foliate face as a symbol of threat. When Norman returned to Exeter House, he conveyed the canon's good wishes and said the clergyman would call upon the Austs that afternoon.

Apollonia and Edward enthusiastically welcomed their friend into the hall, especially thrilled to see that he carried a large leather walet beneath his arm.

"God give you good day, my friends," Canon Chulmleigh greeted them warmly as he entered. "For aught I woot, we shall gain little from these scurrilous sheets, but at your entreaty, my Lady, I have managed to collect them all." With that, he pulled from the walet several very dirty and wrinkled indulgences. "These have been examined by scholars, and little of note has been gained from them."

"You are the most gallant of gentlemen, Canon Baldwin," Apollonia said, while bending over the table where they lay. "I dare never deny your unending courtesy to me. But can you share with me the nature of the scholarly inquiry?"

"Indeed, my Lady, there have been several great minds from our cathedral chapter examine every word, and none has determined meaning in them. It has been our opinion that these are the creations of a mad man!"

Apollonia arranged the fouled indulgences in order, as she remembered precisely how the canon had described their sequence. At the end of the table, she placed the two thrown at the time of the assault and the murder of Wolfson. "In every case, have these been examined for the meaning of their words?" she asked quietly.

"Of course, my Lady, it is the words which define the threat, do they not?"

"But do look closely at their composition, Canon Baldwin. Notice how these, the first threats received by the dean and chapter, consistently display a foliate face with stems streaming from its mouth. The words of the threat continue from the stems. Then, look closely at these last two examples, thrown at the time of the murderous assaults. The foliate face is not well composed, has no stems from its mouth, and the words of the threat are written in an elegant script, but to the side, some distance from the face. Dear friend, I believe we may assume these were not all done by the same hand. Whether sayest thou?"

The canon seemed startled, "I dare not deny it, my Lady. You have discerned significant differences in these designs which we in chapter have not considered as important. I presume you are meaning to say that the sheriff should be looking for two different persons, one who initiated the threats and a second who committed attack and murder?

"Canon Baldwin, my Lady wife and I not only wish to suggest at least two persons were involved," Edward summarized, "we believe the earlier creator of the threats is not a murderer and must not be charged with such crimes."

"By my troth, Master Edward, are you suggesting we have been mistaken in our search for Eric Aunk?"

"No, dear friend, we believe the sheriff was purposefully misled to charge him with the attack on the Green and the subsequent murder of Wolfson," Apollonia said.

By the time the sun had neared setting for the day, Apollonia and Edward had shared with Chulmleigh their convictions that Eric Aunk had been compelled by Wolfson to make fraudulent threats against the dean and chapter, for reasons known only to Wolfson. They both believed that the pitmaker possessed no evil intent against anyone within the Cathedral Close and purposefully designed his threats to be so unspecific as to be meaningless. More importantly, they assured the canon that they could present witnesses to prove Eric was elsewhere at the time of the assault, and especially, though he was in Exeter, Eric Aunk could prove he was not present on the Shilhay when Merchant Wolfson was murdered.

"Again, my Lady, you and Edward have been able to collect the force of truth from the chaos of falsehood and misrepresentation. May we take your witnesses to the dean and the sheriff in Aunk's defence? If he can prove his innocence, the charges of assault and murder may then be withdrawn."

"Canon Baldwin, if you can help us approach the dean and chapter as well as the sheriff," Edward said earnestly, "we shall bring witnesses to the conduct and character of Master Aunk."

"We shall also bring his personal confession to the truth of the green man indulgences, dear friend. Will that not clear the air for once and all within the Close?" Apollonia smiled."

* * *

In the early evening, Apollonia was seated in the hall with Nan, as Gareth brought a wide-eyed and overwhelmed Laston into their presence. "Oi foun im at th baker's shop, m'Lady," Gareth said. "When Oi tol im ye wished a message taken ta a Deadman, ee coom long straightaway!"

As Gareth departed the hall, Laston seemed to shrink. He had never in his young life been allowed inside such a grand place, save for the kitchens, but he held his cap in hand bravely and waited politely until the Lady would give instruction to him.

"Good evening, Laston. My friend, Master Aunk, the pitmaker of the cathedral, has told me that you have been a valued companion and messenger for him. He also said that you would willingly carry a message to him from me. That is why I have asked you here." Apollonia spoke quietly but with encouragement to the boy. She could see that though he felt uneasy and uncomfortably out of place, he remained eager and willing to help his friend.

"Oh aye, m'Lady, Oi be willin ta elp ye, whene'er needs be."

"You seem a bright lad, Laston, and truly faithful to Master Aunk. How is it you know him?"

Laston began to pull himself up to full height, pleased and encouraged to hear the Lady knew Master Aunk by name. "Well, ma'am, Oi coom ta elp im cause, tho ee be a pitmaker now, ee were a squire. Ee's been in real bat'les ma'am, in France. Th turrble scars ee gots, dey cooms from bein wounded by sword."

"I can see that you admire Squire Aunk, Laston, and with good reason. He is a brave and stalwart man. I shan't ask you where he is, but I will ask you to take this message to him from me." And when she placed the small note into his hand, Apollonia added a coin to his palm."

"Ye need'n pay me, Lady. Oi'll do it fur ye, gladly."

"I am asking an important service from you, Laston. Please accept it as my gift.

"Thankee, Lady, Oi'll take it ta moi mum."

With a bow and a swift return of his cap to his head, Laston turned on the spot and fled from the hall.

"My Lady, can you really believe this poor lad will deliver your message?" Nan asked her. "He may very well spend the coin and abandon your note."

"Master Aunk recommended him to be faithful and dependable, Nan. I believe it is always worth investing in the future of a young life."

Apollonia liked Laston. She had already begun to wonder if there may be a place for him in the Aust affinity. She must remember to find a way to speak with his mother.

* * *

Lights burned in an upper chamber within the largest stone building along Exeter Quay. It had been constructed into the side of a high cliff, standing above the river's docks, and included a succession of caves on the cliff face, opening to storage areas far into the underground. By this time in the winter's evening, daylight working hours had ended. Seamen, fullers, and tuckers had all gone to their homes or to the alehouse. The Quay was silent save for two powerful horses whose hooves occasionally stomped in their ground level stable.

"Damn it, why should we give up all access to the pebble beach at Beer? It is the best of smuggling landings and has proven endlessly profitable for us." The tall, well built figure stood near the fireplace in the chamber and gestured at his brother. "Why could you not talk father out of some arrangement for us there?"

"Stedmund, we no longer need it! We have done well, but smuggling in Devon has grown risky, and I am ready to establish my own estates in Cornwall. We have organized the criminal element here in Exeter to do our bidding. You have a sufficient income through protection and manipulation of the cloth industries. I know you are never short of cash."

"But I am bored, Edmund! In the years since returning from Constantinople, I have found life without action to be sheer tedium."

"If you are saying you miss the killing, then damn you, brother, return to the pestilential Crusades! You have already complicated our lives endlessly by your prowling about the town, slicing into anyone who crosses you."

Edmund Falford was now staying in Exeter in his brother Stedmund's hideout, because he had been forced to leave Withycombe

Raleigh Manor. The early arrival of their eldest brother, to claim his inheritance of their father's title and lands, had ended all the advantage they had made of both before their father died. Theirs was a large family that shared no familial affection within it. The new Baron Falford of Withycombe threw his twin brothers out of the manor as quickly as he installed his own household and servants. He wished to clean and air the moated manor house of that which he described as "the putrid remains and odours that still filled its halls." And he made it clear that he regarded his brothers as part of the filth and stench.

"You were the brilliant mind who insisted we should use others to rid ourselves of the miserable aulnage, Edmund. You knew I was determined to put in his place our own man, amenable to me. Had I done the deed, Moreton Molton would be in his grave. But no, brother, the aulnage lives still!" Stedmund Falford shouted.

"And you rendered him vain by maiming his weakling brother, did you?" Edmund spat at him sarcastically. "You have always been the stupid half, but I swear, push me farther, Stedmund, and I shall no longer hang about to sort out your disasters. Thanks to me, another is charged for your crimes!"

"We can still dispatch the aulnage, Edmund, and I shall see it done properly this time. The sheriff has not yet found Aunk, so whilst he runs and hides, we shall employ his incriminating indulgences one last time." Stedmund's lips curled into a sneer. "You may assume yourself to possess intellect and strength, brother, but I know you to be pusillanimously weak!"

Each brother knew well the strength of his twin, and even at the height of their anger, they never resorted to physical attack. Each knew equally well their deeply personal sense of collusion. Edmund and Stedmund Falford needed each other. They were identical twins, but even more since Stedmund's return from Constantinople, they had been inseparable. Edmund asserted he was the brain, and Stedmund was the muscle. But even in the midst of angry threats and hurling insults, both brothers knew they functioned as one.

Chapter Twenty-three

True Pardon

Eric Aunk had gathered his friends, Adam and Friar Francis, to go with him to Exeter House and meet with the Lady Apollonia and her husband. Eric's young friend, Laston, had brought her message to him, assuring Eric that a meeting had been arranged with the dean and chapter of the cathedral, including the Sheriff of Devon. The Austs promised to accompany him, to add their advocacy of Eric as he sought to establish his innocence of murder. The pitmaker had thrown back his hood, as he and his friends walked from the High Street, exposed his honest face, and prayed earnestly for God's guidance. When they reached Exeter House, the group approached the front entrance, rang the bell, and asked to be received by the Lady and Master Edward.

Nan brought them directly into the hall, where Apollonia and her husband awaited them. Apollonia spoke first and greeted their guests with enthusiasm. "Welcome Eric and Friar Francis. Edward and I are pleased to receive you all and especially welcome your friend from Littleham."

Eric responded with a voice that grew in confidence as he presented Adam. "My Lady, Master Edward, I am pleased to introduce you to my lifelong friend. This is Adam Braund of Littleham."

"Greetings, Master Braund," Apollonia said. "Edward and I are very grateful for your willingness to come to Exeter and stand witness in defence of Eric. We both believe in protecting the innocent, but especially in declaring the innocence of a good man who has been wrongly accused."

Adam was a bit taken aback. He had never actually been in the presence of a real English lady. He had never, in his life, acknowledged any superiority in the so-called upper classes, but this Lady approached him with the open friendliness of his own Telitha. And her brilliant smile struck away any anticipation he may have had of her presumption to look down upon him.

To his surprise, Adam found he had no hesitation in responding to both of the Austs. He liked Edward on first sight; his hearty smile and welcoming posture made Adam feel truly well met.

"Master Braund, I understand that you, continuing the work of your father, have provided stone for the building of Exeter's glorious cathedral. Well done. It shall grace the heart of the city for centuries to come," Edward said in honest admiration.

"Yea verily, Mawster Edward, Oi shall ne'er pass th cathedral witout feelin a sense o pride in moi part o its buildin."

Each of the group knew their ultimate purpose that day, so they spent no more time in pleasantries but prepared to make their way to the Cathedral Close. Nan brought cloaks for the Lady and Master Edward, and the larger group left Exeter House to begin their walk on Northgate Street up to the High Street. There was little conversation, but Apollonia continued to smile upon Eric and asked him to tell her more about his daughter, Ariana. He responded with pride, describing her marvelously improving skills in the household, especially in the kitchen.

Adam seconded his comments, "Aye, m'Lady, moi good wife, Telitha, tells me reglar tha Ariana be a'ready a fine on in th kitchen."

Apollonia instinctively knew that speaking of Ariana helped Eric gain confidence in his purpose. He not only had to confess his misdeeds to the dean and chapter of the cathedral; he knew he must defend himself in the presence of the Sheriff of Devon. A loving parent, Apollonia grasped immediately that Eric's first wish in life was to be finally allowed to live together with his daughter. All that he would do this day, Eric wished to do for Ariana towards achieving that hope.

They walked past the west front of the cathedral, whence they found Canon Chulmleigh waiting for them near the entrance to the chapter house. The canon struggled to contain his own excitement, but he truly believed this day would bring solutions to the puzzling problems that had plagued the Close for months. "Greetings, Master Aunk," he said as he led the group towards the chapter house. "We all stand in need of your contributions to our true understanding of green men," he added with a twinkle in his eye.

Apollonia and Edward had never before entered a chapter house and were impressed to find all of the cathedral canons seated along its walls. The Sheriff of Devon, Dean Walkyngton, the treasurer, the precentor, and the chancellor were seated in the centre of the chamber behind a large table. Canon Chulmleigh walked to his seat amongst the other canons. The dean of the cathedral received the Austs, acknowledged their guests, and described the manner in which this hearing would proceed.

To begin, the dean announced that the charges against Eric Aunk would be read in total; then witnesses in his behalf would be heard. "The Lady Apollonia and Master Edward of Aust will be heard first to bring their information and their advocacy of the accused, and then be subject to questions."

Dean Walkyngton continued, "After the Aust testimony, they shall be excused, and we shall hear the testimonies of Friar Francis and Adam Braund, the other witnesses in the pitmaker's defence. They too, will be questioned. Finally, the full confession of the pitmaker, Eric Aunk, will be heard, and he will be examined closely.

The charges against Eric were read out in their awful entirety. Everyone in the chapter house seemed intimidated by their sheer extent: assault, murder, intimidation with intent to harm. But the statements of the Austs returned the tone of the hearing from serious legal charges to advocacy of one whom they regarded as unjustly accused. They began very simply and to the point. The Lady Apollonia spoke first, and Edward added his endorsement. They avowed that they had been personally unacquainted with Eric Aunk. But when their esteemed Friar Francis brought assurances to them that he had been with Eric at the time of Wolfson's murder, the friar proclaimed Eric's innocence of that charge. Each of the Austs stated an earnest desire to protect this man, whom they believed had been falsely charged with crimes against the King's Law that he could not have committed.

Apollonia and Edward urged leniency in the judgement of the dean and chapter, as they heard the confession of Eric Aunk. They called upon the chapter to show mercy for the pitmaker in remembrance of his good works in behalf of the cathedral and his wounds suffered in defence of the kingdom. At the end of their testimonies, they were questioned briefly and then released by the dean with his thanks. The Austs left the chapter house and walked home together. Both knew in their hearts, the next hours of examination would be critical for Eric. They walked, arm in arm, inwardly searching their memories and wondering what more they could do, as silent prayers in his behalf flowed from both of their hearts.

* * *

The Lady and her husband were working with Stafford and several of the managers of their Devon holdings. Everyone in the group knew it had been a good year for them. Their purpose, now that the winter was well upon them, was to discern those things that had been most profitable and which areas of their extended cloth making process still required improvement. Apollonia and Edward were grateful to be at work, to keep their minds occupied, even while their hearts and personal anxieties remained focused in the Cathedral Chapter House.

Apollonia, as was her habit, continued to ask after the conditions of their weavers. She knew they would share in the improved profits this year, but she also wished to maintain some personal insight into their lives, their families, and how they were prepared to face the winter. She was pressing one of their managers for information about the ongoing efforts of a widow in nearby Broadclyst, a capable weaver, but one who frequently struggled to provide for her large family.

"Ah, m'Lady, thou needst nay fret fur th Widow Warren. She be well an as been able ta send er youngest ta th priest fur schoolin. Gossips says she's been walkin out wit a man o der village. Ev'ryone opes fur news o th banns bein published soon."

Apollonia was pleased to make note of these encouraging words from Broadclyst, but she was suddenly aware of the arrival of Phyllis of Bath in the reception area before their front hall. Hurrying towards the main entrance, she gestured to Edward that she and Phyllis would proceed to the solar.

Nan was in process of telling Mistress Phyllis that her Lady and the master were occupied with business when Apollonia entered the passageway and approached their guest.

"Gramercy, Nan, I am free, and I shall speak with Mistress Phyllis in our solar." At that, she took Phyllis by the arm and escorted her to the circular stairs winding to their upper chambers.

Nan accompanied them, following them into the chamber to stir the fire, in an effort to warm the space within the tapestry covered walls of the solar. Apollonia led Phyllis to a comfortable seat near the fire and told her that Edward would join them as soon as he could. "Do you have news for us, Phyllis?" she asked hopefully.

"O aye, m'Lady. Bu Oi'm nay quite certain o wha it means! Did ye an Mawster Edward kno dere be a crim'nal gang doin der evil deeds in Exeter?"

* * *

Edward entered the solar to join them. "Stafford can complete the reports of our managers, Lonia. I am too eager to learn what news our friend has brought." Edward seated himself in a chair to complete their circle, while Phyllis continued her story of the gossip surrounding the unsavoury aspects of Merchant Wolfson's business ventures. Phyllis told them that she had spoken with several reliable people in the wool trade who believed that Raymond Wolfson had sought to employ criminals, organized gang members in Exeter. On one occasion, he used them to see that a rival mill to his fulling operation was set afire late at night. It was also rumoured that he had used the services of the same gang to threaten his weavers, keeping them in line while he paid them far less than the going rate.

"Bu tha ain't all, m'Lady, Mawster Edward. It be said Wolfson used th same gang ta elp im smuggle is reject cloths abroad." Phyllis was wide-eyed in her telling. She regarded herself a woman of the real world, but she had no insight into the criminal activities of gangs. "An worse be said, th gang in Exeter as connexions wit th nobility!"

"Phyllis," Apollonia stopped her, "can you be certain that these folk who told you all of this can be trusted?"

"God be moi witness, m'Lady, Oi kno's ev'ry mann jack o'em. Dey be true an dey ne'er lies ta me. Bu per'aps odders be tellin em wrong?"

"Dear ones," Edward said to his wife and their friend, "I believe we may be beyond our capacity to deal with this news. Mistress Phyllis, we shan't expose anyone with whom you have spoken, but I must return to the cathedral and seek to speak with the sheriff."

* * *

When Edward returned to the chapter house of the cathedral, he saw the hearings therein had been completed, though many of the canons, as well as the sheriff, were still in place, continuing their questions of Eric and his friends. Edward approached Baldwin Chulmleigh and, taking him to one side, indicated that he required a favour of him.

"Canon Chulmleigh, as a dear friend to my family, would you be willing to present me to the sheriff and ask him if we may speak privately on a different matter?"

Without hesitation, the canon strode up to the table where the sheriff remained seated. The sheriff looked up and greeted them both, as he remembered Edward Aust from his earlier testimony. Canon Chulmleigh urged the sheriff to hear Edward's news, so he assured them he would remain until everyone else had departed.

"I would ask you to remain as well, Canon Chulmleigh," Edward said. "I believe you should be informed of a conversation my wife and I shared this afternoon."

While he was waiting for the sheriff to be free, Edward walked towards the pitmaker to speak briefly with him. "I pray thee, Eric, can you tell me anything of the results of your hearing this day? My dear wife and I have been impatient for news."

"I am a free man, Master Edward. Thanks to your confidence in me, I have been cleared of the charges of assault and murder. The dean has declared the extent of the penance that I must do for the evil suspicions I promoted within the Close. But I shall be returned to my position as pitmaker thereafter. I can never thank you enough."

"Eric, if you and your friends will return to Exeter House, my dear wife will be thrilled to share your news. Just now, I must speak with the sheriff, and then I shall follow you to our home."

When the chapter house emptied at last, and its doors were closed, Edward and Baldwin moved to join the sheriff at the large table. Edward explained that he had requested the canon to join them, as he felt the tale he needed to share would be of critical interest to both of them. The sheriff sat back in his large chair, extended his long, booted legs, folded his hands, and encouraged Edward to tell all.

"You must know, sir, that my wife and I are active in the wool trade of Exeter. As such, we have received word that there is a gang of ruffians operating here in the town, robbing, burning, threatening, and forcing men of good conscience to do their will."

At this, the sheriff sat forward in his chair. "And how do you come by this knowledge, Master Aust?"

"I do freely admit it is gossip, but, sir, it is shared by reliable people in the trade whom I am unable to name."

"I shan't require names, Master Edward, but I must ask you if you have personally encountered such threats?"

"No, sir, not as such. But I have one further comment to share with you that I have gleaned from the gossip. The criminals are organized and led by members of an influential noble family in the area. Can that be so?"

"Master Aust, you are an upright man, and I know from the aulnage himself, you are a producer of fine quality cloths. The gossip you describe has come to my ears, and charges have been made against this gang. Although I have been able to charge some of the lesser criminals, I have never been able to put my finger upon the leader. Just when we feel we can prove the presence of a son of the local nobility as leader of the gang, he is consistently able to prove himself as being elsewhere when the crimes were committed."

Canon Chulmleigh interrupted at this point. "Sheriff, do we know who amongst the noble families of Devon is taking part in nefarious activities?"

"I may not reveal the family name upon which my suspicions rest at this point, canon, and I shall depend upon your word to reveal nothing I have told you. But beware the advice of one who wears a distinctive signet ring. On the middle finger of his right hand, the gentleman wears a silver ring displaying an eagle's head, turned to one side with a large ruby as its eye."

Edward absorbed every word the sheriff spoke as gospel. He knew Apollonia would require him to share their entire conversation with her. "Sheriff, I do thank you most heartily for your time and attention, but may I add that several of us within the merchant community of Exeter remain concerned for the protection of the aulnage. My wife is convinced that the safety of Sir Moreton Molton plays a central role in the larger collection of malicious events happening within the city these past months."

"Your lady wife and your friends are wise in their concerns, Master Aust. I shall be grateful to you all for sharing any further information with me. But you will understand that I must have facts." With that, the sheriff stood, bowed to the canon and the merchant, and walked from the chapter house.

"I say, Master Edward, you and your dear wife do seem to find yourselves at the very centre of the investigation of our county's recent adventures." Edward could see that Canon Chulmleigh was smiling, but both knew there was real danger afoot.

* * *

Exeter House was in a state of celebration when Edward returned from the cathedral. Apollonia had not only invited Eric, Friar Francis, and Adam Braund to remain the night with the Aust household; Phyllis of Bath had joined the party, and all members of the affinity had been encouraged to come and meet these extraordinary new friends. The most excited guest of the evening's celebration was Laston, now feeling very grown up and introducing his mum to his good friend, Squire Aunk, the pitmaker to the cathedral.

Edward was thrilled to find Apollonia in the midst of the hall, introducing Adam Braund to Gareth and describing to each the extraordinary skills of the other. "I do hope you will bring your dear wife, Telitha, and your family with you to visit us, Adam," she said. "Our Gareth is a marvelous hand with the horses. Surely your sons would enjoy a chance to experience his skill with the animals. And you, Gareth, may well find with Adam a chance to travel down river to Littleham for your first view of the sea."

Apollonia could see that her husband had returned, and she moved immediately to his side. She took his arm, and they continued their progress through the entire gathering of household and guests, sharing the reasons for their unplanned celebration. They also wanted to help their Exeter household staff to learn to know the good Devon folk who were their guests this day.

Phyllis of Bath easily held the attentions of both Jude and Norman, as she described for them her unwomanly triumphs in the woollen trade. Nan remained near to her Lady but was quietly excited to observe Gareth actually enjoying a social occasion. Unbeknownst to her, Gareth was scheming in his heart that he might take Nan to Littleham. He knew she would be thrilled by the chance of a lifetime to view the Devon sea coast.

But for Eric Aunk, this evening promised far more than celebration. The dean and chapter had been thrilled to learn of his discovery of tunnels beneath the Cathedral Green. In his confession, he told of his use of them to move about unseen within the Close at night. The dean and canons of the chapter had immediately wished to be shown, so he had led them to the grass covered, iron cap in the heart of the Green and lifted it. They marveled to see its entry into the underground. Eric's revelation had captivated them and possibly, he thought, contributed to the relatively mild sentence finally given him.

The pitmaker's confession and plea for mercy had been heard by the dean and chapter. Their sentence against him was that he must do public penance for thirty days. He must appear as a barefoot penitent at the daily masses of the cathedral, holding a five pound candle throughout the mass. Eric was not only grateful for such a mild sentence, he was glad to do the required penance. Once completed, it would be a visible sign of his having achieved forgiveness for evil deeds he had done and knew to have been unworthy.

Eric also rejoiced that once his penance was completed, he could begin immediately to look for lodgings where he and Ariana would be able to renew their lives together. Even more hopeful, Laston's mum had already suggested to him a small dwelling now available near Stepcote Hill and not far from where she lived with Laston and the rest of her brood.

The cheerful, chattering, laughing sounds of their voices filled the hall until at last Master Edward invited all of their guests to join them in the chapel for vespers. Father Anthony led the way, and a truly joyful congregation of worshipers joined the Lady and her husband when they walked into their beautiful new chapel.

Adam Braund moved next to Eric, speaking quietly within his hearing alone. "Oi shall do dis fur ye dis time, Worm, bu Oi shall be offerin moi own prayers fur ye by moi own ways."

* * *

Early the following day, just after morning prayers, Edward had gone into the town with Stafford to a meeting in the Guildhall. The Lady was seated in her solar with Nan, chatting and sharing their truly happy memories of the previous day.

"It was really good of everyone in the household to bring their congratulations to the pitmaker," Apollonia said. "Even if they did not know him, gossip had judged him a criminal. Yet everyone here seemed to rejoice in his ability to declare his innocence. And did you notice, Nan, Eric's face was constantly smiling; no one seemed put off by his dreadful scars." The Lady smiled to herself. It had been such a beautiful evening.

"My Lady, I do not think the pitmaker's face is frightening. Indeed, he must have been terribly wounded, but from the first day I met him, his scars seemed to add an aura of bravery and service to his smile."

Lady Apollonia responded to a knock upon their door in her usual voice but still smiling. "Enter," she called.

Emily came timidly into the solar and announced a visitor awaiting her in the hall.

"Has the visitor given you a name, Emily? Can you tell me whom I shall be receiving?"

"Ee says ye be kno'en im, m'Lady. Is name be Brandon Landow." With that, Emily curtsied and closed the door.

Nan was immediately shocked. "That young man will come for no good purpose, my Lady; shall I see him and send him away?"

"I understand your disapproval of our young pardoner, Nan, but I must receive him, if only in courtesy." The Lady rose from her chair and began to walk out of the chamber. "But would you please find Jude and Norman. I do not fear Brandon, but he must feel there is strength in my purpose."

* * *

As Apollonia entered the hall, Landow made an exaggerated bow, nearly sweeping his arm to the floor. "You need not feel such drama is required, Brandon. I receive you because indeed I do know you, and even you must be accorded every courtesy. Why have you come?"

"Ah, my gracious Lady, you are always straight to the point of the matter. I have called to inquire after your health and, I dare hope, the improved health of your husband?" Landow smiled somewhat awkwardly but seemed to wish to gain some warmth in her response to him.

"Gramercy, Brandon, your concerns are admirable, and my dear husband has returned to his usual state of heartiness. Now what is it that you truly want?"

"As you wish, my Lady, I shall be blunt. In my role as pardoner, I was called to the home of a noble family, the Falfords of Withycombe Raleigh, when their lord, the Baron Brutwald Falford, was near to dying. I had been requested by his son, Sir Edmund Falford, to bring succour to the dying lord in the form of a significant indulgence. After his death, I was to bring ease to the family in the person of a priest to conduct the funeral. I did fulfill both."

"And of course, you were well paid for your services," the Lady added.

"In part, my Lady, but that is not my complaint. You are a lady of influence here in Exeter, and I know personally, you are one who wishes to defend the innocent." At this, Brandon's eyes grew bitter, and Apollonia suspected he wished to use her influence in some way.

"Is it your innocence I am being asked to defend, Brandon?" she asked skeptically.

"No, my Lady, I wish you to know the Falfords are not being honest with you or anyone in this city. I discovered to my distress, there are two of them!"

"But Sir Edmund Falford has already told me there are seven sons amongst them, Brandon. I see no falsehood in that."

Brandon heaved a great aggravated sigh. "No, my Lady, I am trying to tell you that of the many sons of the former Baron Falford, two of them, numbers six and seven, are twins, identical in every way. I saw them together. They possess the same appearance, same height, and same colour of eyes, hair, and skin. They even share the same tone of voice, and if you see them together, you would swear you are seeing double. And, my dear Lady of Aust, together they are doubly evil."

With that, the pardoner began to leave the hall. "I shall delay you no longer." Brandon bowed curtly. "Please forgive my hurried departure, but I am off this day to Wiltshire. Benedicite, my Lady."

Apollonia did not mind his hurried departure, as she was madly trying to grasp all the implications of what he had just told her. When Landow threw open the doors of the hall in his hurried departure, his way was blocked by two sturdy members of the Aust household. Jude and Norman said nothing to him but remained unmovable until the Lady signaled his release. Landow rushed from the house, mounted his horse, and rode back towards the High Street. He had spent enough time in Exeter.

Lady Apollonia called Jude and Norman into the hall. "I shall give you each messages to be delivered straightaway. Norman, you must carry one to the home of Canon Chulmleigh. Then, rush on to the Guildhall and bring your master home to me directly. Jude, you must find the sheriff and deliver my message into his hands alone."

Chapter Twenty-four

Sanctuary and Celebration

It was late in December, and by midmorning, the day had grown bright and sunny, but fierce, chill winds bent the busy folk of the High Street into them. Every man kept a firm grip on his hat, while other folk wrapped their cloaks and scarves more closely to their bodies. The aulnage, Sir Moreton Molton, had begun his daily walk on to the High Street towards the Guildhall, accompanied by two of his household men. Sir Moreton proceeded forthrightly while carrying a tall walking stick, but he frequently took opportunities to bow and graciously greet the citizens he passed. He had repeated his route daily for, in spite of the attack upon him and his brother on the Cathedral Green, he wished all the people of the town to know that the aulnage refused to be intimidated.

Sir Moreton had passed St Stephen's Church when he noticed a remarkably tall gentleman gesturing to him from the other side of the High Street, from a lane just prior to the Guildhall. He gestured to his henchmen to await him and walked across the street to acknowledge the gentleman who sought his attention. He could not recognize the man, as his collar was heightened and his hat pulled down against the frigid winds. Perhaps to avoid the worst of the wind's assault, the unknown gentleman stepped back into the protection of the lane.

The aulnage held his stick firmly in his right hand when he walked into the wind and turned into the lane to offer his greetings. Suddenly, two tall, dark figures, concealed on either side of the lane, violently pulled him by his arms far back into its shadows and threw him to the ground. Even as he landed, the aulnage seemed prepared to strike back. Lying there, he clutched his stick with both hands and began to propel it as a weapon.

The first assailant had drawn a dagger from his belt and rushed at the fallen aulnage with the weapon in his hand. Sir Moreton extended his stick from his fists and brought it crashing across upon the arms of his assailant, sending the dagger flying into the lane behind them.

Without a pause, he swung the stick to his left, striking a heavy blow upon the head and shoulders of the second attacker. That man, though equally tall and muscular as the first, had no stomach for fighting. Stunned by the strength of the aulnage's resistance, he sought to flee from the scene immediately. Without hesitation, Sir Moreton continued to thrust his weapon back and forth before him, all the while shouting his alarm towards the lane opening upon the High Street, "Assassin! Murderer! Help me!"

The first attacker seemed demented in his frustrated anger. Though his dagger had been smashed from his hand, he rushed with both arms extended, reaching towards the throat of the fallen aulnage. Sir Moreton, holding his weapon firmly in both hands, struck again at his attacker. From several points on the High Street, men were drawn to the lane. At first they were distracted by the dark figure that ran past them out onto the High Street. From the entrance to the lane, Sir Moreton's henchmen might have pursued him, but they could see, farther down the lane, a similar dark figure continuing his attack upon their lord, the fallen aulnage. They took up the cry, "Assassin, Murderer!" and ran to the aid of Sir Moreton whilst he never ceased to thrash his great stick at the figure threatening him.

Furiously, the attacker grabbed the stick, pulled it from Sir Moreton's hands, and lifted it over his head to bring its full force upon the now defenceless victim. Swiftly, the aulnage rolled towards the side of the lane and sought protection against the wall of the nearest building. He pulled up his legs, curved his body's length into an oval, while burying his head within the high collar of the padded jupon he wore.

Armed men from the High Street were rushing towards the lane, shouting, and demanding arrest. The first attacker knew he must flee. He hurled the walking stick at Sir Moreton's head and ran in the other direction down the lane. Without the slightest hesitation, he turned into a narrow, dark alley, overhung by extended roofs, and swiftly threw himself over its terminal wall.

At first the assassin thought he had escaped his pursuers, but he could hear the noise of the swearing guardsmen growing closer in their search for him. He pulled off his dark cloak as he continued to run, slung it over his arm, and rounded another corner into an alley which took him purposefully back towards the High Street. He stopped to compose himself before walking out on to Exeter's main thoroughfare, and from his new position, he could look back and see crowds of people gathering on the far side of the Guildhall. He slowed his pace, blended into the crowd of passersby, and moved briskly down the High Street towards the Broad Gate. Once near its looming presence, he dashed towards its open portal and fled into the Cathedral Close.

His mad flight continued until he reached the west front of the cathedral. There he forced his way through its northwest door, ran the full length of the nave, and continued to run until he had crashed into the quire and clambered to the high altar. Grasping the altar cloth in his hands, Stedmund Falford began to shout, "Sanctuary! I claim sanctuary must be granted me!" At last, he lay back upon the stone floor gasping for breath.

The clergy of the quire were astounded by this rabid interruption of their morning mass, but they were all totally stunned to see yet another dark figure erupt into the quire and rush to the high altar. Several members of the chapter recognized this intruder as he threw his great coat to the floor. I am Sir Edmund Falford," he shouted. "My brother and I are gentlemen of this realm, and we demand sanctuary!"

* * *

Baldwin Chulmleigh rushed into Exeter House, just as the Lady and Master Edward were closing the last day's accounts. Edward rose as Nan brought the canon into the hall. "God's greetings, Canon Baldwin, how goeth thy morning, dear friend?"

"My Lady, Master Edward, you have both been close to the expanding tale of disaster within our cathedral community; I come to bring you the most extraordinary tidings!" He hurled himself into his usual chair with a great deep breath. "The villains have come to the cathedral demanding sanctuary!"

"I say, Canon Baldwin, what villains? What drives them to seek sanctuary?" Edward was aghast. A respected franklin, he understood the implications of such an action, but he was more personally moved to discover the identity of the criminals and understand the extent of their offense.

"Faithful friend," Apollonia interrupted, "please do begin at the beginning." She took her husband's arm, and they moved quickly to settle in chairs beside Canon Chulmleigh.

"My Lady, I do apologise for my disarray," Baldwin said more calmly. "You both know all charges against Eric Aunk have been dropped, but the murderer of Merchant Wolfson has remained afoot in

Exeter. As you suggested, my Lady, the life of the aulnage continued to be in danger, and the sheriff put his person under watchful guard. Well, this morning Moreton Molton was attacked in a small lane, just next to the Guildhall off the High Street!"

"Holy Mother, grant us mercy. What is the condition of the aulnage, Canon Baldwin?" Apollonia asked in sincere distress. "Has he survived?"

"Oh yes, my Lady," Baldwin said proudly. "Whereas his brother is a weak and sickly man, Sir Moreton fought them like a caged tiger, even whilst he lay on the ground whence they had hurled him. When the sheriff's men rushed to his side, they chased away those who had attempted to kill him. But the villains had been witnessed in the act of assault, and even though they ran in different directions, both sought the same aim. They ran into the Close to seek sanctuary in the cathedral."

"Dear God, do we know who has done this?" Edward spoke in some exasperation. "Who are these foul creatures?"

"It was the Falford brothers, Master Edward. Edmund Falford has a brother, Stedmund. He was unknown to those of us who thought we knew Edmund, who welcomed him into our homes, and who shared our concerns and our secrets with him. God forgive us, he has a twin!"

"What secrets, Canon Baldwin?" Apollonia asked quietly.

"It was I who shared with Sir Edmund the knowledge of the demented use of indulgences, defaced by a green man, to threaten the dean and chapter. Sir Edmund is a high-born local gentleman; I assumed he could be trusted. And this morning, when the sheriff searched the brothers to be certain they had no weapons concealed upon them, he found yet another indulgence threat in Stedmund's pocket. Presumably they would have left it upon the body of the murdered aulnage to continue their incrimination of Eric Aunk, had their attack been successful."

"And has the sheriff carefully examined the brothers' cloaks to discover a tear in the fabric of either one?" Apollonia persisted.

"Forgive me, again, Lady; I have forgotten myself." The canon sat back into his chair, still shaking his head. "Everything happened so rapidly this morning. I have yet to take it all in."

"Devil take it, Canon Baldwin! This is beyond belief," Edward swore. "I so admired Sir Edmund and found myself flattered by his company. I knew him to be a man of noble birth; he was well informed, widely travelled, and always personable. Lonia, how very deceived we have been."

"My dear Edward, you have always believed the best in people, and I love you for the goodness you grant to others. But I must know more about the twin, Canon Baldwin. How has it been possible for him to be living in Exeter and yet never be noticed?" Apollonia pressed.

"Stedmund Falford, my Lady, is a mirror image of his brother. If people saw either of them on the street, he could be presumed to be Edmund. Stedmund was the Crusader brother whom no one knew had returned from Constantinople, where he developed his proficiency in killing in the defence of Byzantium. He boasts of holding a plenary indulgence from the pope, granted to him by the Holy Father, when he volunteered to go to the East and defend Christianity against Islam." Baldwin paused to mop his forehead.

"But Stedmund returned to England several years ago, and at that time, the brothers decided it was wise to conceal their double identities to assist them in their criminal acts. They arrogantly confessed all this morning to the dean of the cathedral and seemed rather proud of their villainous achievements. They were unaware of Eric Aunk's revelations to the chapter, or the testimony of his witnesses to the Sheriff of Devon, declaring him innocent of assault and murder. Most importantly, my Lady, they had no idea that the aulnage was being guarded by the sheriff's men as he moved about the city."

"How then will their plea for sanctuary proceed, Canon Baldwin?" Edward asked him quietly, still unable to grasp the truth.

"Both brothers will be watched whilst they are maintained inside the cathedral for up to forty days," Baldwin said. "The Sheriff of Devon will set guards about the entire Close to be certain they will have no possibility of escape. But, our Bishop Brantyngham is resolute in his insistence upon the inviolability of sanctuary. The sheriff and his men will not be allowed to apprehend the Falfords. Eventually, the brothers will be assigned a seaport to which they must walk barefoot. From there they will be required to sail away, renouncing England forever and completing their lives as exiles."

"Canon Baldwin, these are extraordinary events, and I am unsure where to begin," Apollonia said cautiously, "but how may we be certain of the Falfords' guilt if they are never put to trial?"

"I do wish you could both have been with the chapter as we gathered around the cathedral's high altar this morning. We were witnesses to the sheriff's display of the fouled indulgence the brothers intended to leave upon Sir Moreton's body. He pointed out the distinctive rings both brothers wear, displaying a silver eagle with a ruby eye. These rings have been reported by several of their victims. We could see for ourselves that the clothes worn by both brothers are identical, except in one detail. The dark woollen cloak worn by Stedmund was shown to have a ragged tear in its back. And, my Lady, the loose threads from Stedmund's torn cloak match those held in Wolfson's hand after his murder on the Shilhay."

The canon seemed to shudder in remembrance, but when he lifted his head, he sought to reassure them. "Soon, my friends, this dreadful business will come to an end. Praise God! But you must pity the cathedral clergy. We shall have to celebrate all of Christ's masses this night with two infamous claimants for sanctuary still clinging to our high altar!"

"Dear fellow, must that be so?" Edward could hardly believe his ears.

"No, Edward, we shall seat them to one side, but I daresay, the Falford brothers remain as desperately in need of Christ's hope of salvation as any men in all of England."

* * *

Late in the evening, Nan and Gareth were organizing all hands from the kitchens and stables to prepare the family's Christmas Crib in the back garden. Friar Francis had come from St Mary Magdalene's Hospital to direct their efforts. He was pleased to do this for Lady Apollonia and Master Edward, duplicating the efforts he designed every year to create a similar crèche for the folk behind the walls of the leprosarium. It was the most exciting celebration of the year for young Francis, chiefly because the friar knew his namesake, Saint Francis, had directed the construction of the first Christmas Crib in Assisi over a century before.

As Saint Francis had done, the friar instructed Gareth to bring a manger from the barn and place it against the garden wall where all members of the household could observe it. They brought hay to fill the manger and form the surrounding stall. Then, the stablemaster and his lads brought a donkey and an ox to stand on either side of the manger and enliven their memories of the original place of the birth of the Holy Child. As they built the crèche, each member of the household could begin to relive in his heart the miracle that had occurred in a stable in Bethlehem.

Nan and the other female servants gathered sturdy candles from every room and brought them to be placed in niches around the crib, lighting the crèche with a flickering halo midst the darkening garden. As midnight arrived, everyone of the Aust affinity had gathered in the garden. Lady Apollonia, her husband, Edward, and their three sons came from the house and seated themselves in the hay.

Friar Francis began by singing the Gospel and then continued to preach a beautiful sermon on the arrival of the Christ Child, first welcomed to earth by the animals in the stable where He lay. Thus it was that the first of Christ's Masses, sung for the Aust household in the year 1380, began not within the beautiful new chapel but in the garden. There, Friar Francis knelt before the manger and stretched his arms towards the heavens in the fervent faith that the Blessed Babe would be born of Mary.

As the midnight mass ended, Apollonia, Edward, and their family led the household silently towards their beds. Except for the movement of their quiet footsteps, nothing was heard in the garden, but a growing spirit of hope could be felt building in each of their hearts. Everyone knew none would sleep long that night, as the second of their services would begin when Father Anthony celebrated the Shepherd's Mass.

* * *

The dawn began to send shafts of grey muted light onto the edges of the eastern horizon when Father Anthony gathered the household once again to kneel near the Christmas Crib, its ox and ass still standing silently but expectantly round the manger. Everyone who knelt round the crib knew the popular legend, that after midnight when they had all gone to their beds, the animals had been briefly granted the gift of speech in thanks for their giving the Infant Jesus His first place of shelter on earth. It was considered bad luck to hear the animals conversing; therefore no one in the household mentioned its happening.

Father Anthony shared the Gospel story of shepherds on the hillsides, frightened by the appearance of angels in the heavens bringing tidings of great joy to all peoples. Many of the servants of the Aust household responded personally to this part of the Gospel message, as many of them felt a closeness of identity with the shepherds. The mere idea that shepherds would leave their flocks and travel to Bethlehem to see the Holy Child brought this, of all Christ's masses, to the day to day understanding of those who know the value of sheep.

Finally, the anticipation of the rest of the day's celebration had, by now, also begun to fire their excitement. For once the Shepherd's Mass had ended, the household retreated to begin their preparations for the most joyfully celebrated holiday of the church year.

By midmorning, Canon Chulmleigh had arrived to represent the cathedral clergy in the Aust household's celebration of the third of Christ's masses, called the Mass of the Divine Word. But even more importantly to Apollonia, he would also officiate in the dedication of the new family chapel. Relatively few members of the household could have defined a specific meaning of "the Divine Word," but everyone knew their lovely new chapel would now officially become the Virgin's Chapel, dedicated to Saint Mary, Mother of God and name saint to their Lady's mother.

Carved niches ranged round the altar; each held a statue of an important saint of the kingdom: Saint Edward, Saint Hugh, Saint Chad, Saint Thomas, Saint Alban, and Saint David. Their images, in many ways like the story of the shepherds, brought the message of the Gospels down to the level of their everyday lives. But for many in the household, it was the aged Saint Apollonia's niche, opposite that of St Edward, whose small altar would always be important to their private prayers. Everyone could see that it was she, whose mature face was that of their Lady who held a pincer in her hand displaying an extracted tooth, and smiling brilliantly upon them all.

* * *

Edward and Apollonia had directed that their Christmas Feast this year would provide a great celebration of the holiday for all their friends, family, and extended household. Edward's preferred role in life was that of host amongst his guests. Of course, this year had gained them the friendship of Canon Chulmleigh and his long time friend, Philip Tropenol, Edward's man of law. Their master mason, William of Wedmore, was pleased to join them, and everyone was prepared to celebrate with enthusiasm when Phyllis of Bath arrived, bringing her boisterous good wishes and hearty greetings of the season.

Eric Aunk and his pretty young daughter, Ariana, were pleased to bring their friends, Adam Braund and his wife, Telitha. The family from Littleham mixed easily with members of the household, especially as Nan and Gareth made a point to introduce them to Edward's hearty yeomen, Jude Dennish, and his good friend, Norman of Salisbury. But Eric was also pleased to bring his friends, Laston and his mother, in response to the Lady's invitation. Laston could be seen taking his mother's arm, leading her into the celebration, while quietly assuring her of their welcome within the Aust household.

The hall was filled with music. Edward had arranged for musicians to take their places upon the upper level of the hall screens passage. The minstrels' leader played a viol. A second minstrel played a tabor, a handheld drum, with his left hand, while his right hand's fingers piped their selected tunes of the season to its rhythms. Their group was completed by a psaltery player whose metal stringed harp was plucked to create striking harmonies with the pipe and the viol. Their instruments played accompaniment to their pure voices, floating majestically down upon all the guests.

As the feast was about to begin, everyone was directed to seats at trestle tables arranged in a giant rectangle stretching out from the head table, all covered in white linen and decorated along their edges with holly and ivy. Mistletoe hung from every entrance and arch, and no one missed a chance to share a sweet kiss in honour of the season. Dishes of soups and stews, with breads and puddings, trays of fowl and fish, were served with ceremony. But the attention of everyone in the hall was immediately arrested by the appearance of the grandest of all presentations, the Yule boar, carried to the head table by four men of the household on its tray. Roasted to perfection, the huge animal appeared with a great apple in its mouth, a large plum in each eye, and a massive crown of pears and cherries circling its head. Edward, as master of the ceremony, saluted this woodland king of the feast and urged all of his guests to savour its royal goodness.

Apollonia rejoiced silently; her heart was full, especially as she could see that Edward seemed completely renewed by the spirit of their celebration. Each of their three sons made a point to visit with their guests. Thomas, Alban, and David took the occasion as a special opportunity to share Christmas greetings with each of their new friends, as well as the staff and all members of the household. During the months they had lived in Exeter, Apollonia could see they had grown, not only into a fuller maturity of their ages, but also in their sense of themselves as young men.

She had been made powerfully aware that they had survived an extraordinary year together, blessed by God's gifts of healing for

Edward and blessed protection for their friends and family. The Lady could not help but smile and glow within herself, while Edward encouraged his guests to eat, drink, and be merry, again and again, in his heartfelt thanks for the goodness of their lives.

The entertainment grew in pitch as a group of mummers paraded into the hall in their gowns and masks. They first strode to the high table to honour their hosts. Then they turned to the larger audience and carried their spectacular masks and disguisings to all those gathered throughout the hall. Two were masked as Gog and Magog; their immense faces caused squeals and shouts when they hovered and threatened. Others bore the large, masked faces of bearded men, some representing wise men and others foolish men, who larked about, displaying the folly of the foolish and the wisdom of the wise. Finally, there were three giant, silver masks of angels, each leading behind them the figures of dragons. As these disguisings continued to parade round the tables, they drew applause and shouts of delight from the guests, but no one was more enthusiastic than their host. The Lady Apollonia preferred to sit quietly at table and observe their entertainment. Edward threw himself into the midst of the show, encouraging all his guests to join him.

After the frumenty and Christmas fruits had been shared, many of the guests rose to sing carols. Several tables were collapsed and pushed to the wall, and though some of the celebrants remained on their benches, many stood to join the circles of carol dance. Each of Apollonia's sons used his voice to lead the carol in the midst of his circle. All the while the guests surrounding him clasped hands and danced to the tune of the carol until they joined together in singing the chorus.

Acrobats and tumblers took centre stage in the middle of the hall. They leaped into their performance with astonishing twists, jumps, and acrobatic towers. Everyone seemed thrilled to sit back and be amazed by the extraordinary feats of the tumblers. But no one applauded them with more enthusiasm than young David Aust.

"This is my gift to the Christ Child, Father," he shouted and joined in tumbling a series of somersaults across the width of the hall.

Edward returned to his wife, slipped into his chair next to her, and leaned his head near to hers. When he lifted her hand to his lips, Apollonia could see his eyes were filled with happy tears. "Thank you, my dearest love. It is a glorious Christmas, Lonia, and my most precious gift is granted in being here with you."

Epilogue

Escape to the Moor

The end of January came at last, and the Falford brothers were to be released from sanctuary in the cathedral, their allowed forty days nearly at an end. A ship of merchant adventurers had arrived in Exeter from Copenhagen. The Falford brothers were sentenced by the dean to board that vessel and depart for their European exile. Their boots were taken from them, for they would be required to walk to the riverside docks on the Quay as barefoot penitents. On the day of their expulsion, each brother was made to carry a ten pound penitent's candle, but they were stripped of all other worldly possessions.

The streets of Exeter, from the Close to the docks, were lined with people. Every man and woman in the city was aware of the Falfords' time of departure from the cathedral, and if he or she was not familiar with their story, someone in the crowds soon supplied the tale. Although Edmund Falford had managed to establish himself as a gentleman of the town, his brother, Stedmund, known to be a Crusader, was regarded as a shadowy figure, gang leader, and major criminal in the shire. Everyone in the town was determined to see them in person, humiliated and sentenced to exile. They had become the major topic of gossip. The Falfords were an ancient and noble Devon family, but these brothers were said to possess devilish similarity. Stories flew amongst the crowds, describing their creation by the demons to look so much alike that they might trick all good folk into their lies and thievery.

Apollonia and Edward allowed none of their household to be present at the anticipated spectacle. The Lady and her husband had no desire to witness the degradation of someone whom they had welcomed into their home, regardless of his guilt. Their sons were kept home from the cathedral school upon this day, and the entire Aust affinity was told of their master's wishes. Therefore, everyone in Exeter House and barns knew that business and chores of the household would remain the foremost concerns of this day.

Apollonia's first care was to see that their sons missed none of their lessons. One of the clerks of the cathedral school was hired to teach Thomas, Alban, and David on that day. In that way, their boys would not be lacking in their studies when allowed to return to classes the following day. The Lady was convinced that David and Alban, surely, and probably also her normally serious Thomas, would return from school with outrageous, malign tales. They would want to share all the gossip of the process of exile for the Falfords and what they had done to deserve it. Apollonia wished to deal with such tales one at a time.

Nan was instructed to keep the household staff focused upon their daily tasks, but the Lady knew whispering had already begun to buzz quietly amongst them. Most of all, Apollonia and Edward wanted their family and household members to remain above the gossip that seemed to rule every shop, craft, and parish church along the main streets of Exeter. None of them were Devon folk, they were reminded, and although they had met some good friends and workmates while living here in Exeter, they were in no position to judge the Falford brothers, and that was to be an end to it.

Yet, every delivery to their door, every merchant come to seek advice on matters of business, and every man on the street brought a voluble description. How far had the process of exile moved? Where were the Falford brothers on their route from the Cathedral Close to the Quay? Stafford, the household steward, was instructed to allow no response to any comments from the outside. He hovered amidst the rest of the staff; his presence enforced a lid of silence upon them.

It was late in the afternoon when no one in the Aust Household could be allowed to feign further disinterest. Phyllis of Bath arrived, crashing through the front entrance, greeting Nan with the blessings of Christ's birth, but insisting she must speak with her Lady and the master.

"Ye mus tell em; dey's fled!"

* * *

Stedmund Falford boiled with fury at the brazenness of these rustics. If he had been armed, he would have gladly cut them to shreds! Exeter folk crowded noisily all along the streets the brothers were required to walk, leading from the cathedral, through the Close, and out by way of its Bear Gate. Stedmund and Edmund had been stripped of their gentlemen's hats, cloaks, and boots or any means of defence. They were forced to walk as humiliated penitents. Each brother struggled to hold before him the massive candle, while the gathered crowds, lining their route, continued to jeer at them, mock their debased state, and hurl slander at their downfall.

"Wher be yer nobility naow, moi lord?"

"Thought ye cou'd git way wit anithin, did ye?"

"Candle go'na lite yer way ta exile, ill it?"

Edmund looked straight ahead, as he moved silently through the clamor of the streets of Exeter. He stood erect and rigidly tall in spite of the stones painfully scraping his bare soles and exposed heels. He held the candle in both hands, acknowledged no face in the crowd, though he could see many whom he knew, and repeated to himself, "It will soon be over. I shall endure this infamy, but only whilst I must."

During the long days of their sanctuary in the cathedral, the Falford brothers had been on display to the quiet taunts and low sneers of the common people. But the contacts with local people had also allowed Edmund and Stedmund to send secret messages to members of their gang. They had given instructions that their own horses were to be waiting for them in an arranged location near the River Exe. Edmund felt certain that once they had struggled down Stepcote Hill and finally made their way out of the city through the West Gate, they would soon be able to achieve their escape.

In the midst of the shouting disarray, Edmund was aware that his brother was burning to lash out at these common pigs who dared to humiliate them. He quietly urged Stedmund to be calm. They both knew they must maintain their pretence of penitence. They must continue to appear helpless, defenceless, and full of remorse, just until they could reach their horses. They knew they would find their swords attached to their saddles, and God help any peasant who sought to belittle them then!

The mocking and scoffing continued unabated, even as they finally turned onto Stepcote Hill. Some bystanders from the side of the road pushed them from behind, forcing them into the sewage flowing down its drains. Their bleeding feet were forced to walk midst garbage as well as animal and human faeces. Edmund steadily reminded his brother, "We shall return to correct these humiliations, Stedmund; pay them no heed."

Stedmund said nothing, his face contorted in hatred, but he continued to walk with more urgency and angry determination in his step. "Yes," he assured himself, "I shall find revenge. I shall wipe my wounded feet on their faces, by God, and it will be bloody fine."

The crowds lined their path all the way through the West Gate of the city wall. Some gentler bystanders stood quietly, shaking their heads, aware they were witnesses to the downfall of greatness. How the mighty had fallen, they clucked amongst themselves. Indeed, they assured each other, they were seeing a major turn of the wheel of fortune. "Pride always goeth before a fall," the moralists in the crowd reminded each other. Many of those who watched the spectacle from the side streets enjoyed making use of this once in a lifetime opportunity to remain unseen, while they mocked fallen gentlemen. They increased the volume of their sneers. No officials were on the streets to inhibit them.

Edmund continued to speak calmly to his brother, ignoring the collection of scoffing faces. "Pay them no mind, Stedmund. They are not worthy of your anger. Our time approaches, brother."

When at last they had passed through the West Gate, the Falfords continued walking towards the river, as if they were truly proceeding to board the ship docked at the Quay. They paused briefly before taking the turning towards the docks and looked rapidly about them until they saw a copse of trees, standing along the banks of the Exe. With an informed glance, one towards the other, the brothers acknowledged this was the place. Heaving their candles into the roadway, they ran as the athletes they were to the copse where both of their mounts stood waiting for them. The brothers grasped reins into their hands; they sprang into their saddles and kicked their horses to a gallop, not towards the Quay but on to the great stone bridge arched across the River Exe.

The crowds of bystanders could not believe their eyes. These men were required by law to take ship, leave England, and never return. But their contempt for their role as penitents had now been openly displayed. Their candles lay broken and abandoned on the ground, while the Falford brothers galloped across the bridge, scattering bystanders and carts in their way. Guards on the city wall could see them going first towards St Thomas. They had not the slightest intention of accepting exile!

Within minutes, the Falfords reached the far bank of the river and continued to gallop furiously through St Thomas. Once outside the village, they turned their mounts uphill and searched for the turning onto the path leading into Dartmoor. Stedmund was beside himself. "We have done it, Edmund! Dammit man, we are free!"

"Hold, brother," Edmund shouted back to him, "we must find the provisions. Once on the moor, we shall never be discovered, but we must be prepared to survive."

They slowed the pace of their horses slightly in an effort to locate their next important stop and moved cautiously up the trail towards Dartmoor. Two miles beyond St Thomas they found it, an old, abandoned barn with its main doors fallen open. They rode into its ruined walls and found waiting for them a pack horse, loaded with clothes, boots, and provisions to maintain them in the months ahead. The brothers dismounted quickly and walked gingerly to the collections of their gear. Each of them eagerly snatched from his pack a pair of boots! Once their feet were properly covered and warmed, they began to feel returned to their presumed positions of superiority. Surely they would accomplish their escape, but they must not waste precious time.

"No one will stop us now, Edmund; we shall outwit them all, the fools!" Stedmund laughed out loud. Escape would be first, he told himself, but he would find ways to enact his personal longings for revenge.

The brothers hurriedly pulled great cloaks upon their shoulders and strapped their swords to their belts. But as they rushed to clothe and arm themselves, a familiar, deep voice spoke to them from the back stalls of the ancient barn. "I am eternally grateful that you may now fulfill your promise to your father, Sir Edmund."

"Damnation, Rauf, how in hell's fury came you here?" Stedmund was irritated and angry once again. He had been convinced that their escape route had been cleared of all interruption.

"Your men in the cave on the Quay know me to be a servant of your family, Sir Stedmund. I told them I should be happy to bring your pack horse to you on their behalf because I had a message for Sir Edmund," Rauf continued to speak very reasonably.

"If thou hast, complete thy task and begone, man! We have no further need of ye."

"Oh, I shall not hinder you, Sir Stedmund; I only wish to assure that your brother fulfills the last wishes of your honourable father. My Lord Brutwald died in such pain and misery, I feel bound to see to it that he rests, at last, in peace." Rauf spoke somberly but could be seen to address himself specifically to Edmund.

"You dare to make demands of me, servant?" Edmund sneered. "Remove yourself! I know my eldest brother, the simple-minded

Falford heir, has thrown you out of his household. I have no desire to keep you about. You still stink of father's disease."

"It is not my position in question here, Sir Edmund; it is your solemn promise to see that your father is properly buried as a Knight of the Garter in the parish church. I saw him give you your mother's jewels to pay the costs. Now it must be done," Rauf's voice grew cold, but his insistence wavered not at all as he walked up to stand before Edmund's horse.

"Well, I shan't tarry about here for the Sheriff of Devon's arrival," Stedmund muttered. "If you have business with this peasant, I shall leave you to it." With that, he climbed into the saddle of his horse and reached down to pull away the reins of the pack horse.

"Oh no, dear brother, you shan't leave without me," Edmund shouted, pulling the reins back from his brother's hand. "I have no business with him, and he has no claim upon me. Let us away!"

Edmund, full of frustrated anger, leaped into his saddle and prepared to ride over Rauf, if need be. He would not be seen to accept any of this servant's impertinence, though he knew in his heart, Rauf spoke only truth.

The manservant of his father grabbed the halter of Edmund's mount and said again, "You may not leave until you have fulfilled your promise to grant your father's deathbed wish!"

Edmund kicked Rauf furiously in his chest, forced the servant out from his horse's path, and began to turn his mount, pulling the packhorse with him towards the open door. Stedmund, seeing his brother was preparing to leave, trotted his horse to the lead and rode out of the barn. Once outside the ruined barn, neither of them looked back to see that Rauf had picked up a large portion of a block of stone from the collapsing wall in his powerful right hand. He hurled it directly at Edmund's head, and its crushing impact resounded with the fragmenting bone of his skull. Edmund's hand limply let loose of the packhorse's reins when his arm collapsed to his side. His body crumpled forward, then slid to the left of his mount's head and fell to the ground. His startled horse trotted a few paces ahead, unconstrained by the hands of its fallen rider.

Stedmund turned to see his brother fall, pulled his sword from its sheath, and roared back into the entrance of the barn, crashing to a halt where Rauf stood unmoved, his face boldly forward.

With one fracturing sword's blow, Stedmund's weapon sliced through Rauf's neck, sending the servant's head flying from his shoulders. Spurting fountains of bloody currents began to pump rhythmically out from the gaping wound that had been his neck. Rauf's body slowly sank to the earth, whence he had stood.

Stedmund turned his horse away from the heap of Rauf's body, urged his mount back out through the ruined barn door, and paused only to look down upon the crushed, distorted skull of his dead brother's body. He seized up the reins of the pack horse, grazing quietly next to Edmund's horse, and, pulling it sharply to follow his lead, galloped into the descending fog of Dartmoor.

Glossary

Abbey: monastery supervised by an abbot.

Affinity: medieval concept of loyal household, wearing the livery or heraldic badge of one's lord and granting full allegiance and acceptance of his rule in one's life.

Ague: a fit of fever.

Almoner: a person whose function is the distribution of alms in behalf of a noble person.

Ambit: circuit, limits.

Ambulatory: in architecture, an aisle surrounding the end of the chancel of a church. A processional way around the sanctuary, frequently used by pilgrims but also used for liturgical procession.

Areopagite: member of the council of the Areopagus Hill in Athens.

Assize: usually "assizes" meaning a trial session civil or criminal, held periodically in certain locations in England: judges travel the counties on six circuits, trying all the criminals they encounter.

Aught I woot: as far as I know.

Aulnage: royal official whose duty it was to examine all cloth offered for sale and see that it conformed to the requirements of English law.

Bay: architectural term for divisions of an interior wall; ex. Nave was divided into six bays.

Benedicite: fourteenth century usage, meaning (the Lord) blesses you.

Benedictine:	member of the Order of monks founded by St. Benedict at Monte Casino, about AD 530.
Bishop:	member of the clergy who supervises a diocese, governing many parish churches and whose main seat or throne is found in his cathedral.
Cadet branch:	branch of a noble family of one of the younger sons.
Canon:	member of the clergy chapter attached to a cathedral or collegiate church.
Canon law:	the body of ecclesiastical or church law.
Cap-a-pie:	from head to foot.
Carding:	the process by which wool fibers are manipulated into sliver form prior to spinning.
Carpe diem:	Latin phrase, "seize the day."
Cathedral:	principal church of a diocese containing the bishop's throne.
Cathedral chapter:	general assembly of the canons of the cathedral.
Cathedral Close:	confined walled area attached to the cathedral that could be closed off from the public.
Cathedral dean:	the member of clergy who is head of the cathedral chapter.
Cathedral Green:	grassy area within the cathedral close.
Cathedral Yard:	the burial area by the cathedral.
Celts:	Indo-European tribal peoples occupying England at the time of the Roman invasions and before the arrival of the Anglo-Saxons. Now Celts are represented chiefly by the Cornish, Irish, Gaels, Welsh and Bretons.
Chantry chapel:	a chapel attached to a church, endowed for the saying of masses for the souls of founders or specified persons.

<u>Charnel house:</u>	building where the bones of the dead are stored.
<u>Chevet:</u>	the apsidal end of a Gothic cathedral.
<u>Chivalry:</u>	rules and ideal qualifications of a medieval knight: courage, courtesy, generosity, valor, and dexterity in arms.
<u>Cistercians:</u>	members of an order of monks founded in 11th century France near Citeaux.
<u>Clerk:</u>	in Chaucer's day, a person who is able to read and write; a scholar, frequently in minor holy orders.
<u>Cloister:</u>	a covered walk, usually opening onto a courtyard, within a religious institution, monastery or convent.
<u>Cloth of assize:</u>	cloth of 24 twenty-four yards by two yards.
<u>Commons:</u>	commonality, the common people, as distinguished from those with authority, rank and station.
<u>Compline:</u>	the final service of the round of daily prayer, took place around 7:00 p.m. See *opus dei*, round of daily prayer.
<u>Confraternity:</u>	a lay brotherhood devoted to a religious or charitable purpose.
<u>Coracle:</u>	small round boat made of wicker work covered in oiled cloth or tarred skin or canvas.
<u>Corbel:</u>	architectural stone bracket projecting from a wall usually meant to support roof beams or ribs.
<u>Corrupcioun:</u>	in Chaucer's day, a description of decayed matter, or place of dissolution. Corrupcioun Cave in the chapter title refers to a place of corrupt activities.
<u>Courtesy:</u>	In the understanding of those followers of Julian of Norwich from about 1400, courtesy is not meant to be understood as excellence of manners or polite behaviour. Courtesy means loving respect implying not only indulgence of another but also goodness granted freely regardless of sinful behaviour. Mother

Julian describes God as our "Courteous Lord".

Crossing: intersection of the nave and transcepts in a cruciform church building.

Curate: any ecclesiastic entrusted with the cure of souls.

Custor: a custodian.

Deanery: the residence of a dean.

Deformity's descant: phrase from Shakespeare's Richard III, meaning a variation upon the state of being deformed.

Dextra: in the right side or to the right direction.

Diocese: ecclesiastical district under the jurisdiction of a bishop.

Dozens: in the 14th century, sellers of cloth made available various sizes of cloth. The dozens were small cloths, twelve yards long by one wide.

Druids: members of religious order of priests in pre-Christian Britain.

Effigy: human image representing the deceased, sculpted upon a tomb.

Expresse: in 14th century, "expresse" meant clearly, explicitly.

Foliate face: in 14th century architecture, a carved face composed, covered, or shaped by leaves, more commonly known as a green man.

Franciscans: members of the mendicant order founded by St. Francis of Assisi, also called the Grey Friars.

Franklin: in the 15th century, a wealthy freeholder who was not of noble birth.

Friary: a monastery of friars of a mendicant order, such as the Franciscans.

Frumenty: in the 14th century, a dish of hulled wheat boiled in milk and seasoned with sugar, cinnamon, and raisins.

Fuller: one who was involved in the finishing of woollen cloth. Woven woollen cloth was first soaked in urine and fuller's earth to remove oils and other impurities, later they would soap them, then put them into the fulling mills.

<u>Garderobe:</u>	medieval privy often built into the walls of a castle or manor house.
<u>Garter knight:</u>	a member of the Order of the Garter, founded by King Edward III.
<u>Gentry:</u>	well-born, well-bred people, an aristocracy; in England, the class under the nobility.
<u>Gramercy:</u>	an expression of thanks, "grand merci."
<u>Green man:</u>	a sculpted face surrounded by or made from leaves, or having branches or vines sprouting from any part of a face.
<u>Grey Friar:</u>	a brother of the Franciscan order.
<u>Guildhall:</u>	ancient hall built by and for members of the guilds, a place for civic functions, celebrations and markets.
<u>Guildsman:</u>	member of medieval association of merchants or tradesmen.
<u>High Street:</u>	main street in the centre of the town.
<u>Holy Orders:</u>	the rank or status of ordained Christian ministry.
<u>Image screen:</u>	a collection of carvings of saints, kings, angels or Fathers of the Church displayed across the front of a major church. In the 14th century these images and their niches were usually brightly painted.
<u>Indulgence:</u>	a document containing a partial remission of punishment in purgatory, still due for sin after absolution.
<u>*In loco parentis:*</u>	Latin phrase meaning in place of a parent.
<u>Jackanapes:</u>	derisive term to ridicule or mock.
<u>Jack o' th green:</u>	a figure of a tower of leaves about eight feet high, escorted by green men.
<u>Lady Chapel:</u>	a chapel dedicated to the Virgin Mary attached to a church at the eastern extremity, usually behind the high altar.

Lauds:	a service of the church marked especially by psalms of praise; in monastic life, Lauds is the first daytime office of the daily round of prayer called the *opus dei*.
Leprosarium:	hospital for the treatment of leprosy.
Liripipe:	the tail or pendant part of the back of a hood or hat of the 14th century.
Malignity:	The state or character of being maligned; malevolence; intense ill will; spite.
Manliness meene:	14th century words meaning to signify qualities proper to a man.
Man of law:	14th century barrister or lawyer.
Mass of Separation:	mass, spoken by a priest, performed at a leper's hut, forbidding him to have any human contact in religious or civil society, to drink at any stream or fountain, or to touch anything belonging to another human being.
Mendicant:	a person who lives by begging; a mendicant friar is a member of a brotherhood who lives by begging.
Meschaunce grave:	Chaucer's words referring to a misfortunate or mis-conducted burial.
Minstrel's Gallery:	in the 14th century, a balcony or top of a screen from which music could be performed.
Missal:	book of prayers or devotions.
Moor:	tract of open wasteland, common in high altitudes. There are two in Devon, England Dartmoor and Exmoor.
Moor:	a Muslim of mixed Berber and Arab peoples who conquered Spain in the 8th century.
Morderour expresse:	14th century words meaning explicit or clearly murder.
Murrain:	any of various diseases of cattle or sheep.
Nave:	principal longitudinal area of a church extending from main entrance to the chancel.

Nave aisle:	in a major church, the architectural longitudinal division of the public space, extending from the main entrance to the chancel. The nave aisle is the central aisle. In the 14th century, the nave had two aisles, separated by the colonnade.
Noble:	distinguished by birth, rank or title.
Noblesse oblige:	the moral obligation of the rich or highborn to display honourable or charitable conduct.
Noblewoman:	a woman of noble birth or rank.
Nonage:	any period of immaturity.
Normans:	natives of Normandy.
Nosy Parkers:	nick name for a prying person, a busybody.
Novitiate:	novice of a religious order.
Opus dei:	literally the "work of God" but referring specifically to the services for the divine offices of the church; eight services or offices required by St. Benedict including Matins, Lauds, Prime, Terce, Sext, None, Vespers and Compline.
Oratory:	small chapel or room for private prayer.
Palfrey:	a saddle horse particularly suited to a woman.
Pardoner:	an ecclesiastical official charged with the granting of indulgences.
Patrimony:	one's heritage, or an inherited estate.
Physic:	in the 14th century, any medicine or drug, especially one that purges.
Pilaster:	a shallow architectural feature projecting from a wall having the shape of a pillar with capital.
Pitmaker:	grave digger.
Plague:	epidemic disease of high mortality, pestilence.
Portal:	door, gate, or entrance.
Pother:	commotion or uproar.

Poulaines: 14th century excessively long, pointed shoes that
                    often had to be tied round the calf to enable the
                    wearer to walk.

Precentor: canon of the cathedral who is in charge of the music
                    and singing.

Prie-dieu: piece of furniture especially designed for kneeling
                    upon during prayer.

Prioress: a woman holding the position equal to that of a prior.

Priory: religious convent governed by a prior or prioress.

Quadrangle: a square space or court surrounded by buildings.

Quaestores: Latin word used as title for church official known as a
                    pardoner.

Quay: wharf or landing place constructed along a body of
                    water.

Quire: archaic spelling of 14th century area in a medieval
                    church for the choir stalls. This ancient spelling is
                    still in use in Exeter Cathedral today.

Quire aisle: main space between the rows of choir stalls.

Quire screen: a stone or wooden screen or structure of division
                    separating the choir from the nave of a great church.

Rayonnant: term used to describe a style of window tracery in the
                    development of French Gothic architecture from
                    about 1240-1350.

Refectory: dining hall in a religious house.

Relic: ecclesiastical term referring to the body, a part of the
                    body or a personal memorial of a saint or members of
                    the Holy Family and worthy of veneration.

Reliquary: beautifully crafted receptacle for a relic.

Roof boss: key stone at the intersection of roof supporting ribs.

Rose window: circular window decorated with symmetrical tracery.

Sanctuary: (the place) the part of a church around the altar

Sanctuary:	(the act) a church or other sacred place where fugitives were formerly entitled to immunity from arrest.
Saxons:	Germanic tribes, a group of which invaded and occupied parts of Britain in the 5th and 6th centuries.
Scriptorium:	room in a monastery set aside for the writing or copying of manuscripts.
Sext:	service of the church, the fourth of seven canonical hours.
Sinistra:	to the left.
Solar:	a private or upper chamber in a medieval English house or castle.
Sovereignty:	the status of authority and independence.
Squire:	the first degree of knighthood, squire as servant to a knight; a country gentleman, especially the chief landed proprietor in a district.
Steward:	one who serves as manager of financial and business affairs, serving as manager or agent for another.
Sumptuary laws:	In the 14th century, laws were passed in England which regulated ornateness of dress.
Table tomb:	a sepulchral structure with a flat, slab-like top.
Thatched roof:	a roof make of straw, rushes, leaves or other thatching material.
Tierceron vault:	in a ribbed Gothic vault, a collection of ribs springing from a single point of support.
Tithe barn:	a barn built on church or parish property to hold the tenth part of agricultural harvest.
Tracery:	ornamental work within a Gothic window.
Transept:	the cross-like arms of a major church extending out from the intersection of nave and choir.

<u>Treasury of Merit:</u>	a treasury of the goodness, the merits of Christ and the saints, left to the keeping of the Church and which is the source of Indulgences. In the later Middle Ages, the sale of Indulgences became a significant means of raising funds.
<u>Truckle bed:</u>	low bed usually pushed under another bed.
<u>Tucker:</u>	a person active in the medieval cloth industry.
<u>Vain:</u>	meaning without effect or significance; to no purpose.
<u>Veil of Veronica:</u>	a pious woman at the time of Christ's crucifixion wiped His face leaving the image of his face on the cloth she used. A veil of Veronica has been preserved at St. Peters in Rome since the 8th century and was highly venerated in the 14th century.
<u>Vicar:</u>	person acting as priest in place of the rector.
<u>Vicars Choral:</u>	those in holy orders serving as members of the choir.
<u>Virger:</u>	an Exeter Cathedral spelling of verger, a church official who carries the verge or symbol of office.
<u>Votive:</u>	something offered or given.
<u>Voussoir:</u>	in architecture, any piece of stone in the shape of a truncated wedge which forms an arch or vault.
<u>Walet:</u>	14th century expression of a bag for carrying small articles.
<u>West front:</u>	the ecclesiastical western face of a church, in the case of a great church or cathedral, may contain an image screen portraying kings, saints, angels and apostles.
<u>Wimple:</u>	a 14th century woman's headcloth drawn in folds about the chin.
<u>Yeoman:</u>	subordinate in a great household in the 14th century, the yeomen were lesser freeholders below the gentry level who cultivated their own land.

References

The Riverside Chaucer

    Larry D. Benson, General Editor
    Houghton Mifflin Company
    Boston. 1987

Exeter Cathedral A Short History and Description

    Audrey Erskine, Vyvyan Hope and John Lloyd
    Published by the dean and chapter of Exeter Cathedral
    A. Wheaton and Co. Ltd., Exeter. 1988

Devon

    W. G. Hoskins
    Devon Books
    Tiverton, Devon. 1992

The Time Traveler's Guide to Medieval England A Handbook for

    Visitors to the Fourteenth Century
    Ian Mortimer
    A Touchstone Book published by Simon & Schuster
    New York, NY. 2008

Exeter Cathedral The First Thousand Years, 400-1550

    Nicholas Orme
    Impress Books Ltd. Exeter. 2009

A Distant Mirror The Calamitous 14th Century
    Barbara W. Tuchman
    Alfred A Knopf New York 1978